An Atlas of Irish History

An Atlas of Irish History

Second edition

RUTH DUDLEY EDWARDS

Routledge
London and New York

First published in 1973 by
Methuen & Co. Ltd
Second edition 1981
Reprinted 1986

Reprinted 1989
by Routledge
11 New Fetter Lane, London EC4P 4EE
29 West 35th Street, New York, NY 10001

Phototypeset in Linotron 202 Meridien by
Western Printing Services Ltd, Bristol
Printed in Great Britain by
Richard Clay Ltd, Bungay, Suffolk

British Library Cataloguing in Publication Data

Edwards, Ruth Dudley
An atlas of Irish history. – 2nd ed. –
(University paperbacks).
1. Ireland – Historical geography – Maps
I. Title   II. Series
911'.415   G1830   80–41921

ISBN 0–416–74820–1
ISBN 0–415–03980–0 Pbk (University paperback 505)

Contents

Foreword

There is an inevitable arbitrariness about attempting to represent history or politics cartographically. It becomes necessary to concentrate on those aspects which can most usefully be displayed visually. Therefore, while I have attempted to deal with the more important features in the development of the Irish people, the medium lends itself to the portraying of facts rather than ideas, and some bias will be discernible. Any imbalance in the choice of material is conditioned by the aim of using the medium as effectively as possible, rather than of forcing a strict pattern.

Let the nature of the beast therefore be the excuse for inadequate treatment of areas of Irish history which could claim extensive coverage in any general survey. By way of compensation, the cartographic format lends itself to a less insular approach. If one defines Irish history as being the history of the Irish people rather than simply of the island, one must look to most of the world for material. The Irish abroad merit a complete section within this book, as does Irish trade, since they are both susceptible of visual representation.

My debt to historians of Ireland will be evident throughout the book, and will be acknowledged in the bibliography. I owe many other debts. Mr W. H. Bromage drew the maps; his skill and forebearance in the face of enormous odds made the project possible. Professor G. R. Elton bears the responsibility for involving me in this venture, and has been my teacher and friend. My parents have given me moral, intellectual and practical support at all times; the book could not have been written without their help. Miss Vanessa MacErlean has been a precociously efficient assistant and a constant

11

provider of moral support. Mr Patrick Taylor has been a model among publishers and Mrs Vanessa Mitchell a most helpful editor. Many others have rendered assistance, including Dr Patrick Cosgrave, Dr Ronan Fanning, Dr Dermot Fenlon, Mr Liam Hourican, Mr James McGuire and Mrs Una O'Donoghue. To them, and others, I extend my gratitude.

I have sectionalised the book with the object of increasing its coherence. All sections are prefaced by a general introduction. Cross-references are shown by a numeral in brackets, and refer to the relevant map and its accompanying text. Roman numerals refer to sectional introductions. Each section, and indeed each map and accompanying text is intended to form an independent unit, but cross-referencing to other parts of the text should not be ignored.

R.D.E.   1973

Note on Second Edition

In preparing a new edition I have acted where possible on the constructive criticisms made by reviewers and users of the first. The scope of the book has been enlarged, new maps, graphs and charts have been added, several others have been improved, updated or replaced, and the text has been extensively revised. I am grateful to my publishers (particularly my encouraging, constructive and efficient editor, Miss Mary Ann Kernan) for agreeing to substantial expansion and alterations.

I am grateful to Dr Michael Laffan for some very helpful suggestions; to Mr Oliver Snoddy for map 78a; to Mr Neil Hyslop for so ably taking over as cartographer; to the staff of the Irish Embassy in London who answered promptly, efficiently and courteously my many requests for information; to the Northern Ireland Office and the British Library.

My father deserves a paragraph to himself. He spent over a week reading and annotating the book in fine detail, spotting errors and anachronisms, bringing me up to date on the last decade of Irish historiography, making countless useful suggestions for improvements and generally giving me that selfless and invaluable help which I am lucky enough always to have on call from my parents, husband, household and friends.

R.D.E.   September 1980

I Reference

The six maps in this section have been included primarily for reference purposes. In addition to the political and physical maps, which follow a traditional format, there are included maps of the provinces of Ireland split into baronies. The importance of such maps for reference purposes will be appreciated by any student of Irish history, especially in dealing with political, military or social history.

1. POLITICAL GEOGRAPHY OF IRELAND

The political geography of Ireland can be traced with some accuracy from the seventh century. At that time the country was divided into about 150 units of government, or small kingdoms, called *tuatha*. A *tuath* was an autonomous group of people of independent political jurisdiction under a king. Larger units, comprising several *tuatha*, were built up by local kings whose families maintained their ascendancy traditionally. Some thirty such larger units existed by the early twelfth century when the diocesan system was established, and it was upon these that the new ecclesiastical organisation was based (V).

Larger historic units developed, dominated in the north west by the Uí Néill and in the south by the Dalcassian descendants of Brian Ború (IV). This in the twelfth century led to the proposed division of the whole country into two ecclesiastical provinces – Armagh and Cashel. When the Uí Néill and the O'Briens failed to maintain their hegemony in the west and east, two other provinces – Tuam and Dublin – were added. In this way four greater kingdoms came

1. *Political geography of Ireland: present county divisions*

to be distinguished which were described by ancient titles as Ulster, Leinster, Munster and Connacht. In fact the Uí Néill and the O'Briens had previously held no territorial rights to be rulers of Ulster and Munster. The areas of these provinces comprised those territories not claimed by the newly-expanding kingdoms of Connacht and Leinster. Clare was conceded to Munster and Breffny to Ulster. Leinster was confined to the historic Laigin lands to which Ossory and Dublin were conceded. On the other hand, the Viking towns of Waterford and Limerick appear to have preferred to be associated with Munster.

The Normans adapted their methods of government to suit the conditions which they found in Ireland, and therefore did not interfere with the provincial divisions which they encountered there. They were, however, concerned to superimpose on those parts of the country over which they had control the political divisions which had obtained in England since the Anglo-Saxons. During the Norman period, therefore, began the division of Ireland into shires, later called counties. Although only Dublin was a shire before 1200, by the early fourteenth century there were twelve shires, Dublin, Waterford, Cork, Kerry, Limerick, Tipperary, Kildare, Carlow, Louth, Roscommon, Connacht and Meath, and four liberties, Wexford, Kilkenny, Trim and Ulster. After the Bruce invasion, some of the shires became liberties.

To correspond with the sub-division of shires known in England as the hundred, Irish counties were subdivided into cantreds – later known as baronies, which in turn were sub-divided into townlands. Although the baronies initially denoted feudal and military jurisdictions, eventually they were used for fiscal and administrative purposes only. These divisions proved an essential administrative aid to the process of colonising land, and later provided the basic units for the collection of census statistics.

Mainly because of political weakness, there was little attempt to extend the shiring of the country during the late middle ages. Apart from Mary's colonisation of Queen's County and King's County (50), there was little opportunity for the Dublin government to extend its control until the military and political advances of the Elizabethan period. Between 1570 and 1585 Munster was divided into counties and Connacht, which in the fourteenth century had been called a county, was sub-divided. During the

Map labels:

Ulster

N.E. LIBERTIES of COLERAINE

KILMACRENAN · INISHOWEN · E · W

DL · DUN-LUCE · CARY · U

GLENARM · L

COLERAINE · KEEN-AGHT · TIR-KEERAN · ①

KILCONWAY · ANTRIM · L · U

DONEGAL · BOYLAGH · RAPHOE · N · S · L

LONDONDERRY

TOOME · U

ANTRIM · L · BELFAST

CARRICK-FERGUS

BANAGH · TIRHUGH · OMAGH · STRABANE · U · LOUGHIN-SHOLIN

MASSEREENE · U · L

Lough · Neagh · L · U

CASTLE-REAGH · ARDS · U · L

LURG · MAGHERABOY · TIR-KENNEDY

CLOGHER · DUNGANNON · E · M · L

ONEILLAND · W · E

LIVEAGH · L · U

DUFFERIN

DOWN · L · U · LECALE

FERMANAGH · CLAN-AWLEY · MAGHERA-STEPHANA · CLAN-KELLY

ORIOR · L · U

KINELARTY · UR IVEAGH · U

TULLYHAW · KNOCKNINNY · COOLE · MONAGHAN · TROUGH

ARMAGH · FEWS · L · UFEWS

② · L · MOURNE

MONAGHAN · DARTREE · CREMORNE

TULLYGARVEY · CLANKEE · FARNEY

CAVAN · LOUGHTEE · L · U

TULLYHUNCO · CASTLERAHAN · CLANMAHON

① N.W. LIBERTIES of LONDONDERRY

② LORDSHIP of NEWRY

BARONY MAPS
U —— UPPER
L —— LOWER
N —— North
S —— South
E —— East
W —— West

W. Bromage

2. *Ulster: counties and baronies*

reign of James I, Ulster was shired at the time of its plantation
(51).

The divisions of the four provinces of Ireland are now as follows:

2. ULSTER

Ulster covers 26·3% of Ireland and consists of nine counties: Londonderry, Antrim, Tyrone, Armagh, Fermanagh and Down, which are
within Northern Ireland, and Cavan, Donegal and Monaghan,
which are in the Republic.

16

3. *Leinster: counties and baronies*

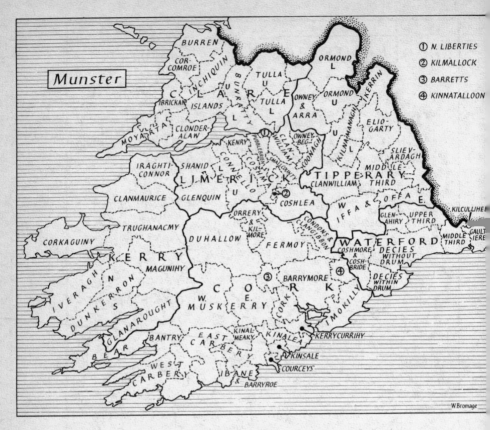

4. Munster: counties and baronies

3. LEINSTER

Leinster covers 23·4% of Ireland and consists of twelve counties, Louth, Dublin, Kildare, Carlow, Kilkenny, Leix (formerly Queen's County), Offaly (formerly King's County), Meath, Westmeath, Wicklow, Wexford and Longford.

4. MUNSTER

Munster covers 29·3% of Ireland and consists of six counties, Cork, Kerry, Clare, Limerick, Tipperary and Waterford.

5. CONNACHT

Connacht covers 21% of Ireland and consists of five counties, Galway, Leitrim, Mayo, Roscommon and Sligo.

18

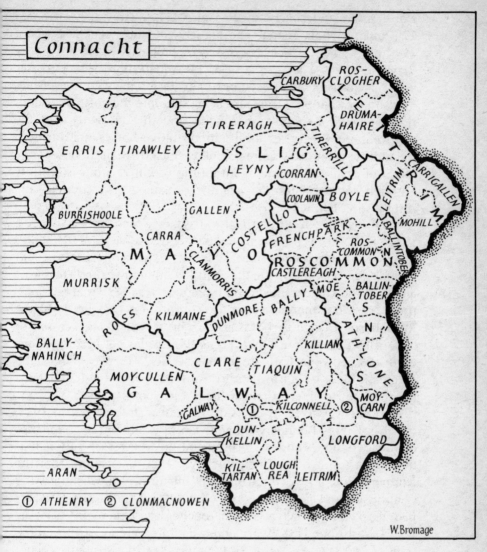

Connacht

CARBURY · ROS-CLOGHER
DRUMA-HAIRE
TIRERAGH · TIRERRILL · CARRIGALLEN
ERRIS · TIRAWLEY · SLIGO · LEITRIM
LEYNY · CORRAN · MOHILL
COOLAVIN · BOYLE
BURRISHOOLE · GALLEN · BALLINTOBER
CARRA · COSTELLO · FRENCHPARK · ROS-COMMON N
MAYO · CLANMORRIS · ROSCOMMON
CASTLEREAGH
MURRISK · MOE · BALLIN-TOBER S
ROSS · KILMAINE · DUNMORE · BALLY · N
BALLY-NAHINCH · ATHLONE
CLARE · KILLIAN
MOYCULLEN · TIAQUIN · S
GALWAY · MOY-CARN
GALWAY · ① · KILCONNELL · ②
DUN-KELLIN · LONGFORD
ARAN · KIL-TARTAN · LOUGH REA · LEITRIM
① ATHENRY ② CLONMACNOWEN

W. Bromage

5. *Connacht: counties and baronies*

The only difference between the contemporary divisions and those of the sixteenth century are that Connacht, as befitted its historical importance, was then much larger, comprising in addition to its modern counties, those of Cavan and Longford.

The main contemporary political feature of Ireland is partition.

Northern Ireland covers an area of 5,452 square miles, or about 17% of the whole island. The border with the Republic is about 250 miles long, which poses severe problems of security. The Republic covers a total area of 27,136 square miles. For purposes of local government the country is divided into twenty-seven administrative counties (Tipperary being split into the north and south ridings) and four county boroughs, and the department of the environment supervises local administrative bodies. In Northern Ireland the position is more complex, since there are five separate kinds of local government authorities: county councils, county borough councils, borough councils, urban district councils and rural district councils.

The original constitution of the Irish Free State was enacted in 1922. In 1937 a new constitution set up a *de facto* Republic; it was so worded that a repealable act (External Relations) could provide for relations with the British Commonwealth. Therefore, although the king retained certain prerogatives in external relations, these were not mentioned in the constitution (23). In 1948 the Republic of Ireland Act was passed, by which Ireland ceased to be a British dominion; however, its citizens did not become aliens in Britain. Anyone born in Ireland before 1948 was granted the automatic right to opt to be a British subject, and any Irish citizen has the right to enter Britain without a passport.

Partition was fixed by the Government of Ireland Act of 1922, which set up a Boundary Commission to examine the boundaries of the two states and to recommend any necessary rationalisation. As a result of the Irish Civil War (22), opposition from the Northern Ireland government and dilatoriness in London, the Commission did not begin work until 1924. Although its members had reached internal agreement on border changes in 1925, its report was suppressed. Its recommendations were to have been the transfer of 183,000 acres and 31,000 people from Northern Ireland to the Free State and the transfer of 50,000 acres and 7,500 people from the Free State to the north. Before the Commission could publish its report, a leak of information to the *Morning Post* caused Eoin MacNeill, the Irish government's representative, to resign. The boundaries of the two countries therefore remained as they had been in 1921.

Ireland is remarkable for a topographical variety disproportionate to her size. The coastline is dramatic, and often inaccessible. Its most notable features are the high cliffs of north Antrim, famous for the legendary Giant's Causeway, a promontory made up of pillars of basalt, some nearly 40 feet wide and 20 feet high, and the spectacular cliffs of Donegal, Clare and Kerry. Most of the south-west coast is an alternation of sandy bays and high cliffs.

Many of the coastal waters are dangerous, which is why the main harbours have all been established in river estuaries – Dublin on the Liffey, Wexford on the Slaney, Waterford on the Suir, Cork on the Lee, Limerick on the Shannon, Londonderry on the Foyle and Belfast on the Lagan.

Near the coastline are situated most of the uplands of Ireland, although the so-called 'Central Plain' of Ireland is dotted with numerous low hills, known as drumlins (8). Much of this land is uneven and diverse, varying in quality from rich pasture land to bare peat bogs.

Ireland covers an area of 32,588 square miles, averages 110 miles in breadth and 220 miles in length. The climate is bland, there being relatively little seasonal variation in temperature, but there is a great deal of rain, averaging 30–50 inches annually over most of the country for up to 250 days in the wettest parts. Professor Macalister contended that the climate in all but the north-eastern corner was the most enervating in Europe, and claimed that 'To this quite irredeemable vice of the Irish climate is due the notorious fact that Irishmen always do better in any country but their own.'

Much of the history of Ireland is the story of how invaders coped with the physical problems posed by the island. The Norse, for example, were uniquely equipped to adapt to the demands of the environment, and made generous use of the rivers and lakes of Ireland to penetrate its inner fastnesses (11). Other invaders found the country more inhospitable.

More significant perhaps, than the physical problems of the country is its location. The close physical relationship between Ireland and Great Britain is symbolised by the fact that the minimum distance between the two is only thirteen miles. Difficult of access by her western neighbours, and protected from the twelfth century by

6. *Physical features of Ireland*

22

the intimate interest of her nearest neighbour from attacks from the north, south or east, Ireland has nevertheless been locked in a struggle for some kind of independence for the last thousand years. Immune from the Homeric clashes raging across the Continent over the centuries, since the twelfth century the Irish people have concentrated on one enemy, not recognising that without that enemy she would have been faced with unwelcome advances from others (10).

II Cartography

The development of cartography owes a great deal to many disciplines. The early map-makers could not have functioned without the material provided to them by traders and travellers. Later map-makers were given encouragement and an impetus towards accuracy by the increasing military requirement for scientific maps. Early maps were concerned mainly to indicate routes and landmarks: they were visual representations of itineraries. Accuracy in indicating direction or distance was of lesser concern. Imagination played an important part in map design, and artistry was a necessary feature.

Soldiers, however, needed to have an accurate idea of distances and locations, and the skills of mathematicians, and of astronomers, were incorporated into the science of cartography. Trigonometry aided the establishing of distances. Astronomers established that the earth was spherical and that any location could be pinpointed by the use of concepts of latitude and longitude. At a later stage, scientists found ways of accurately finding longitude.

Map-making began in the Middle East, notably with the Egyptians, but by the sixth century B.C. the Greeks were pre-eminent. From an early stage they constructed maps of their trading routes, including descriptions of the coasts known to their sailors. Obviously, accurate data were not available, since myth and hearsay formed a major element in the material brought back by travellers. By the second century A.D. the science of cartography had advanced considerably; Claudius Ptolemy of Alexandria and Marinus of Tyre made dramatic contributions.

Although no examples of Ptolemy's work remain extant, alleged copies exist, and his writings give enough information to enable maps to be based on them. Ptolemy did not gain recognition in Europe until the fifteenth century, but his influence was then profound for over a hundred years. Of the maps illustrated here, the first is based on the findings of Ptolemy in the second century, and the second was drawn fourteen hundred years later by a cartographer known as the Argentinian Ptolemy.

The discovery of Ptolemy in Europe in the fifteenth century heralded a cartographical renaissance. Hitherto, map-making had consisted largely of inaccurate copying of earlier maps, although Italian navigators and cartographers introduced portolans or sea charts to aid traders. Simultaneously with the discovery of Ptolemy came the increase in data forthcoming from the great explorers, the Italian, Spanish, French, Dutch, Portuguese and English sailors who reached India, Brazil, the West Indies, southern Africa and many other undiscovered parts of the globe during this period. Subsequently, the advance of the science was steady. Crucial advances in instrument-making led to the creation of maps of real accuracy during the late eighteenth and early nineteenth century. Britain, which had hitherto followed rather than led cartographical advances, illustrated this new development by establishing the Ordnance Survey in 1791, which formalised the work being done in surveying by army engineers. From 1745, when the army initiated scientific surveys of the Scottish Highlands, their contribution to map-making was considerable, and engineers took a leading part in the whole Ordnance Survey enterprise. By 1870, one inch to a mile maps for the whole of England, Scotland, Wales and Ireland had been produced.

7. IRELAND AND HER CARTOGRAPHERS

As far as Ireland was concerned, her isolation restricted cartographical activity. For a considerable period she was considered to be the westernmost outpost of the world. The map constructed from Ptolemy's data, however, shows that some trading contacts existed even in the second century which enabled an attempt to be made at describing the Irish coastline and the location of some of the tribes. By the fourth century, there were no longer any attempts to record tribal distribution; the inhabitants of Ireland were known simply as Scotae (40).

25

Hyperborean Ocean

Maleus
Epidium
Ebuda
Ricina
Monaceda
Vennicnium Cape
R. Vidda
R. Argita
Robogdium Cape
ROBOGDII
Northern Cape
ERDINI
VENNICNII
R. Ravius
Regia
DARINI
R. Logia
Western
Nagnata
R. Vinderius
Ocean
NAGNATA
VOLUNTII
Isamnium Cape
R. Libnius
Raeba
R. Ausoba
Regia
Eblana
R. Buvinda
R. Senus
Laberus
Edrus
BLANI
Limnus
AUTINI
CAUCI
R. Oboca
Ituna Aest
R. Dur
Macolicum
Dunum
R. Modonnos
MENAPII
Menapia
Ivernian
GANGANI
Ivernis
CORIONDI
Ocean
R. Ternus
VELLEBORI
BRIGANTES
Mona
IVERNI
VODIÆ
Southern Cape
R. Birgus
Sacred Cape
Seteia Aest
R. Dabrona
Deva
ORDOVICES
Vergivian Ocean
NOVANTÆ
BRIGANTES

W. Bromage

7. Ireland and her cartographers: maps
by Ptolemy and Argentinian Ptolemy

Laionel
Libains purgatoriu Sancti Patricii
C. Ligra Abram
Drosso
Donsobry
moneth
Verfordo
Chevein
Estonford
HIBERNIA
Dairbe
Drozda
ordes
Rebi
Irlando Denvelim
Bie
Ardroim
Vicello
Artello
Iacacis Confrenclom
Otorum Oram
Rove
Orforda
Risate
elebnift
fredit
iondal
Regi
Lamerich
Castrembre
Sanbrandari
le deng
Gana forda
granan
minarit
Braschei
fertonia
Drauert andelitadi Domberg granarg
floles godefida
icandal
Antquo
drosey
C. Cauena

The Argentinian Ptolemy · 1513

26

The later map shown here indicates that although cartography had advanced little by the sixteenth century, trading knowledge of Ireland had become much more extensive (62) and important contemporary ports such as Drogheda, Dublin, Cork and Limerick were located with reasonable accuracy. In fact French, Spanish and Italian seafarers show in their maps a better geographical knowledge of Ireland than does the first English map of Ireland, produced in about 1483, which greatly exaggerates the importance of the Pale.

A number of detailed maps of Ireland were produced during the Tudor period, many of which, however, though beautiful, relied more on hearsay than on facts, on imagination than on investigation. The Elizabethans took a more pragmatic interest in cartography, largely because of the contemporary concern with exploration, and the maps produced in the late sixteenth century were a considerable improvement on earlier work. Technical developments improved the accuracy of surveying, and with the recognition of the important contribution to be made by cartography to political and military activity, the science was encouraged. The work that ensued, though hampered in Ireland by war and appalling communications, is nevertheless a tribute to the dedication and ability of the map-makers.

The Elizabethans had practical, political and military reasons for encouraging good map-making. Inspired by the greatest map-makers of the age, the Flemings, and by the publication of Mercator's map of England and Wales in 1564, English surveyors and draughtsmen worked together to produce maps of great artistry and increasing accuracy, though they excelled more in the former than in the latter. Ptolemy is said to have believed that a map without artistry did not convey any message, and Elizabethan cartographers too were preoccupied with the beauty of the finished product. Two of the great cartographers of the period were John Norden and Richard Bartlett, both of whom produced fine maps of Ireland. Bartlett was employed to produce a series of military maps, many of which had to be researched and drawn during the Nine Years War (15). Bartlett made use of information gathered by the English army during this war and incorporated it into his maps. His knowledge grew with the increasing success of the English forces.

The major breakthrough in accurate cartography in Ireland was made by Sir William Petty in his atlas of Irish maps, published in 1685. In 1654 Petty proposed to the commissioners responsible for the land survey which was to provide the basis of the Cromwellian land settlement (52) a scheme for mapping the relevant parts of the country. This survey, known as the 'Down Survey', literally because the results were being noted down, formed the basis of his later atlas. He used soldiers to do the necessary surveying fieldwork, and the resultant maps were pioneering in their accuracy. His maps were not surpassed until the Ordnance Survey maps of Ireland in the 1840s, which were surveyed by army engineers and drawn by draughtsmen, using techniques which ensured accuracy and good representation.

III Military developments

Professor Hayes-McCoy calculates that there were more than 200 military engagements of varying degrees of importance and size in Ireland from the medieval period to 1798. The more important of these are shown in map 9; they demonstrate that with the coming of the Norman invaders (12) the Irish began a military struggle which was to continue over four centuries. Before the Norman invasion Irish military history was dominated by confrontations with the Norse invaders (11), although internecine strife between Irish aspirants to kingship was a feature of Irish life from the beginning of recorded history.

The major engagements of the medieval period are, however, those of defenders against invaders. Most of them were fought in an attempt to prevent further Norman penetration of the country. The fact that the Irish succeeded in preventing the Normans from completely overrunning the country was due not only to their stout resistance, but also to the isolation of the invaders from their homeland and the impossibility of gaining sufficient reinforcements to maintain and consolidate their position. Additionally, the importation by the Irish of Scots mercenary soldiers called galloglas (from *gall óglach* – foreign warrior) from the thirteenth century onwards, was to strengthen their resistance considerably. At first confined to Ulster, galloglas later spread throughout Ireland in the service of the great families. These mercenaries prolonged the life of the independent Gaelic kingdoms for more than two centuries after the defeat of Edward Bruce (14). Four centuries after the conquest the O'Neills and O'Donnells were still ruling most of Ulster according to the customs of their ancestors. It was not until their defeat in the Nine Years War (15) in 1603, that all of Gaelic Ireland finally fell to the invaders.

During the seventeenth century, Irish military history was to a considerable extent an offshoot of the English history of that period. The alliance between the Catholic Old English and the Gaelic Irish was to develop in the 1640s into a confrontation with the English parliamentary forces (16). When James II landed in Ireland in 1689 in a desperate bid to regain his throne, he was using Ireland as an outpost in an English struggle for supremacy between Stuart and Orange (17).

With the triumph of William of Orange and the emigration of a large number of Irish soldiers throughout the last decade of the seventeenth century (17) and much of the eighteenth, any serious resistance was finally crushed. Ireland was totally subdued, and any future resistance was to take the form of rebellions of varying ineffectiveness. Despite the setbacks of the sixteenth and seventeenth centuries when Ireland had looked to Spain, France and the papacy for help against England, the dissident elements of the Irish people continued to hope that ultimately foreign intervention would give them independence (10). During the sixteenth century, Ireland had become a country whose fortunes were of interest to Continental powers, and to some extent she became a pawn in the military and ideological conflicts of Europe. During the reign of Elizabeth, three invasions occurred in support of the Munster rebellion and the Nine Years War. The Continental confrontation between William of Orange and Louis XIV had its echo in Ireland, whither Louis sent men, arms ammunition and money, less in an effort to secure a decisive victory for James, than in order to deflect William's attention from the Continent to a long drawn-out war in Ireland.

After William's victory there was no further Continental intervention in Ireland until after the French Revolution. The United Irish leaders, inspired by concepts of universal brotherhood, managed to involve the French in the 1798 rising (19). This new defeat deterred the Continental powers from giving any further help, and during the nineteenth century Irish revolutionaries had to go it alone, their only foreign help being in the form of financial support from Irish-Americans (47).

In 1803, Robert Emmet led an abortive rising, which in many

ways was merely a continuation of the 1798 rising. Bad communications led to a confusion of orders, and when the rising eventually broke out on 23 July 1803, instead of involving 3,000 men, as planned, he was left with a rabble of only 80. He and 21 others were executed.

Even more ineffective was the Young Irelanders' rising in 1848 (30). They had made few preparations or plans for a rebellion, which was precipitated by an acceleration of government coercion and the arrest of many of their leaders. The main organiser was William Smith O'Brien, but no amount of rhetoric could persuade the starving Irish peasantry to rebel against the advice of their clergy in favour of intangible political ideals. The country scarcely noticed the rebellion or the subsequent transportation to Van Dieman's Land of the leaders of the movement, including Smith O'Brien and Thomas Francis Meagher, John Mitchel having been sent there for treason before the rebellion.

The other Irish rebellion of the nineteenth century owed something to the 1848 rebellion. A number of Young Ireland followers were to become Fenian leaders later, including James Stephens and Charles Kickham, and although their rising in 1867 (47) affected only a few scattered areas of the country, nevertheless the Fenian movement was to be a potent force in Irish revolutionary circles until independence.

Irish revolutionary activity during the twentieth century has again brought in a Continental element. The 1916 leaders (20) received help from Germany and subsequently I.R.A. groups negotiated during the 1930s and 1940s for German aid. As was the case with earlier Continental help, German aid was given with the object of embarrassing Britain rather than of helping the Irish. Currently, the I.R.A. receives money, equipment or moral support from a variety of sources, including Libya, international terrorist groups and unofficial Irish-American sympathisers (47).

There is a coherent pattern in Irish military activity. Until the seventeenth century, when the woods were cut down and roads improved, military encounters were dominated by physical considerations (8) – by problems of terrain. For almost four centuries there was a continuous struggle between invaders and defenders, which broadened during the late sixteenth century to involve Continental armies. During the seventeenth century military activity

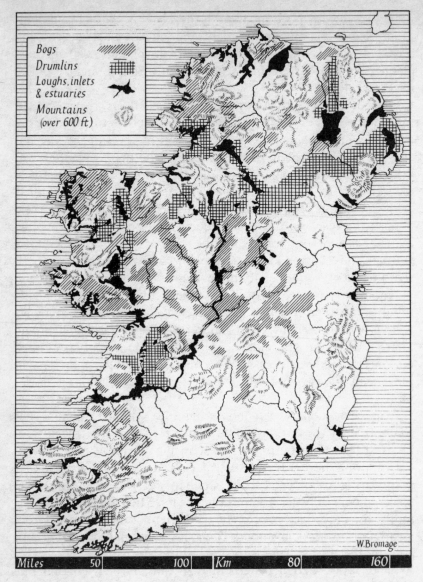

8. *Strategic considerations*

was mainly concerned with the reverberations of English politics. From the eighteenth to the twentieth centuries militarism became a concern of a small section of the population. At no time until the war of independence were more than a tiny minority involved in the various armed rebellions, which until 1916 had little political impact. With the outbreak of the civil war there developed an ugly confrontation which was to prove a divisive force in Ireland until the present day (32). Recently the I.R.A., its off-shoots and its para-military opponents have introduced a pattern of vicarious violence and destruction into Irish military activity.

8. STRATEGIC CONSIDERATIONS

Ireland's natural barriers have always posed problems to invading forces. Only the Vikings, with their skilful command of internal rivers and lakes (11), were equipped to meet competently the physi-cal hazards of the country. For other invaders, a country so liberally supplied with rivers, lakes, mountains, bogs, drumlins (small hills) and an inhospitable coastline, posed almost insuperable difficulties. Additionally, until their commercial exploitation in the seventeenth century, vast areas of woodland covered the country, forming vir-tually impenetrable barriers to effective progress. In the early seven-teenth century, about 15% of the total area of the country was affor-ested. Vast tracts of woodland made most of north-east Ulster and south-west Munster almost totally inaccessible, while extensive detours were necessary to reach many parts of Connacht.

Ulster posed the most serious problems of accessibility, and its physical defences explain why Gaelic rule continued throughout most of the province until 1603. There were only three entry routes. Two were close together in the south-west, where Ulster and Con-nacht are separated by the river Erne, the approaches being over the river near Ballyshannon, and another between the lakes at Enniskillen. In the south-east of Ulster there was the Moyry Pass, the gateway to Ulster – known as the Gap of the North and said to have been defended by the mythological Cuchulainn. Moyry is the gorge in the hills between Dundalk and Newry through which the Slighe Mhidhluachra (57) ran, 'where the Irish might skip but the English could not go'. The importance of commanding these vantage-points, from a military standpoint, was obvious, and the

33

earlier neglect of forts in Ulster had severely handicapped the English army in the Nine Years War (15).

In the west of Ireland, the Shannon posed a formidable obstacle to an advancing army, although it could be forded at some points, and the country beyond was inhospitable and unfamiliar. Leinster was familiar territory, but even there, before the seventeenth century, the English were never at home in the mountainous and wooded areas of Wicklow from which the Irish chiefs launched frequent attacks on the Pale (27). The most favourable part of Ireland from the military point of view was south-east Munster, which had rich land, numerous towns and good communications.

The Irish were successful in resistance while they used the Fabian tactics suitable to their difficult terrain. The Normans settled in good land, and while the Irish avoided direct confrontation and stuck to forays from their mountains, woods and bogs and the use of guerrilla tactics, they could hope to compensate to some extent for their inferior military skill and equipment. O'Neill was successful as long as he stayed in Ulster; it was only when he moved out of there to Munster that he met defeat.

The English learned well the lesson taught them by O'Neill, and by 1610 a chain of garrisons and forts had been set up around the whole country. Twenty-six garrisons and thirty forts established government control throughout Ireland, and guarded trading towns and landing places from foreign invasion.

9. BATTLE SITES

This map is a reference point for the main battles or sieges in Irish history. So many different protagonists are found in Irish battles, including Irish, Norse, Normans, Old English, Scots, English, royalists, parliamentarians, Protestants and Catholics, and there is such a bewildering mixture of these elements, that it is impossible to convey more than a general indication of the main bodies on each side.

1014   **Clontarf:** Victory of the high-king, Brian Ború, over his challenger, Máel Mórda, king of Leinster, the Norse of Dublin and Norse allies from Orkney, Scandinavia, Iceland and Normandy (11).

1171   **Dublin:** Strongbow took Dublin in 1170, but in 1171 was

34

Irish v English --------- ⊞
Irish v Normans -------- ⊗
Parl. = Parliamentarians
Roy.= Royalists Or.=Orange

× Farsetmore
1567
Irish v Scots/Irish

⊞ Derry
Siege·1689
Stuart v Or.

Benburb
) 1646
Irish v Eng./Scots ×

⊗ Downpatrick
·1260

⊞ Yellow Ford
1598

Diamond 1795 × ×
Catholic v Or.

Clontibret
1595 ⊞

Moyry Pass
⊞ 1600
×
Faughart 1318
Scots/Irish v Norman

× Castlebar
(1798
French/United Irish v Govt.

Knockdoe
1504
×
Norman v Norman

Dungan's
Hill·1647 ×
Roy v Parl.

Drogheda
⊞ 1649

× The Boyne 1690-91
Stuart v Or.

Clontarf
1014 ×
Irish v Norse

1171
⊗

Athenry ·1316 ⊗

× Aughrim
1691
Stuart v Or.

●DUBLIN
[1534
Old Eng./Irish
v English

Rathmines
·1649
Roy. v Parl.

Dysert O'Dea
⊗ 1318

×
Arklow
1798
United Irish
v Govt.

⊞ Limerick
Siege 1690-91
Stuart v Or.

× Vinegar Hill
1798
United Irish v Govt.

Knocknanuss·1647
Roy. v Parl.
×

Pilltown
1462 ×
Norman v
Norman

⊗ Callann
1261

⊞ Kinsale
Siege· ⌐ 1601

W.Bromage

Miles   50   100   Km   80   160

9. Battle sites

35

threatened from the east by a fleet of 1,000 Norse under the displaced king of Dublin, Asgall, and from the west by a much larger army led by the high-king, Rory O'Connor. Instead of launching a united attack, the Norse attacked in May and were decisively defeated by the Normans. The high-king continued to build up his forces and besiege Dublin, but in September a surprise raid on his camp by a small Norman army resulted in a complete rout (12).

1260 Downpatrick: As part of the attempt to revive the O'Neill claim to the high-kingship, Brian O'Neill of Tirowen led an attack on Norman settlers in Down, and was defeated (14).

1261 Callann: In 1259, a royal grant of Desmond and Decies was made to John FitzThomas. This provoked a rising of the MacCarthys, who at the battle of Callann won a total victory over FitzThomas and the justiciar, and confirmed for a time their control of south-west Ireland (26).

1318 Dysert O'Dea: Contemporaneously with the Bruce invasion occurred the last stages in the war in Thomond between the native rulers, the O'Briens, and the Norman settlers, the de Clares. In May 1318 came the final confrontation, with a total victory for the O'Briens and a recovery of their kingship, which in 1540 became an earldom (14).

1318 Faughart: Total defeat of Edward Bruce and an army of Scots, native Irish and Norman rebels, by a Norman force led by John de Bermingham (14).

1462 Pilltown: Ireland was very largely Yorkist in sympathy during the Wars of the Roses, giving support to Richard, duke of York, when he fled from England. The only notable Lancastrian supporters were the Butlers, whose attempt to prolong the struggle led to their defeat at Pilltown in 1462 by a force led by Thomas, earl of Desmond, and their subsequent exile (26).

1504 Knockdoe: In August 1504 was fought the battle of Knockdoe between the Lord Deputy, the Great Earl of Kildare, and his son-in-law, Ulick Burke of Clanrickard, ostensibly because Burke was challenging the royal authority in Galway, but really because his increasing power was becoming a threat to the Kildare balance of power; Kildare was not prepared to countenance any rival. Kildare's army consisted of his own men (including galloglas), and the forces of his Ulster allies – including O'Neill, O'Donnell, Magennis, MacMahon, O'Hanlon, O'Reilly; from Connacht MacDermott, O'Farrell, O'Kelly and the Mayo Burkes; he also had the support of the great Pale families, including the Prestons. St Laurences and Plunketts (26). To set against this force, Ulick Burke had the support of the O'Briens of Thomond, the Macnamaras, the O'Carrolls and the O'Kennedys, and his own force of galloglas. The precise numbers cannot be estimated, but they were substantial with the Great Earl having a numerical advantage, and using, for the first time in an Irish battle, firearms. Kildare's victory was total, and smashed the power of the south-east Connacht/north-west Munster alliance.

1534 Dublin: In February 1534, Kildare was summoned to London and imprisoned in the Tower; his son and deputy, Thomas, Lord Offaly, on hearing a rumour of his death, led an unsuccessful rebellion in Dublin in which the Archbishop of Dublin was killed. Although Offaly took the city he was unable to take Dublin Castle. Under Sir William Skeffington, the new Lord Deputy, a large army arrived which suppressed the rebellion and in March 1535 took Offaly's Maynooth stronghold by the use of heavy cannon (26).

1567 Farsetmore: Shane O'Neill's attempts at territorial aggrandisement in Ulster continued until 1567, when they were ended by the battle of Farsetmore, brought about by his unsuccessful attack on the O'Donnells. The O'Donnells relied mainly on galloglas, while O'Neill had a force which largely comprised his own people, whom he had militarised over the years to compensate for the shortage of mercenaries (50).

1595 Clontibret: In May 1595, Marshal Sir Henry Bagenal set out to relieve the English outpost of Monaghan, under attack from Hugh O'Neill. He marched with 1,750 men to Monaghan, suffering some harrassment on the way. While returning he encountered several ambushes, culminating in a battle at Clontibret where severe losses were sustained. Only a relief force from Newry prevented total disaster (15).

1598 Yellow Ford: At the Yellow Ford, on the Blackwater, in July, Sir Henry Bagenal marched with about 5,000 men to relieve the Blackwater fort, and was defeated and killed in an ambush by an army led by O'Neill and O'Donnell (15).

1600   Moyry Pass: In September 1600, Lord Mountjoy, attempting to reach Armagh to establish a garrison, found the Moyry Pass barred by a series of trenches. Several attempts to break through resulted in serious losses by the English forces. Until later in the year when O'Neill chose to cease defending the pass, the English were unable to penetrate it (15).

1601   Kinsale: In September 1601, a Spanish force of less than 3,500 landed at Kinsale. Mountjoy began a siege of Kinsale with a force which by December had reached 7,500, by which time O'Neill and O'Donnell were threatening his position with an army of about 6,500. At the ensuing battle, Mountjoy secured a decisive victory which effectively ended the Nine Years War (15).

1646   Benburb: Owen Roe O'Neill, at the head of an army of about 5,000, largely formed of Gaelic Irish, defeated an army led by General Robert Monro, composed of Ulster planters, English and Scots, and numbering about 6,000, at Benburb in June. Monro suffered huge losses, largely as a result of O'Neill's superior tactics (16).

1647   Dungan's Hill: The leader of the Old English Catholic forces, Thomas Preston, besieged Trim in July, and in August, his army, which included Catholic Scots, was heavily defeated by the parliamentary commander, Michael Jones, at the nearby Dungan's Hill (16).

1647   Knocknanuss: With Dungan's Hill, Knocknanuss proved to be a death blow to the Confederation in Munster. In November 1647, Murrough O'Brien, Earl of Inchiquin, at the head of a parliamentary force, destroyed the Confederate army, which included a large number of Catholic Scots, under Lord Taaffe (16).

1649   Rathmines: In an effort to recover the royalist cause, after the execution of Charles I, the Marquess of Ormond marched on Dublin with his old enemy and new ally, Lord Inchiquin, who had changed sides. On August 2, they were defeated by the parliamentary leader, Michael Jones, at Rathmines, leaving the way clear for Cromwell to land at Dublin thirteen days later, without opposition (16).

1649   Drogheda: Drogheda proved to be Cromwell's first objective in Ireland; with a force of about 8,000 he besieged and took Drogheda, massacring all the soldiers and clergy found within the city, and causing the garrisons of Trim and Dundalk to flee without resistance (16).

1689   Derry: In March 1689, James II arrived from his French exile to attempt to establish a base in Ireland from which to regain his kingdom. On April 17 he began the siege of Derry, which lasted until July 30. During this period, despite near starvation, the Protestant inhabitants of the city maintained their defiance until a foodship, the 'Mountjoy', forced its way through a barrier on Lough Foyle to relieve the city (17, XII).

1690   The Boyne: William of Orange, with an army of about 36,000, including English, Scots, Dutch, Danes, Germans and Huguenots met James II, with an army mainly of Irish and French – numbering about 25,000, at the Boyne in July. William's victory opened the way to Dublin, led to James's flight and ultimately won the war (17).

1691   Aughrim: On July 12 a desperate attempt was made at Aughrim to halt William's general, Ginkel. About 20,000 men were on each side. Marquis de St Ruth, the French general, was killed and the Jacobite troops were routed (17).

1690–1   Limerick: A siege of Limerick in August 1690, by William, was repulsed and raised; after Aughrim a siege began led by Ginkel, from September 4 to October 3, when Lieutenant-General Sarsfield surrendered (17).

1795   Diamond: From the 1780s there were constant skirmishes between Ulster Catholics and Protestants competing for land. In 1795, in September, at the Diamond, in Armagh, in a battle between the Catholic 'Defenders' and the Protestant 'Peep O'Day Boys', over twenty Catholics were killed. The Protestant group founded the Orange Order after this incident (18, XII).

1798   Arklow: On June 9, an army of rebels numbering about 20,000, of whom only about 5,000 were armed, under the leadership of Anthony Perry and later of Father Michael Murphy, attacked Arklow. The town was defended by General Francis Needham, with 1,500 troops, mostly militia. Needham repulsed the insurgents effectively (19).

1798   Vinegar Hill: The Wexford insurgents established their headquarters at Vinegar Hill near Enniscorthy. On June 21 they

39

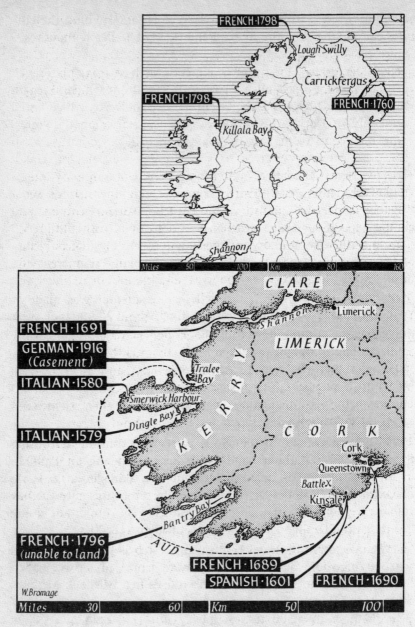

FRENCH·1798
Lough Swilly
Carrickfergus
FRENCH·1760
FRENCH·1798
Killala Bay
Shannon
Miles   50   100   Km   80   160

CLARE
FRENCH·1691
Shannon   Limerick
GERMAN·1916
(Casement)
LIMERICK
ITALIAN·1580
Tralee
Bay
Smerwick Harbour
Dingle Bay
ITALIAN·1579
K E R R Y
C O R K
Cork
Queenstown
Battle X
Kinsale
FRENCH·1796
(unable to land)
Bantry Bay
A U D
FRENCH·1689
SPANISH·1601
FRENCH·1690
W.Bromage
Miles   30   60   Km   50   100

10. *Continental interventions*

40

were heavily defeated there by a large force of militia and yeomanry – effectively ending the rebellion (19).

1798   Castlebar: On August 22, an expedition of 1,000 troops, led by the French General Humbert, landed at Killala. Marching east, Humbert met and defeated a force of yeomanry and militia before finally meeting defeat at Ballinamuck (10, 19).

10. CONTINENTAL INTERVENTIONS

There were two features common to all Continental military interventions in Irish affairs. Firstly, none of them was disinterested. Whether launched by France or the papacy, by Spain or Germany, all the expeditions were sent less to aid Ireland against England than to further the military, religious, political or ideological cause of the government which financed them. Secondly, they were all unsuccessful. The map shows the more important of these interventions, which are here described briefly.

1579   Dingle Bay: On July 18, Sir James Fitzmaurice, leader of the Munster rebellion, landed at Dingle with a force of about 300 soldiers, mainly Italians and Spaniards, financed by Pope Gregory XIII, who had declared Elizabeth deposed, and also privately by Philip II of Spain. This invasion was announced as a religious crusade, being accompanied by Spanish and English papal commissaries. Its defeat ended in Fitzmaurice's death (50).

1580   Smerwick: In September a papal force of 700 landed at Smerwick, led by Colonel San Joseph. Besieged in the fort of Dún-an-óir, this army was defeated by Lord Grey de Wilton, the earl of Ormond and Sir Walter Raleigh in November, and most of the Italians were massacred.

1601   Kinsale: On September 21, a Spanish force of less than 3,500 landed at Kinsale, led by Don Juan del Aguila. In December, a small force of Spaniards, under Pedro de Zubiar, landed in Castlehaven 30 miles to the west. They were defeated with the Irish at the battle of Kinsale (15).

1689   Kinsale: On 12 March 1689, James II landed at Kinsale with the Comte D'Avaux and a French fleet of 22 ships, ammunition, money, Irish, English and French officers, but no troops, to attempt unsuccessfully to regain his crown (17).

1690   Cork: In March, Louis XIV sent an army of 7,000 French infantry and some gunners under the Count de Lauzun to aid James, in exchange for 5,387 Irish soldiers under Lord Mountcashel, who went to France as part of the Wild Geese and later formed the nucleus of the Irish Brigade. These French troops were with James at the Boyne and were recalled shortly afterwards (17).

1691   Limerick: In May 1691, Marshal St Ruth arrived with arms and money, but no men, to aid the Jacobite army (17).

1760   Carrickfergus: In February a small invading force under the French commander Thurot, captured Carrickfergus. Securing only opposition locally, however, he withdrew and was defeated by a British force.

1796   Bantry Bay: Wolfe Tone, with a French fleet of 43 ships, and 15,000 well-armed troops led by Hoche, left Brest on 15 December 1796. Less than half the force ever came within sight of the coast, owing to bad weather, and no landing could be attempted even by those ships which had reached Bantry Bay. They returned to France (19).

1798   Killala Bay: On 22 August 1798, three French ships containing 1,100 men led by General Humbert landed in Killala Bay. Despite success at Castlebar, they were forced to surrender at Ballinamuck where they were defeated by Cornwallis (19).

1798   Lough Swilly: In September a French expedition of about 3,000 troops and with Wolfe Tone on board, sailed from Brest. Many of the ships were captured off the Donegal coast, Tone's ship, the Hoche, being forced to surrender in Lough Swilly. Tone was captured, condemned to death, and almost certainly committed suicide (19).

1916   Kerry: On April 20 a German ship containing arms and ammunition for the rebels arrived off the Kerry coast. Due to a communications failure, she found no contact awaiting her and when captured by a British ship and brought into Queenstown harbour two days later was scuttled by her captain (20).

1916   Tralee Bay: On April 20 Sir Roger Casement arrived in Tralee Bay, on Banna Strand, on a German submarine, was put ashore and captured (20).

42

During the ninth and tenth centuries, Europe was threatened militarily on all sides: from the south by Moslems, from the east by Magyars and from the north by the Vikings of Scandinavia.

The name 'Viking' probably comes from the Old Norse word *víkingr*, a sea-rover or pirate, and it is a generic term given to the Danish, Swedish and Norwegian farmers, fishermen and merchant sea-men who became raiders during the eighth century. The Vikings (often called Northmen or Norse), were great warriors and sea-farers; they used the same military tactics wherever they turned their attention. Their brilliantly designed ships were suitable for sailing on oceans, lakes or rivers. They launched raids along the coasts of the British Isles and Ireland, and elsewhere, including the Netherlands, France, Spain, North Africa, Greenland, America and as far east as Moscow and Constantinople. They penetrated the interior of each country by the use of inland waterways. Initially, they came only to pillage, but ultimately they stayed, were converted to local beliefs and absorbed into the community. Their trading expertise made them valuable members of society.

Vikings are first recorded in Ireland in 795, when they sacked Lambay Island. Sporadic raids continued until 832, when a new phase of systematic and large-scale raids began. The map shows the dates of the first raids. From this period the Vikings began to build fortified settlements throughout the country. Attracted by the wealth of the monasteries and churches, they plundered and ravaged them steadily. Many monks and scholars fled to the Continent, taking with them their most precious possessions.

The invaders established fleets on the main rivers and lakes. In the later part of the ninth century, and the beginning of the tenth, the Viking threat receded for a time, those living in Ireland establishing their settlements and becoming less aggressive, while those outside concentrated their attentions elsewhere. In 914 a new phase of attack and consolidation began with the arrival in Waterford of a great fleet. For much of the century the Vikings ravaged the country and founded new settlements. In the second half of the century, however, the Dál Cais, an east Clare sect, began its rise to power, culminating in Brian Ború's achievement of the high-kingship in 1002. Brian benefited from the serious weakening of

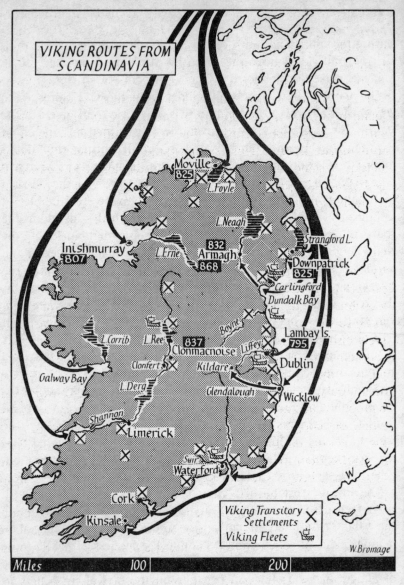

11. *Viking invasions*

Viking power which had been brought about by his predecessor as high-king, Malachy II, who had inflicted a number of defeats on them. In 1014, Brian broke the power of the Vikings permanently at Clontarf (9).

The Vikings continued to develop their role in the Irish community. Although the independent kingdoms which they had founded in Dublin, Waterford, Wexford, Cork and Limerick did not survive the Norman invasion, the towns continued to grow and to dominate internal and external trade. As a people, the Vikings quickly became fully absorbed into the religious and political life of Ireland, although their commercial interests kept them centred in their traditional locations in the coastal towns.

12. THE NORMAN INVASION ·

By 911, the Vikings, or Northmen, had established themselves so powerfully in a large area round the lower Seine, that the territory was formally granted to them as the Duchy of the Northmen – later to be called Normandy. They achieved a reputation as warriors in their disputes with their neighbours, and in 1016 were invited to southern Italy as mercenaries. By 1030 they had created a principality of their own at Aversa; in 1059 Pope Nicholas II granted them Sicily, Calabria and Apulia. In 1066, William, duke of Normandy, with only 5,000 men, took the crown of England by force. By 1166, when Dermot MacMurrough, in need of allies to restore him to his kingdom, outlined to Henry II and his barons the profits to be gained from involving themselves in Irish affairs, the Normans had established a strong kingdom in England and were firmly rooted in Scotland and Wales.

On 1 May 1169, Robert FitzStephen, Meiler FitzHenry and Robert de Barry, with 30 knights, 60 other horsemen and 300 archers, 'the flower of the youth of Wales', landed at Bannow Bay, in three ships. A contemporary chronicler, Robert Wace, described typical Norman landing tactics. First ashore were the archers, with bow bent and quiver ready, taking up a position on the beach ready for immediate action. Not until a reconnaissance had been completed and the all-clear given, would the men-at-arms, all in full equipment, be allowed to disembark with their horses. The cavalry would then ride inland through the screen of archers. Such tactics were typical

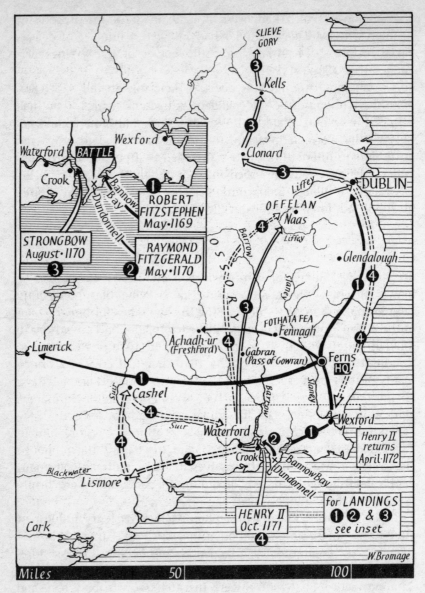

The map contains the following labels:

SLIEVE GORY

③ Kells

③

Clonard

③

Liffey

DUBLIN

OFFELAN
④ Naas
Liffey

Glendalough

④

①

④

③
FOTHATA FEA
Fennagh

Achadh-ur
(Freshford) ④

Gabran
(Pass of Gowran)

Slaney

Barrow

Ferns
HQ

④

Limerick

① Cashel

④

Suir

Suir
Waterford

④

Blackwater

Lismore

Cork

Barrow

Slaney

② Crook
× Dundonnell
Bannow Bay

① Wexford

Henry II
returns
April·1172

HENRY II
Oct. 1171
④

for LANDINGS
① ② & ③
see inset

W. Bromage

Inset:

Wexford

Waterford
BATTLE
Crook
×
Bannow Bay
Dundonnell

① ROBERT
FITZSTEPHEN
May·1169

STRONGBOW
August·1170
③

RAYMOND
FITZGERALD
May·1170
②

Miles   50   100

12. *The Norman invasion*

of the military sophistication of the Normans, which was to bring them to military victory in Ireland despite their inferior numerical strength (13).

On May 2 arrived Maurice de Prendergast with ten men-at-arms and about 200 archers, in two ships. The map shows the landing places of the main invading armies, and traces the more important invasion routes; it should be emphasised that only an indication of direction can be given – not precise itineraries.

The two Norman armies were joined by Dermot MacMurrough, with 500 men, and together they took Wexford. After resting at Ferns, the invading force, now about 3,000 strong with the addition of a number of Leinstermen and Norse from Wexford, launched an attack on Ossory, which met with success, despite a spirited defence. Successful expeditions were launched against Offelan and Omurethy (24). Another expedition into Ossory resulted in the defeat of MacGillapatrick at Achadh-ur. At this stage Prendergast seems to have lost heart in the enterprise and he attempted to return to Wales with his men. When prevented from doing so by MacMurrough, he allied himself with the king of Ossory and caused a great deal of trouble to his erstwhile allies before finally leaving the country.

At this stage the high-king, Rory O'Connor, showed unexpected strength in marching into Leinster and forcing MacMurrough to submit to him. He contented himself with taking hostages and exacting from MacMurrough a promise to bring no more foreigners into Ireland and to expel his Norman allies when Leinster should finally be subdued. This was to prove to be a promise which Mac-Murrough had neither the inclination nor the power to keep.

Late in 1169, two more ships arrived in Wexford, bearing Maurice FitzGerald, FitzStephen's halfbrother, with 10 knights, 30 mounted retainers and 100 archers. Shortly after this MacMurrough marched towards Dublin and secured the submission of the citizens. Meanwhile FitzStephen led an army to Limerick to attempt an attack on the high-king, but was forced back to Leinster.

In May 1170, Raymond FitzGerald (le Gros) arrived with 10 knights and 70 archers. Landing at Dundonnell, he there defeated the men of Waterford in battle, and awaited Strongbow, who arrived in August with 200 knights and 1,000 other troops, accompanied by Maurice de Prendergast, who had been persuaded to return. Up to his arrival, the invasion had been only partially successful; his intervention was to lead the Norman forces to military triumph. Richard FitzGilbert de Clare, called Earl of Striguil and popularly known as Strongbow, was a leading Welsh baron. It had been his original agreement with MacMurrough in 1168 to lend military support in exchange for the succession to the kingship of Leinster which laid the foundations for the Norman invasion and gave it its Welsh character. Landing at Crook, Strongbow and le Gros attacked and took Waterford. They then joined MacMurrough, who confirmed the alliance by giving his daughter to Strongbow in marriage. Together, they captured Dublin in September. Attacks were launched on Meath and on O'Rourke's territory, as far as Slieve Gory. MacMurrough then retired to his palace at Ferns, where he died the following year, and Strongbow spent the next year consolidating his military position. After MacMurrough's death the high-king besieged Dublin, but was defeated in a surprise attack in September and forced to retire (9).

By the autumn of 1171 Strongbow was master of Dublin, Waterford and Wexford. He was, however, uncomfortably aware that Henry II was intending to intervene and curb his power. Strongbow had already defied an order from Henry to return from Ireland, and had hoped to stave off his wrath by sending a message of loyalty. When Henry arrived in October at Crook with about 4,000 troops in 400 ships, he had two objectives – firstly to secure the submission of the Irish leaders and secondly to impose his authority on his own barons. He was successful in both his aims. He secured the submission of many of the Irish kings, including MacCarthy, O'Brien and O'Rourke. Although O'Connor and many of the northern kings refused to submit, the high-king's resistance was to prove temporary. At a council of Irish bishops in Cashel, fealty was sworn to Henry, and the Irish church was pledged to conform to the practices of the English church (V, 35). Henry restricted Strongbow's power in two ways. Although he granted Leinster to him, Dublin, Wexford and Waterford were removed from his jurisdiction. He also indicated his determination to control Strongbow's pretensions to power by appointing Hugh de Lacy justiciar and granting him Meath.

With these grants the conquest became a political reality. Although the military struggle was to continue for centuries, by 1172 the Normans were so strongly entrenched in the east and south-east of the country that there could no longer be any hope of their eventual expulsion. The next century was to prove to be a century of consolidation (13, 25).

13. NORMAN CONSOLIDATION

The contemporary historian, Giraldus Cambrensis, Gerald of Wales, says of the Irish that they 'pay no regard to castles, but use the woods as their strongholds and the marshes as their entrenchments'. The Normans, on the other hand, saw castle-building as a fundamental element in their military strategy. When they took over an area, instead of following the Irish practice of then devastating and abandoning the neighbourhood, they consolidated their position by the building of a castle. During the initial stages of the conquest of Ireland, these structures were not castles in the traditional sense, but motes, wooden buildings placed on mounds of earth, surrounded at the base by a ditch. Usually a stockade was constructed beside the mote. The map shows the distribution of motes, castles and walled towns throughout the country at the end of the thirteenth century. It can be seen that the motes are mainly concentrated in the east and centre of Ireland because they were built during the early stages of the Norman invasion. They were intended only as temporary structures, being easy to erect, and almost all of them were later replaced by stone castles. The Normans appreciated the necessity of ensuring rational distribution of their castles. They constructed them according to a pattern which aimed at close inter-communication and avoided building isolated castles.

Following the erection of stone castles came the development of surrounding communities. Around the castles were built houses and churches, and from these grew many of the towns of Ireland (68). The Vikings had established the main coastal towns; other towns had developed from major religious centres, but the main contribution to setting up towns came from the Normans. It is interesting to see the connection between the major castles on the map and many of the towns which grew round them, for example, Carrickfergus, Kildare, Nenagh, Athenry and Athlone. The walled towns marked on the map all had important castles and were either existing towns fortified by the Normans or new foundations.

The gradual incastellation of Ireland symbolised the steady

Greencastle

Carrickfergus

Dundrum

Dundalk
Greencastle

Ballymote
Carlingford

DROGHEDA

Roscommon
Trim
Randown
Athlone
Maynooth
DUBLIN
GALWAY
ATHENRY
Drunnagh

Clonmacnoise
Newcastle
Kildare
Black Castle
Roscrea
Carlow
Arklow
Nenagh

Ferns
LIMERICK

Kilkenny
Enniscorthy
Adare

Carrick
NEW
ROSS
WEXFORD

WATERFORD

CORK

Walled towns
Major castles
Motes

W. Bromage

Miles   50   100   Km   80   160

13. *Norman consolidation: late thirteenth century*

progress of the Normans in taking over the country. Despite setbacks, they had little difficulty in achieving rapid conquest. Their numerical inferiority was more than compensated for by their military sophistication. In battle they relied on mailed cavalry wielding long swords, skilled Welsh archers armed with the cross-bow and experienced Flemish infantry. Against these the Irish could pit only their inadequately clad infantry, who were as inferior in arms as in military strategy.

For the first century after the Norman invasion, the Irish fought a losing battle against the conquerors. In 1175 the Treaty of Windsor between Henry II and Rory O'Connor recognised Henry as lord of Ireland and O'Connor as king of Connacht. In 1177 Henry's son John was named 'dominus Hiberniae', lord of Ireland. Simultaneously Henry granted the kingdom of Desmond to Robert FitzStephen and Milo de Cogan and of Thomond to Philip de Braose, although he reserved the cities of Cork and Limerick to himself. De Braose was unsuccessful in implementing his grant, but FitzStephen and de Cogan captured a considerable area of land in the south, around Cork city.

In 1177 John de Courcy led a small army on Ulster and took a large part of the north-east, having defeated its king, MacDonlevy. He failed at any time, however, to penetrate beyond the Bann. Despite considerable native opposition he quickly built castles in Downpatrick, Dromore, Newry, Coleraine and Carrickfergus. During twenty-seven years as ruler of Ulidia, de Courcy founded monasteries, towns and castles and kept the peace.

In 1185 Prince John arrived in Ireland with an army of over 2,000; with him were Theobald Walter, his butler and founder of the Butler family, William de Burgo, founder of the Burke family, and Bertram de Verdon. To Walter John granted land in Clare, Offaly, Limerick and Tipperary; to de Burgo he granted land in Tipperary and Connacht; to de Verdon and Roger Pipard he granted land in Uriel. Walter failed to conquer Clare, but he set up the foundations for the later lordship of Ormond in Tipperary. De Burgo established himself in south Tipperary and his claim to Connacht was not taken up in that generation.

By 1200 the FitzGeralds had received grants of lands in Limerick and Kerry and were building up their Munster possessions at the expense of the MacCarthys.

King John operated on a principle of reducing or diluting the power of his barons in Ireland; he balanced grantees against each other and gave some concessions to the native Irish. In 1205 he confiscated de Courcy's territory and awarded it to the younger Hugh de Lacy as an earldom (though he was later to defeat de Lacy in battle). Throughout his reign he reduced liberties and he also made some grants to the native Irish, like that of Connacht to the O'Connors and Thomond to the O'Briens. He succeeded in altering the purely feudal nature of the Norman occupation by setting up a royal administration.

During the thirteenth century the Normans made continuous attacks on the territories remaining in native Irish hands. In 1235 Connacht was taken by Richard de Burgo, and throughout the country the Normans continued to advance and consolidate. They failed, however, in their attempts on Tirconnell and Tirowen. In Connacht the O'Connors kept the King's cantreds, later called Roscommon. During the second half of the thirteenth century, the native lords began a fight back which flared up in different parts of the country at different times. Connacht was constantly in a state of unrest from about 1280, Leinster from 1283, Meath from 1289. The underlying weakness of the Norman colony was to be strikingly demonstrated by the Bruce invasion in the early fourteenth century (14).

14. THE BRUCE INVASION

One effect of the Norman invasion was to show to Irish leaders the necessity for unity in the face of a common enemy. The growing acceptance of this was symbolised in 1263 when a number of Irish chiefs offered the crown of Ireland to King Haakon IV of Norway. Although Haakon's death prevented any follow-up to this, it showed that determination to fight back which from the mid-thirteenth century slowed up and even reversed the trend of the Norman advance. The fourteenth century was to see an even more concentrated struggle for control of the country.

In 1314 when the Scots under Robert Bruce decisively defeated the English at Bannockburn, Bruce was in a position to follow up his plan to set up a united Celtic kingdom, by providing a kingdom for his restless and ambitious brother Edward in Ireland. Before Edward's landing in May 1315, Robert had secured the support of

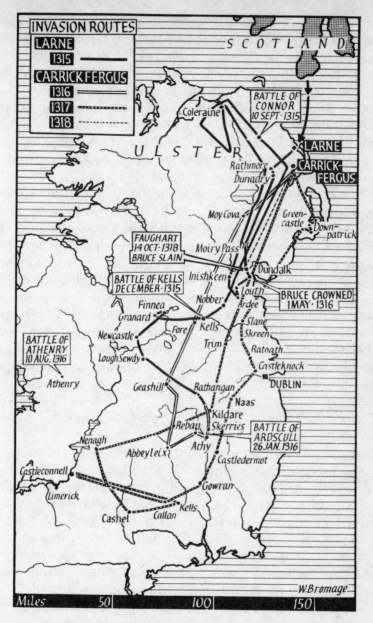

INVASION ROUTES
LARNE
1315 ────
CARRICK FERGUS
1316 ═══
1317 ∙∙∙∙∙∙
1318 ------

SCOTLAND

ULSTER

Coleraine

BATTLE OF
CONNOR
10 SEPT·1315

LARNE
CARRICK-
FERGUS

Rathmore
Dunadry

Moy Cova

Green-
castle
Down-
patrick

FAUGHART
14 OCT·1318
BRUCE SLAIN

Moiry Pass

Inishkeen

Dundalk

BATTLE OF KELLS
DECEMBER·1315

Nobber

Louth
Ardee

BRUCE CROWNED
1 MAY·1316

Finnea
Granard

Fore

Kells

Slane
Screen

Newcastle

Trim

Ratoath

BATTLE OF
ATHENRY
10 AUG·1316

Lough Sewdy

Castleknock

DUBLIN

Athenry

Geashill

Rathangan

Naas

Kildare
Skerries

Reban

BATTLE OF
ARDSCULL
26 JAN·1316

Nenagh

Abbeyleix

Athy

Castleconnell

Castledermot

Limerick

Gowran

Cashel

Callan

Kells

W.Bromage

Miles   50   100   150

14. *The Bruce invasion*

Irish chiefs for the venture and Edward and his 6,000 Scots troops were joined by O'Neill, O'Kane, O'Hanlon, O'Hagan and MacCartan. Marching south, they sacked Dundalk, Ardee and neighbouring towns. A gathering of 50,000 opposing forces, led by Richard de Burgo, Earl of Ulster, with Felim O'Connor and the Justiciar, Edmund Butler, proved abortive, since de Burgo insisted on meeting Bruce independently of Butler, with only 20,000 men. After no more than a brief skirmish, Bruce retreated to Coleraine, where he succeeded in persuading O'Connor to desert de Burgo, whom he defeated shortly afterwards at the battle of Connor.

Bruce now marched south again, taking Nobber and defeating Roger Mortimer, lord of Meath, at Kells. He was joined by many deserting Norman-Irish. He burned Granard, Finnea and Newcastle and advanced to Kildare, where at Ardscull he defeated Butler, Fitz-Thomas and Power.

In Ireland 1316 was a year of famine and disease, exacerbated by the devastation of war. Although the time was propitious for attacking Dublin, Bruce chose instead to return north, taking Athy, Reban, Lea, Geashill, Fore and the castle of Moy Cova on his way, and being crowned king of Ireland. He then besieged and took Carrickfergus, which he used from then onwards as his headquarters.

In this same year, Gaelic leaders were making simultaneous attacks on Norman power in Ireland. Aodh O'Donnell and Felim O'Connor had initial success in Connacht, supported by the O'Briens, O'Rourkes and other local chieftains. However, at Athenry in August, the de Burgos won a complete victory, which established permanently their pre-eminence in Connacht. The simultaneous attacks of the O'Mores, O'Tooles and O'Byrnes in Leix and Wicklow were inconclusive, but irritating to the Dublin government.

Robert Bruce arrived in Carrickfergus with a large army, to aid his brother; in February 1317 they set out to march south. On their route they devastated Downpatrick (where they destroyed the monastery), Greencastle, Slane, Skreen and Ratoath. In the latter area they were challenged unsuccessfully by the Earl of Ulster. Advancing to Castleknock, the Scots were discouraged by the defences of Dublin from attacking and instead they marched, leaving the usual legacy of destruction, through the south-east as far south as Cashel and as far west as Castleconnell, and back to Carrickfergus, from whence Robert returned to Scotland. Their progress had been virtually without incident, although it had inspired sporadic Gaelic risings in the south. Roger Mortimer, who had been appointed justiciar, had landed at Youghal in April with a large force, but had proffered no opposition to the Bruces.

During 1317 Mortimer concentrated on strengthening his position in the south, regaining conquered lands and making peace with Gaelic chiefs. Pope John XXII supported Edward II by excommunicating Bruce's allies. In 1318, in September, tired of inaction and intending another southern march, Bruce advanced on Dundalk, where he was defeated and killed by an army led by John de Bermingham and the Primate of Armagh.

With Bruce's death ended the dream of an independent Celtic kingdom – a dream which had brought so much economic and social disaster to Ireland. Nevertheless, his invasion had shown how vulnerable was the Norman colony and had prevented its exploitation by Edward II for the war against Scotland. Tactically, however, Bruce had shown little ability. He failed to consolidate his successes and contented himself with inflicting widespread devastation on the country he hoped to rule. Few even of his allies mourned his death.

15. THE NINE YEARS WAR

Queen Elizabeth was determined to anglicise Ireland and she proceeded steadily throughout her reign towards this objective. By the end of the sixteenth century Leinster, Munster and Connacht had been subdued and the Ulster lords, who had maintained almost total independence over the centuries, began to feel threatened. They were not prepared to see their lands subject to English law and administration and their power reduced. Their anxiety was exacerbated in 1591 by the government's completion of a surrender and re-grant treaty with the neighbouring MacMahons and MacKennas in Monaghan (50), on which from 1593 Hugh Maguire and Hugh O'Donnell began sporadic raids. In August 1594 they defeated an English army at the 'Ford of the Biscuits' and thereby declared themselves to be in open revolt.

Ulster was uniquely situated for such a rebellion. There were only three ways into the province, the Moyry Pass and the fords of the Erne. Hugh O'Neill, Earl of Tyrone, who joined the rebellion openly

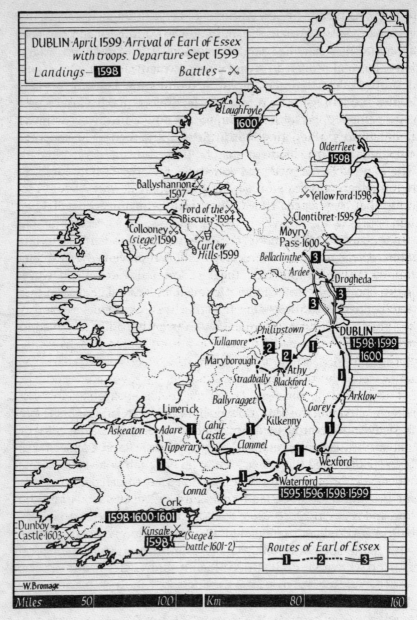

DUBLIN·April 1599·Arrival of Earl of Essex with troops. Departure Sept 1599

Landings— **1598**   Battles— ✕

Lough Foyle **1600**

Olderfleet **1598**

Ballyshannon 1597 ✕

Yellow Ford·1598 ✕

'Ford of the Biscuits'·1594 ✕

Clontibret·1595 ✕

Collooney (siege) 1599 ✕

Curlew Hills·1599 ✕

Moyry Pass·1600 ✕

Bellaclinthe **3**

Ardee

Drogheda **3**

3

Philipstown

Tullamore **2**

2

DUBLIN **1598·1599 1600**

Maryborough

Athy

Stradbally Blackford

1

Ballyragget

Kilkenny

Gorey

Arklow

Limerick

Cahir Castle

1

1

Askeaton

Adare

Tipperary

Clonmel

1

1

Wexford

1

1

1

Conna

Waterford **1595·1596·1598·1599**

Cork **1598·1600·1601**

Dunboy Castle·1603 ✕

Kinsale ✕ **1598** (Siege & battle·1601-2)

Routes of Earl of Essex
1 ----- **2** ═══ **3**

W. Bromage

Miles 50   100   Km   80   160

15. *The Nine Years War*

in 1595, had built up an efficient army with, in addition to his own men, Scottish mercenaries (galloglas) and Irish mercenaries (bonnachta). At Clontibret he defeated an English force under Sir Henry Bagenal (9) and in June he was proclaimed a traitor. Despite this, he made a truce with the government which lasted from October 1595 to April 1596, when peace was declared, all the rebels being pardoned. While paying lip-service to the peace, O'Neill was simultaneously negotiating for Spanish aid and securing the support of several southern chiefs.

In May 1597 the war was renewed, with the Dublin administration suffering defeats on the northern front at Ballyshannon so severe that they agreed to a further truce, which lasted until June 1598.

In August O'Neill and O'Donnell, with Ulster and Connacht troops, defeated Bagenal decisively at the Yellow Ford (9) and thus inspired risings throughout the country. Until April 1599, the English hesitated to make any move against the rebels, but in that month arrived Sir Robert Devereux, Earl of Essex and favourite of the queen, with an army of over 17,000. His first action was to march south, and on this march his army suffered from guerrilla attacks and disease, a combination which served to reduce his active troops by three quarters, although it proved uneventful in that it yielded no opportunity for the major engagements which he sought. Simultaneously O'Donnell was increasing the extent of his sway in Connacht, successfully besieging the O'Connor Sligo at Collooney and having a major victory over English forces at the Curlew Hills.

A second brief expedition by Essex had an equal lack of success and in August he marched to the Ford of Bellaclinthe where he made a truce with O'Neill which lasted until the end of 1599. Essex returned discredited to England and eventual execution.

By January 1600 O'Neill, having again made use of the period of truce to rearm and strengthen his army, descended on the barony of Delvin in Westmeath and ravaged it. In February 1600 arrived the fateful figure of Charles Blount, Lord Mountjoy, Lord Deputy, with an army 20,000 strong. With the aid of the new President of Munster, Sir George Carew, the Munster rising was soon crushed and Leinster and Connacht quieted. The English generals could now concentrate on the north. Many of the minor chiefs, scenting defeat, deserted O'Neill's cause and he found himself under severe pressure from new and reinforced garrisons. The English troops were gaining ground in their assaults on Ulster and at the Moyry Pass they succeeded in forcing the retreat of Irish troops (9). Meanwhile O'Neill anxiously awaited the promised troops from Spain for which he had so long been negotiating.

The Spaniards, when they eventually arrived, landed at Kinsale in September 1601 with a force of only 4,000 (10). O'Neill and O'Donnell marched to join them securing the help of O'Sullivan Beare and O'Driscoll of Kerry. At the battle of Kinsale, Mountjoy, with inferior numbers, won a decisive victory over the combined Spanish and Irish forces, after which O'Donnell fled to Spain. Some of the Irish made a last stand at Dunboy Castle, not yielding until 1603, and O'Neill, who had returned to Ulster to stand his own ground, eventually submitted to Mountjoy in March 1603.

O'Neill's submission symbolised the end of the Gaelic lordship and a new period of complete English domination of Ireland. Although the Irish had fought with determination and uncharacteristic unity, and although in O'Neill they had a leader of unusual diplomatic cunning and military ability, the English had proved to be indefatigable in warfare. Elizabeth succeeded where her predecessors had failed in securing the subjection of Ireland. Although she was normally parsimonious in her dealings with the country, she was sufficiently pragmatic to see the need in the 1590s for enough money and manpower to ensure victory. Over a seven year period more than a dozen massive troop landings were made (see map) and Elizabeth's best generals were sent to lead them. She appreciated the strategic importance of Ireland at a time of Continental warfare (10) and acted accordingly.

16. THE 1640s: THE CONFEDERATION AND CROMWELL

By the 1640s, Ireland was ripe for rebellion. During the reign of James I (1603–25) his plantations (51) had resulted in the dispossession of many Gaelic and Old English families and the introduction of a new colonial population to Ulster. With the accession of Charles I, the Catholic Old English hoped to reach an agreement with the king which would guarantee them secure possession of their lands and a measure of religious freedom. In 1627 an agreement

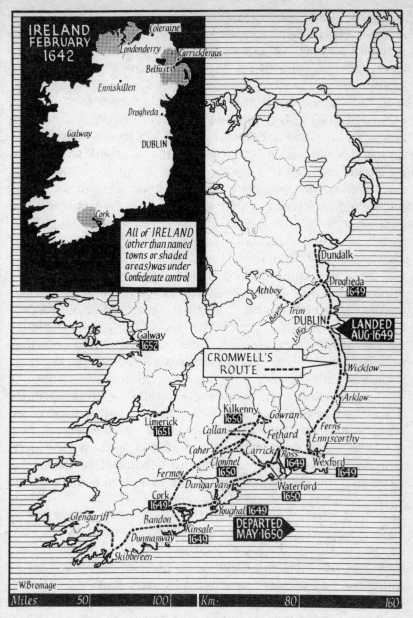

IRELAND FEBRUARY 1642

Coleraine
Londonderry
Carrickfergus
Belfast
Enniskillen
Drogheda
Galway
DUBLIN
Cork

All of IRELAND (other than named towns or shaded areas) was under Confederate control

Dundalk
Athboy
Drogheda 1649
Boyne
Trim
DUBLIN
Liffey
LANDED AUG·1649
Galway 1652
CROMWELL'S ROUTE - - - -
Wicklow
Arklow
Kilkenny 1650
Gowran
Callan
Fethard
Ferns
Limerick 1651
Caher
Carrick
Ross 1649
Enniscorthy
Fermoy
Clonmel 1650
Wexford 1649
Dungarvan
Waterford 1650
Cork 1649
Youghal 1649
DEPARTED MAY·1650
Glengariff
Bandon
Kinsale 1649
Dunmanway
Skibbereen

W.Bromage

| Miles | 50 | 100 | Km· | 80 | 160 |

16. *The 1640s: the Confederation and Cromwell*

was made by which, in exchange for £120,000 a number of concessions on land and religion known as the 'Graces' were to be made by the king. Although the money was paid, the Graces were never legally confirmed and this was to prove a serious source of discontent.

In 1633 a new Lord Deputy, Sir Thomas Wentworth (later Earl of Strafford) arrived in Ireland. His mission was to make Ireland economically viable and this he achieved in considerable measure through his encouragement of industry and mercantile shipping and the virtual eradication of piracy (IX, X). Despite these successes he succeeded in alienating almost every element in Irish society. His refusal to grant the Graces in their agreed form alienated the Catholic Irish and Old English, as did the threat to their lands posed by his abortive plans for a plantation in Connacht and Clare. Members of the Church of Ireland were affronted by his radical ecclesiastical reforms and his importation of Englishmen to fill important ecclesiastical offices. Scots dissenters suffered considerable harassment, which was all the more resented because of the degree of toleration then being extended unofficially to the Catholics. Additionally, he imposed heavy fines and confiscations upon those of the colonial settlers who had infringed the terms of the plantation settlement.

When Strafford's enemies finally united to bring about his downfall and execution, Charles attempted to placate the dissident elements in Ireland by a number of conciliatory measures, including the granting of many of the Graces and the abandonment of the proposed plantations. The increasing importance of the puritan elements in the Irish parliament, however, coupled with the attitude of the two powerful puritan Lords Justices, Sir William Parsons and Sir John Borlase, were to negate the effect of these measures, especially when in 1641 the prorogation of parliament by the Lords Justices prevented the legalisation of the Graces. Simultaneously, the severe rifts between Charles and his parliament became known in Ireland, and Charles's abortive secret negotiations with Ormond and the Earl of Antrim to secure military aid against parliament set the scene for a rebellion designed to take advantage of a confused situation.

In October 1641 a rising of native Irish began, led by Sir Felim O'Neill, Rory O'More and Lord Maguire. Although their plans to take Dublin failed, there was a widespread rising in Leinster and a take-over of the whole province of Ulster. The resulting bloodshed and destruction was considerable, although it was subsequently exaggerated out of all proportion by the Dublin government for propaganda purposes.

The government responded with panic and incompetence. Although they were promised reinforcements by the English parliament, the time-scale was too great to enable them to take effective action. By December 1641 many of the Old English, despising the inept administration and conscious of being viewed as disloyal because of their religion, joined with the Irish rebels, having secured from them a declaration of loyalty to the crown. The English parliament passed an act known as the 'Adventurers Act', which provided for the repayment in Irish land of money advanced to help quell the Irish rebellion (52). During the course of 1642 Scottish troops under General Monro arrived to aid in the suppression of the rebellion, but for a time the military success of the rebels continued. By February 1642, virtually all of the country was in their hands (see inset map) and later in the year they formalised matters by setting up a provisional government, with elected representatives, at Kilkenny. From that time they were known as 'the Confederate Catholics of Ireland', their motto being 'Pro Deo, pro rege, pro patria Hibernia unanimis'. Despite this lip-service to unity, there were deep divisions among the Confederates. The Old English were dominated by their loyalty to the king, and wished for a quick ending to the war, while the Irish were more concerned to recover lands long since confiscated, and wished to see the war through to the bitter end. This disunity was symbolised by the divided command which ensued when Owen Roe O'Neill and Thomas Preston, who had been serving abroad, arrived to aid the rebels; their mutual jealousy accentuated the divisions of the Confederates and prevented any real cooperation between them. O'Neill commanded a Gaelic-Irish army in Ulster and Preston an Old English army in Leinster.

Throughout the rest of the decade the Confederates were never again to equal their earlier successes. Ormond, on behalf of the king, succeeded in negotiating a truce with them in 1643 for one year, which was, however, rejected by the Ulster Protestants and the Munster parliamentarians under Murrough O'Brien, Lord

61

Inchiquin. The disunity among the Confederates was matched by the disunity among their enemies. The war was waged on a provincial rather than on a national basis.

In August 1645 a secret treaty was made between the Confederates and an emissary of King Charles, Lord Glamorgan, which promised full religious toleration in exchange for military support against the English parliament. When the treaty became known, however, Charles repudiated it, and negotiations came to an end, although Ormond continued to negotiate for peace.

In October 1645 the papal nuncio, Giovanni Battista Rinuccini arrived in Ireland; he was to destroy all Ormond's hopes of a peaceful settlement. He maintained an intransigent attitude, insisting that throughout areas under Confederate control the Catholic church should be the only established church, and he gave support to O'Neill and the extremist clerical party. O'Neill's victory at Benburb (9) against Monro gave hope of ultimate victory, but he failed to follow this success effectively. Ormond, under severe pressure in Dublin saw that he would have to surrender the city either to the Confederates or to the English parliament; it was to the latter that he transferred his command in June 1647 before leaving Ireland and going into exile.

Subsequently the Confederates had increasing setbacks. Preston was defeated at Dungan's Hill (9) and Inchiquin scored a great victory at Knocknanuss (9). The Confederates agreed to a truce in May 1648 and were excommunicated by Rinuccini, who, however, was discredited and left Ireland early in 1649. A realignment then occurred. Inchiquin adopted the royalist cause and with the Confederates agreed to serve the monarchy under Ormond, who returned from abroad. Despite some initial successes, Ormond's defeat at Rathmines by Jones (9) was to pave the way for the Cromwellian conquest.

Cromwell arrived in Ireland impatient to end the civil war, and determined to punish the rebels. His initial expedition was northwards, where after a successful siege of Drogheda his army massacred the garrison, the clergy and some of the townspeople. The Dundalk and Trim garrisons fled on hearing the news. He turned south where he met initial resistance from the Wexford garrison. The slaughter which again followed a successful siege broke the spirit of the resistance. The remainder of his campaign lasted only seven months, until May 1650. Before the end of 1649 he had taken several towns, including New Ross, Youghal, Cork, Kinsale and Bandon. His only check came in Waterford, which, with the help of reinforcements, successfully resisted his siege. In the spring he moved northwards again, taking Kilkenny and Clonmel. By May he felt sufficiently confident of victory to leave the rest of the conquest of Ireland to his lieutenants, Broghill in Munster, Coote in Ulster and Henry Ireton at the head of the main army. By May 1652 the last royalist stronghold, Galway, had surrendered and the whole country was subdued.

This subjugation had been bought at a heavy price. Famine and disease were rampant throughout the country. Ormond, Preston and Inchiquin had left Ireland in 1650; O'Neill was dead. The decade had seen the collapse of the rebellion due to the most characteristic Irish military and political failings. The members of the Confederacy were disunited in their objectives and military strategy; their leadership suffered from personal jealousies; they overestimated their resources. The intervention of Rinuccini exacerbated all the divisiveness of the situation and ruined any chance of an early alliance with Ormond. By the time Cromwell arrived in Ireland the war was already lost and resistance was half-hearted. In the face of a determined and disciplined enemy, defeat was inevitable.

17. STUART AND ORANGE

After the restoration of the monarchy in 1660, the Catholics in Ireland hoped not just for toleration but for preferential treatment. They felt threatened by the fast-expanding Protestant community, which was being swelled by a steady influx of dissenters (38). Under Charles II (1660–85), Catholics had a limited degree of toleration, but with the succession to the throne of James II, the position of Catholics changed dramatically. In Ireland a Catholic, Richard Talbot, Earl of Tyrconnell became commander of the army in 1685, and later chief governor. By 1688 Roman Catholics were dominant in the army, the administration, the judiciary and the town corporations and by the end of that year Protestant power in Ireland was seriously weakened. When William of Orange landed in England in November 1688 to relieve his father-in-law of his throne, James

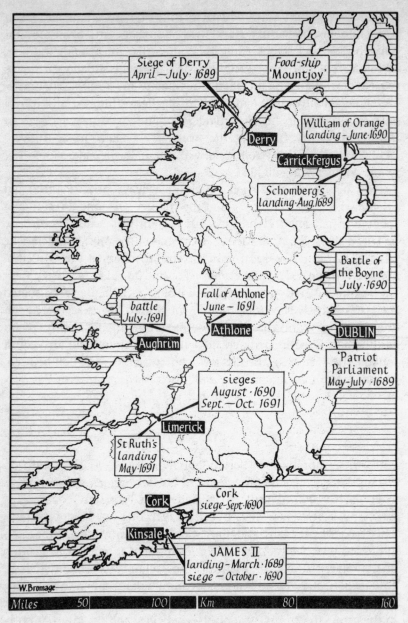

Siege of Derry
April — July · 1689

Food-ship
'Mountjoy'

William of Orange
landing — June · 1690

Derry

Carrickfergus

Schomberg's
landing · Aug. 1689

Battle of
the Boyne
July · 1690

Fall of Athlone
June — 1691

battle
July · 1691

Athlone

DUBLIN

Aughrim

'Patriot
Parliament
May-July · 1689

sieges
August · 1690
Sept. — Oct. 1691

Limerick

St Ruth's
landing
May · 1691

Cork
siege-Sept · 1690

Cork

Kinsale

JAMES II
landing — March · 1689
siege — October · 1690

W. Bromage

Miles   50   100   Km   80   160

17. *Stuart and Orange*

64

fled to France but soon left for Ireland which by now was for him a natural base from which to launch his counter-attack.

By the date of James's arrival in Ireland, in March 1689, only Londonderry and Enniskillen were in Protestant hands. Derry had repulsed an attempt of Tyrconnell's to garrison the town with a royal army the previous December when a group of apprentice boys, in a famous incident much heralded in Orange songs, shut the gates in the face of the garrison. It was James's first objective, and he besieged it in April. The townspeople proved indomitable in their resistance. Militarily unequipped to force the siege, the Jacobites hoped to starve the city into surrender. The inhabitants were 30,000 in number, and food supplies were low. Nevertheless, despite numerous deaths from starvation during the fifteen weeks of the siege, the city held out; on July 28 the foodship Mountjoy forced its way through the barriers built across the Foyle. This military and moral victory was of enormous significance in the campaign.

Shortly after this, Marshal Schomberg, William's general, landed near Belfast, besieged and took the Jacobite-held city of Carrickfergus and settled to await reinforcements. He concentrated on consolidating his position in Ulster and avoided any direct confrontation with James. Apart from holding a parliament in Dublin which repealed the Penal Laws against Catholics and in effect transferred almost all the land of Ireland back to Catholic ownership (29), James was inactive during this period. He remained in Dublin until William's arrival at Carrickfergus in June 1690, when he decided to confront him at the Boyne (9). William's triumph in this battle was a result of his military superiority, which was based both on strategy and on numbers.

James left Ireland with maximum speed, leaving Tyrconnell in command of the army. The Jacobite forces had to retreat westwards to Limerick where they were unsuccessfully besieged by William, who returned to England leaving General Ginkel in command. Ginkel took little action until June 1691, during which time the Williamite commander Marlborough had captured Cork and Kinsale, and the Jacobite commander St Ruth had landed with arms and supplies at Limerick. Ginkel took Athlone and Aughrim in June and July, after two military engagements in which famous stories of courage on the Jacobite side have provided inspiration to patriot Irish poets and musicians. The second siege of Limerick resulted in an early Jacobite surrender and the signing of the Treaty of Limerick (53).

An important military result of the defeat was the mass exodus of Jacobite officers and men to France. Eleven thousand sailed to France and joined the army, in which they formed the famous Irish Brigade. This Brigade and others formed in European armies were reinforced throughout the next century by thousands of Irishmen, known in song and legend as the Wild Geese.

The Stuart/Orange war is of particular contemporary interest in Ireland. The siege of Derry and the battle of the Boyne have a present-day significance enjoyed by no other military encounters in Ireland. They are being refought in the streets of Belfast and Derry in every clash between Catholic and Protestant; they are symbolised in every Orange parade.

18. THE IRISH MILITIA

After the defeat of the Jacobites in 1691, there was little active resistance remaining in Ireland. The military-minded left the country to fight in foreign armies – almost half a million Irishmen joined the French army alone between 1691 and 1791.

During the eighteenth century, however, indications of aggression emerged from secret societies formed by peasants throughout the country. This began largely because of resentment at the loss of common land to pasture for cattle raising, which was encouraged by the lifting in 1759 of restrictions on the export of Irish cattle to England (65). The Whiteboys were the most widespread of these groups, although the Hearts of Oak and the Hearts of Steel were also important. They were all concerned with local agrarian problems, and were swift and brutal in meting out their particular ideas of justice. In Ulster, peasant movements were dominated by sectarian land disputes – the Defenders being the main Catholic society and the Peep-O'-Day Boys the Protestant group – and later the nucleus of the Orange Order (XII).

Despite the lack of any other signs of military activity in the country, fears of invasion by France and Spain, coupled with agrarian crime and the absence of any militia led to the formation of a number of volunteer forces throughout the country. By 1783 the Volunteers had reached a strength of 100,000; they were unpaid

Part of LEITRIM and CAVAN

Ballinamore • Belturbet·2 • Cootehill·6
Killashandra·1
Carrick·2 • Cloone • Cavan·6
on Shannon • Mohill • Crossdoney·1

Coleraine·5
LONDON-DERRY **10**
ANTRIM **8**
DONEGAL **10** Strabane·5 Magherafelt·1 Carrickfergus·8
Ballyshannon·5 Omagh·1
TYRONE **10**
Manor Hamilton·1 Monaghan·3 ARMAGH **8** DOWN **12**
Sligo·3 LEITRIM **6** FERMANAGH **6** MONAGHAN **8** Newry·6
Ballina·1 SLIGO **6** Clones·1 Dundalk·9
MAYO **14** Carrick Carrick-macross·1 LOUTH **9**
on Shannon·2 CAVAN **6** Drogheda·8
Newport·2 Boyle·3 Kells·2
Castlebar·2 Elphin·1 Castlerea·2 Castle pollard·1 Navan·1 Balbriggan·1
ROSCOMMON **8** LONGFORD Trim·4
Roscommon·1 Mullingar·7 MEATH **8** DUBLIN **14**
GALWAY **10** WESTMEATH **6** Charlesfort·8
Tuam·1 Athlone·8 KILDARE
Galway·17 KING'S C[o] **5**
Kildare·5 Kilcullen·1 WICKLOW **6**
Parsonstown·7 QUEEN'S C[o] Ballitore·1
CLARE **6** Maryborough·6 **6** Carlow·4
TIPPERARY **10** CARLOW **5** WEXFORD **10**
Limerick·8 KILKENNY **8** Enniscorthy·1
LIMERICK **14** Cashel·8 New Ross·1 Wexford·6
Tralee·2 Charleville·6 Mitchelstown·7 Waterford·7 Taghmon·1
Dingle·2 Castleisland·1 Mallow·1 WATERFORD **8** Geneva·1
Killarney Millstreet·2 Midleton·2
&Rosscastle·3 Macroom·2 Youghal·10
KERRY **8** Cork·18 Cloyne·2
Dunmanway·2 CORK **24** CorkHarb[r]·4
Bantry·2 Kinsale·6 Spike Is.&
Skibbereen·2 Haulbowline Is.·5

Companies of Militia
drawn from each County···· **13**
The numbers of Companies
& where quartered··Mullingar·7

W.Bromage

Miles 50 100 Km 80 160

18. *The Irish Militia, 1794*

and equipped themselves with arms and uniforms. After the lapsing of the Continental military threats of the 70s and 80s, they turned their attentions to political reform (29). By the mid 80s, however, their influence was on the wane and they ceased to be a significant force in Irish politics.

In the early 1790s, alarmed by the French Revolution, fearing foreign invasion, but unwilling to risk a resurgence of Volunteer activity, the government determined to set up a proper militia. The force had a proposed complement of 16,000, and was virtually full-time, being composed mainly of Irish peasants and artisans, although there was a significant number of English non-commissioned officers. Officers were usually Protestant, although overall, Catholics were in a majority of about three to one.

As an aid to discipline, units were quartered away from the county of their origin, and these quarters were changed frequently. The map shows the distribution of militia companies in 1794 and the number raised in each county. It is interesting to see, for example, that although Dublin contributed fourteen companies, it quartered only one, while Cork, which contributed twenty-four, quartered seventy-one. The disruption caused by such companies in many rural communities was considerable.

In 1796, responding to doubts about the loyalty of the militia, the government set up a part-time yeomanry force of about 37,000, which was mainly made up of landlords and their own tenants, and was therefore largely Protestant.

When in 1798 the rising put both the yeomanry and the militia to the loyalty test, there appears to have been little difference in their performance. Allegations of brutality were made against both forces, and it is clear that the rebels received no mercy from their co-religionists (19).

Despite its loyalty, the militia did not survive long. In 1801 recruitment and re-enlistment were stopped, and in 1802 the force was disembodied. Although it was later re-embodied and survived until its eventual dissolution in 1816, the changes in policy caused a great deal of hardship to members of the militia. Many of them joined the British army, which had about 150,000 Irish recruits from 1793 to 1815. The army, like the yeomanry and the militia, was a useful source of employment for landless peasants.

The virtual disbandment of the Volunteers (18) and the consequent political frustrations felt by many of its members was a major reason for the formation of the United Irishmen. The French Revolution had had a considerable influence on Irish popular opinion, many elements of which wanted religious equality and radical extension of the franchise. Under the leadership of Theobald Wolfe Tone, the Society of United Irishmen was founded in Belfast in 1791, to pursue these policies. The society contained the rump of the Volunteers, mainly middle class. Other societies were founded throughout the country. The leadership included Lord Edward Fitzgerald, Thomas Addis Emmet, James Napper Tandy and Henry Joy McCracken.

Various government attempts at conciliation were ineffective. The outbreak of war between France and England and the suppression of the Volunteers in 1793 led to a hardening of attitude among the United Irishmen, many of whom favoured an alliance with France. By 1795 the society was pledged to republicanism. In 1796 the government introduced a number of repressive measures to attempt to prevent rebellion or invasion, including the suspension of *habeas corpus*. Tone had been exerting pressure on the French Directory to mount an invasion of Ireland and in December the unsuccessful Hoche expedition (10) was launched. Increasingly brutal attempts were made by the militia and the yeomanry alike to stamp out sedition. In Ulster, under General Lake, efforts were made to set the United Irishmen against the Orangemen, many of whom joined the yeomanry.

The continual pressure forced the society to plan for an early rebellion. However, government spies were effective and two months before the proposed date, many of the leaders, including Emmet, were arrested; Fitzgerald was captured later and died in prison.

Martial law was declared in late March and the brutality of the troops became worse. On May 23 the rebellion broke out. The United Irish leaders had planned a rebellion believing that they could count on an army of over a quarter of a million, of whom over 100,000 would be from Ulster. In the event, in the absence of the leadership and a central plan, risings broke out locally without coherence. The first risings were in Leinster, in Meath, Dublin,

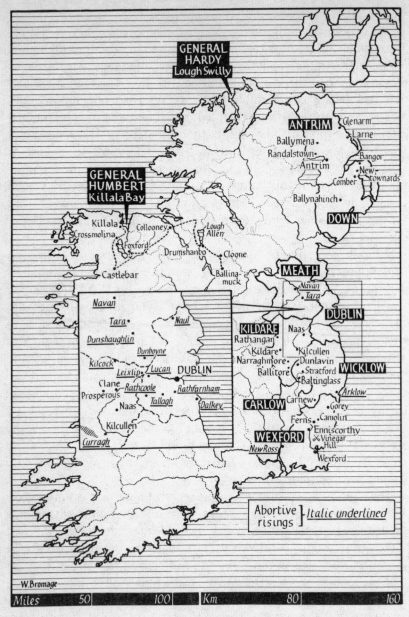

GENERAL
HARDY
Lough Swilly

GENERAL
HUMBERT
Killala Bay

ANTRIM
Glenarm
Larne
Ballymena
Randalstown
Antrim
Bangor
Comber
New-
townards
Ballynahinch
DOWN

Killala
Crossmolina
Collooney
Lough
Allen
Foxford
Drumshanto
Cloone
Castlebar
Ballina-
muck

MEATH
Navan
Tara
DUBLIN
KILDARE
Naas
Rathangan
Kilcullen
Kildare
Dunlavin
Narraghmore
Stratford
Ballitore
Baltinglass
WICKLOW
Arklow
Carnew
CARLOW
Gorey
Ferns
Camolin
Enniscorthy
×Vinegar
Hill
WEXFORD
New Ross
Wexford

Navan

Tara
Naul

Dunshaughlin
Dunboyne

Kilcock
Lucan
Leixlip
DUBLIN
Clane
Rathcoole
Rathfarnham
Prosperous
Naas
Tallagh
Dalkey
Kilcullen

Curragh

Abortive
risings
}
Italic underlined

W.Bromage

| Miles | 50 | 100 | Km | 80 | 160 |

19. *The 1798 rising*

Kildare, Carlow and Wicklow; many of these local actions proved abortive, but even those which achieved some success were quickly crushed. The most significant outbreak was in Wexford, where under the leadership of local clergy a rebellion lasted from May 25 to early July. The most notable incidents were the capture by the insurgents of Enniscorthy and all county Wexford except New Ross, but the beginning of the end came with the battle of Vinegar Hill where the rebels were defeated (9).

In Ulster there were two main risings, neither of which lasted more than a week; in Antrim about 6,000 men were led by McCracken, but they were quickly defeated. In Down Henry Munro led an army of about 7,000 in another unsuccessful action. Both McCracken and Munro were executed.

On August 23 the French landed at Killala Bay and had some shortlived success (10). In late September another unsuccessful French expedition with Tone on board entered Lough Swilly (10).

The rising was expensive in terms of lives and property. About 30,000 people died and over a million pounds worth of property was destroyed. After this rebellion and that of Robert Emmet in 1803 (III), the government extended its military precautions. Among defensive measures taken was the building of military roads, including one across the Dublin mountains. During the Napoleonic wars, increased fears of foreign invasion led to the widespread construction of Martello towers along the Irish coast-line.

Apart from the destruction of the revolutionary movement which resulted from the rising and the consequent discrediting of the ideals of fraternity and religious equality which had been at the base of its thinking, an immediate result of the rising was to increase pressure for Union between Ireland and Britain. The final irony was that the main result of the 1798 rising was to be to bind Ireland closer to Britain for more than another century.

20. THE 1916 RISING

In 1912 Prime Minister Asquith introduced the third Home Rule Bill for Ireland; this eventually received the royal assent in September 1914, although it was suspended for the duration of the war. By this time, however, the Ulster Unionists had established the Ulster Volunteers with the aim of using 'all means which may be found

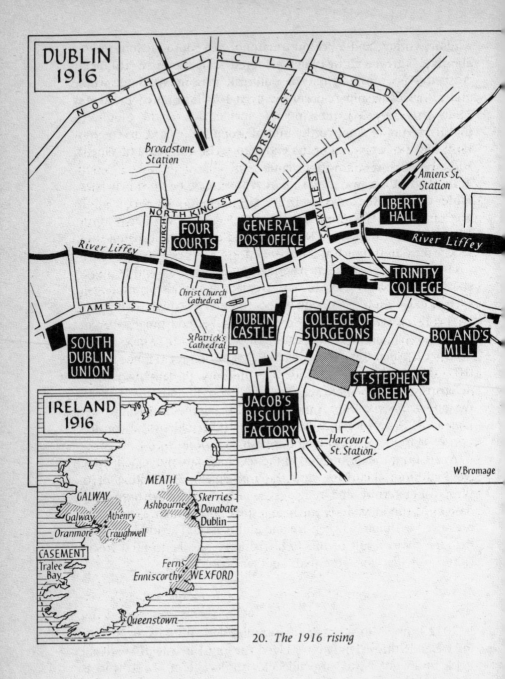

20. *The 1916 rising*

necessary to defeat the present conspiracy to set up a Home Rule Parliament in Ireland'. In 1913 Eoin MacNeill had founded the Irish Volunteers as a counter-force and John Redmond and his political party (31) had become closely involved with it. Both forces were armed with smuggled weapons.

With the outbreak of war Redmond urged the Irish Volunteers to join the British army. In protest, 10,000 men under MacNeill split the movement, retaining the name Irish Volunteers; the 170,000 who remained became the National Volunteers. Fears of conscription led to increased support for the Sinn Féin movement (31) and gave a fresh impetus to the activities of the secret society, the Irish Republican Brotherhood (I.R.B.), many of whose members were in key positions in the Irish Volunteers. I.R.B. leaders began talks with German leaders and both Sir Roger Casement and Joseph Plunkett visited Berlin. A rising was planned for Easter 1916, for which German arms were promised.

In April Casement left Germany in a submarine, which was to rendezvous with the German arms ship, the Aud. The plan failed and when Casement landed on Banna Strand on April 22 with two companions, they were captured. On the same day the Aud's captain scuttled her to avoid capture.

MacNeill then banned the Volunteer parade which had been intended to provide the opportunity for the rising. However the Military Council of the I.R.B. – Eamon Ceannt, Thomas Clarke, James Connolly, Sean MacDermott, Thomas MacDonagh, Patrick Pearse and Joseph Plunkett – decided to go ahead with the rising; on Monday April 24 at 12:00 the action began. There were five battalions in Dublin, MacDonagh being Brigade Commandant.

1st Battalion: Commandant Daly, at the head of about 120 men, occupied the Four Courts and set up barricades to the north and west.

2nd Battalion: Commandant MacDonagh occupied Jacob's Biscuit Factory, while some of his men joined the force in the General Post Office (GPO). They failed to follow the plan which required them to place barricades to the north-east.

3rd Battalion: Commandant de Valera, at the head of about 130 men, occupied Boland's Mill and Westland Row

	Railway Station, and set up barricades and outposts to the south, one being at Mount Street Bridge.
4th Battalion:	Commandant Ceannt, at the head of about 130 men, occupied the South Dublin Union Workhouse and set up outposts to the east and south-east.
5th Battalion:	Commandant Ashe led a force drawn from north county Dublin, which operated outside the city, took Skerries and Donabate and attacked Ashbourne.

The Irish Citizen Army split into three sections.

Section 1:	Commandant Mallin and Countess Markiewicz, at the head of about 100 men, occupied the College of Surgeons and set up outposts in Harcourt Street Station and at Portobello Canal Bridge.
Section 2:	About 50 men launched an abortive attack on Dublin Castle.
Section 3:	About 70 men joined with some 60 Volunteers, under the leadership of Connolly, Pearse and Plunkett and occupied the GPO.

When Pearse proclaimed an Irish Republic from the GPO, he styled himself President of the Provisional Government and Commandant-in-Chief of the army, with Connolly becoming Commandant-General of the Dublin districts.

Throughout the course of the insurrection, fewer than 2,000 insurgents were involved at any time in Dublin. There was little action elsewhere. In Leinster there were only Ashe's skirmishes outside the city and some activity in Wexford, led by Paul Galligan. In Galway, there were some unsuccessful skirmishes caused by the force of about 500–600 led by Liam Mellows.

From the start the rebellion had no chance of success. The insurgents were underarmed, and poor communications and contradictory orders had virtually restricted the action to Dublin and drastically reduced the number of men taking part. With the failure to take Dublin Castle, the strategy of the Dublin plan collapsed.

Although at the outbreak of the rebellion there were only 2,500 troops in Dublin, reinforcements brought in from other parts of Ireland and from England brought about a speedy conclusion to the insurrection. Pearse ordered a surrender on the 29th.

The casualties of the rising were about 500 deaths (300 civilians, 132 troops and police and 76 insurgents) and 2,500 injured (2,000 civilians, 400 troops and police and 120 insurgents). Sixteen of the rebels were executed, according to the following time-scale:

May 3 Thomas J. Clarke Thomas MacDonagh P. H. Pearse	*May 8* Eamonn Ceannt Cornelius Colbert Sean J. Heuston Michael Mallin
May 4 Edward Daly Michael O'Hanrahan William Pearse Joseph Mary Plunkett	*May 9* Thomas Kent *May 12* James Connolly Sean MacDermott
May 5 John MacBride	
	August 3 Sir Roger Casement

The executions were to rebound on the British government in the 1918 election, since they swung the sympathy of the electorate behind the revolutionaries rather than the constitutionalists (31,32). Another action which was to secure sympathy for the rebels was the arrest of about 3,000 men and women following the insurrection. Most of them were interned in prison camps in Britain, though many of them were released by the end of 1916. The appointment of the uncompromising Lord French as Viceroy in May 1918 alienated public opinion still further. He placed a number of revolutionary leaders under arrest, including de Valera, Arthur Griffith and Countess Markievicz, many of whom had been in prison from May 1916 until their release a year later. Their reimprisonment was extremely unpopular with the country as a whole. He also suppressed Sinn Féin, Cumann na mBan, the Volunteers and the Gaelic League. All these measures were to contribute directly to the sweeping victory of Sinn Féin in the election of December 1918.

75

In 1918 the Irish Volunteers, reorganised since the 1916 rebellion, were about 100,000 strong. There were divisions within the movement between those who though prepared to resist conscription by use of force hoped for a negotiated settlement of the claim to independence, and those who believed that only physical force could bring about separation from Britain.

The threat of conscription disappeared with the conclusion of the armistice in November 1918, and, coupled with the political success of Sinn Féin in the December election, led to a dwindling of the numbers of Irish Volunteers. Some of the physical force men took matters into their own hands: on 21 January 1919, under the leadership of Séan Treacy and Dan Breen, a handful of Tipperary Volunteers killed two Royal Irish Constabulary (R.I.C.) men in an ammunition raid at Soloheadbeg. Others followed suit and during 1919 sporadic arms raids and murders of policemen were carried out.

By the end of 1919 morale in the R.I.C. was low and numerical weakness was forcing the evacuation of outlying barracks. The British government encouraged the recruitment of ex-servicemen into the R.I.C. and by March 1920 these were beginning to arrive in Ireland. Inadequately trained and badly disciplined, these British recruits in the early days had not even a proper uniform. Their mixture of khaki and black outfits earned them the nickname of Black and Tans. They were joined in August by a force of ex-officers, known as the Auxiliary Division, R.I.C. They met terror with counter-terror, raids with reprisals. During 1920 and 1921 the violence and brutality escalated on both sides.

By June 1921 the Volunteers (by now commonly referred to as the Irish Republican Army) had only about 3,000 active members, matched against almost 40,000 troops, 12,500 R.I.C. and 1,500 Auxiliaries. While they could not hope to win a military victory, their pertinacity had finally convinced Lloyd George of the need to compromise. In July 1921 a truce was declared; treaty negotiations began in October (32).

During the two years of the war a number of popular heroes had emerged. Terence MacSwiney, Lord Mayor of Cork, had died on hunger strike in an English jail. Kevin Barry, an 18-year-old medical

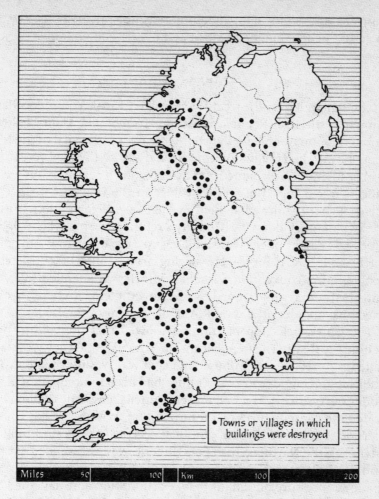

● Towns or villages in which
buildings were destroyed

| Miles | 50 | 100 | Km | 100 | 200 |

21. *The Anglo-Irish war: reprisals by British forces, September
1919–July 1921.* (Source: *E. Rumpf and A. C. Hepburn (1977)*
Nationalism and Socialism in twentieth century Ireland)

student, had been hanged for his part in a raid in which six soldiers
were killed. Michael Collins had waged a vicious war but had shown
fine leadership and great personal courage. The cost of the war had
been considerable and both sides had specialised in gratuitous destruction, for instance the burning of a large part of the centre of Cork
city by the Black and Tans and the burning by the I.R.A. of the

Customs House in Dublin and numerous fine private houses. More than 700 people had been killed and over 1,200 wounded.

22. THE CIVIL WAR

As the Dáil split over the treaty (32) so did the Irish Volunteers (later known as the Irish Republican Army). To men like Liam Mellows, Rory O'Connor and Liam Lynch, the treaty was a denial of the Irish republic they had fought for. On 7 January 1922, the final vote in the Dáil brought the acceptance of the treaty; one week later anti-treaty officers asked the Minister of Defence in the Provisional Government, Richard Mulcahy, to hold a general army convention. During the two months following Mulcahy's refusal, the split widened. The Free State Government were building up a separate army and police force while I.R.A. men were staging arms raids. On 26 March a general army convention assembled which was attended solely by anti-treaty men and banned by the government; it chose its own executive and declared the I.R.A. independent of the Dáil.

The general election of June 16 showed that the country was behind the treaty. The Republicans (or 'Irregulars', as they were later called) refused to compromise, and civil war was inevitable. A Republican force under Rory O'Connor had been in occupation of the Four Courts since April, their presence unchallenged by Collins, who feared the consequences of a confrontation. Within five days of the election, Sir Henry Wilson, who had accepted the post of military adviser to the Northern Irish government, was assassinated in London. Believing this to be the work of the I.R.A. the British government put pressure on Collins to take action; the same day, the Four Courts garrison seized General J. J. O'Connell of the Free State Army. On June 28, O'Connor having ignored an ultimatum to leave the Four Courts, the Republicans were besieged by Free State forces armed with British artillery. Before the Republicans surrendered, the Public Record Office, part of the Four Courts complex, was destroyed. Simultaneous fighting was going on in O'Connell Street, where Cathal Brugha and 63 others were killed, and there was over £5 million worth of damage. Fighting broke out in the country. The map shows how the I.R.A. divisions split, most Republican strength being in the south and west.

Within a month the 'Irregulars' had been forced back into what

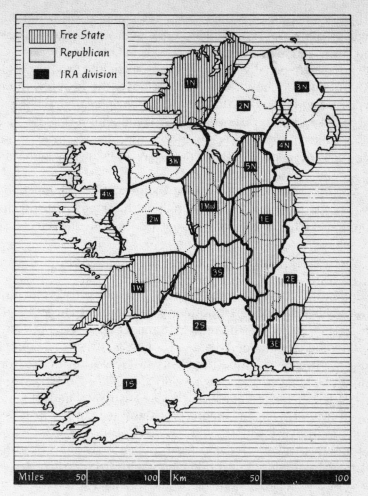

22. *The civil war: the allegiances of the I.R.A. divisions, 1922*
(Source: *F. O'Donoghue (1954)* No Other Law)

was known as the Republic of Munster, behind a line running from Limerick to Waterford. The Free State forces, led by Collins, showed initiative, skill and determination in their assault on their opponents and their large stock of British artillery gave them a tremendous advantage. By August 11 the Free State forces were in control of Munster and the Republicans had to fall back on the guerrilla tactics of the Anglo-Irish war.

The civil war was viciously and ruthlessly conducted by both sides, with assassinations, beatings, arms raids and arson common. In August, Collins was shot dead in a Cork ambush. In October the Free State army was given emergency powers to hold military courts and order the death penalty. 77 Republicans, including Erskine Childers, O'Connor and Mellows, were executed over the next few months. By April it was clear that the Republicans were beaten. Having tried and failed to secure a cease-fire on favourable terms, de Valera, whose military role had been very minor, but who was still their political leader, ordered them on 24 May 1923 to give up the struggle.

Casualties were about 600 killed and over 3,000 wounded; damage to property amounted to £30 million; the extent of the psychological damage to the young state was beyond calculation.

23. IRELAND AND THE SECOND WORLD WAR

Under Articles 6 and 7 of the Anglo-Irish treaty of 1921, the British government retained certain military and naval privileges in southern Ireland. However, in April 1938, under an agreement between the Chamberlain and de Valera governments, Britain renounced all these privileges, including her rights to the use of the Irish ports of Cobh, Berehaven and Lough Swilly.

This development made it practicable for Ireland to adopt a position of neutrality on the outbreak of the war between Britain and Germany. However, in regaining control of the ports, Ireland had also lost her rights to the defence of her coast line by Britain. Despite her strong political differences with Britain their ties were too strong to make it desirable to have Ireland used as a base for enemy attacks on Britain. De Valera maintained Ireland's precarious neutrality successfully throughout the war, although the country was divided on the issue. A number of Fine Gael politicians and supporters, notably James Dillon, were unhappy about neutrality and pressed for Irish involvement in support of Britain. Right-wing Republican elements favoured an alliance with Germany, and although most members of the Blue Shirt fascist movement (32) were pro-British, some believed that Ireland should become part of an alliance of Germany, Italy, Spain and Vichy France. In the event, a large number of southern Irishmen joined the British army, while only a handful joined the German army, although one of their

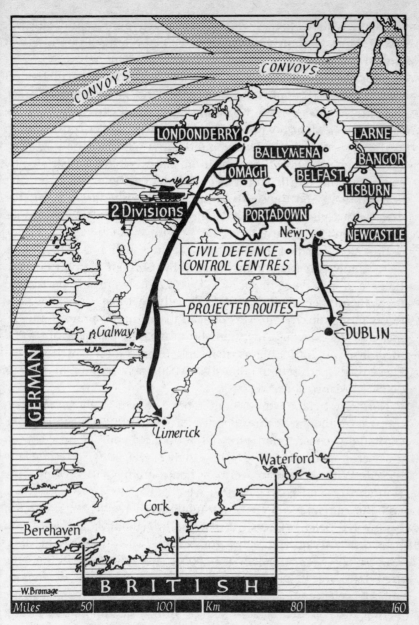

23. *Ireland and the second world war: invasion plans*

number, William Joyce, who had been active in Oswald Mosley's fascist movement for years, was to secure widespread notoriety as 'Lord Haw Haw'.

After the fall of France fears of a German invasion of Ireland became very real, both to the Irish and British governments, since the latter could not afford to allow such an occurrence. The map shows the German invasion plans which were under consideration at the time, and the British counter-plans. While the only realistic German plan involved invasion from the west, the British already controlled the north, and could take the east and west from her northern base and the south from the sea. While no invasion ever materialised, the existence of detailed plans indicate how precarious was Ireland's neutrality.

De Valera handled the diplomacy of the situation skilfully. There were some embarrassments caused by German support for the I.R.A. and also, later in the war, by American pressure on Ireland to abandon her neutrality. Additionally, without British defence forces to rely on, Ireland was obliged to attempt to provide an adequate defence against invasion. From an establishment of 26,000 men in 1940, including regular and reserve forces, by 1941 the figure had increased to almost 250,000 men serving in various defence organisations.

Northern Ireland, on the other hand, was actively involved in the war. Although mainly because of resistance from the Catholic community conscription was not introduced, the country was of great economic and military importance. Her ports were crucially placed. With France in German hands from 1940 onwards the Northern Ireland coastal waters were essential for ocean convoys, and the ports for repairs and supplies. There were also aircraft bases. Civil Defence forces were strong throughout the province, and had to face serious problems from air raids. In two raids in 1941, 850 people were killed and 10,000 made homeless. Despite the importance of Belfast shipyards and factories to the war effort, military defences such as anti-aircraft guns were totally inadequate. During the war Belfast built 10% of all British shipping, including 140 warships, and she also manufactured tanks and weapons. Additionally, from 1942, Northern Ireland became host to thousands of American troops.

IV Politics

Until after 13,000 B.C., Ireland, like the rest of Europe, was in the grip of the Ice Age. With Britain she was physically joined to the Continent – not becoming a separate entity until about 6,000 B.C. It was at about this period that the first immigrants arrived in Ireland – the Mesolithic people – who were primarily fishermen who spread from Scotland into northern Ireland in search of flint. They travelled by water as far south as Carlow. Some traces of the Mesolithic people remain, but our first extensive knowledge of our early ancestry comes with the advent of the New Stone Age and Neolithic man, who arrived about 3,000 B.C.

Neolithic men did not have their predecessors' predilection for water. Where Mesolithic men had used the seas, lakes and rivers of Ireland for food and transport, and had dwelt beside the waters, Neolithic men were farmers. They made effective tools from stone and learned to till the soil and raise domestic animals. The forests which covered most of the country, and which had discouraged the earlier inhabitants, with their primitive flint tools, from venturing away from the water, began to be cleared. During this period, the whole country was gradually inhabited by successive waves of settlers, some of whom brought with them a rich and mature culture. Their most spectacular legacies were megalithic ('built of great stones') tombs that are spread throughout Ireland in their thousands, the largest of them being the massive passage-graves, many of them ornately carved. Newgrange, the most famous of these, is over 40 feet high and covers nearly an acre of ground.

By about 2,000 B.C., yet another race had made their mark on Ireland. These were miners and metalworkers. Following them, in about 600 B.C., came a tribe who brought to Ireland an expertise in the use of iron, a well-defined religion, complex tribal laws, a war-like tradition and a Celtic language. Although by this date the Celts had established their dominance throughout central and western Europe, it was in Britain and Ireland that their influence was to prove most lasting. Until the Norman invasion, the pre-eminence of the Celts was not seriously challenged. By the first century B.C. they were fully established in Ireland.

The tribal law of the Celts, like their culture, was highly developed and was transmitted orally by professionals. Jurists interpreted and adjudicated on a most complex and rigid legal code, basically protective in character, which restricted a man to his own tribe and affected every aspect of his life. This tribal law, in modified form, functioned for as long as Gaelic Ireland maintained its identity – right up to the Tudor conquest (15). The other professionals, the poets, historians, druids and musicians travelled between tribes and were greatly honoured – a practice which also continued as an integral part of Gaelic society. It was not until the ruin of the Gaelic landed proprietors in the seventeenth century that the itinerant poets lost their position of privilege and prosperity (82).

The political divisions of Ireland at this time have been described elsewhere (1). Basically it was divided into 150 little kingdoms called *tuatha*. There were three classes within each kingdom, the professionals (*aos dána*), the free (*saor aicme*) and the unfree (*daor aicme*). The free owned land and cattle and were warriors, while the unfree were slaves. Many of the unfree were prisoners or descendants of prisoners, many of them having been captured from Roman Britain. During the fourth and fifth centuries, at the height of Irish raids of Britain (40), many prisoners were captured during raids abroad, including the boy who was later to become St Patrick.

From an early stage the *tuatha* were grouped into larger tribal organisations. In the north-west the main tribe was that of the Northern Uí Néill and in the north-east the Dál Riada, who had earlier been founders of a Scottish kingdom (40), while the Airgialla occupied a large part of the centre of Ulster. In Meath the Southern Uí Néill were the chief family and throughout Leinster the various branches of the Laigin alternated as overlords of the province. The Eóganacht dynasty in Munster was divided into a number of groups throughout the province and dominated all other tribes. In the west the Connachta were the chief tribe, among whom the Uí Fiachrach, Uí Briúin and Uí Maine were important. The Uí Briúin were powerful in Breffny. (See 24a for the position in the ninth century.)

The chief family of Ireland for over a thousand years were the Uí Néill, who were named after their ancestor, Niall of the Nine Hostages, whose legendary exploits at home and abroad gave his family a status which was exaggerated in poetic and genealogical tracts. The Uí Néill spread from Connacht over most of Ulster, Meath and Westmeath and launched continuous attacks on southern families; in doing so they destroyed the tribal structure of the country. Ultimately they claimed to be high-kings of Ireland, although at no time did they succeed in achieving recognition from all the other ruling families. Nevertheless, their claim to the high-kingship was not seriously challenged until the tenth century, when Brian Ború of the east Clare Dál Cais tribe overthrew the established order.

24. IRELAND BEFORE THE NORMANS

Brian Ború's struggle for the high-kingship of Ireland was symbolic of the political violence of the centuries before the Norman invasion, although it was typical of an age of centralisation. Devastating as had been the attacks of the Viking invaders, the internecine warfare of the Irish provincial kings proved equally disastrous. Brian overthrew the traditional Uí Néill high-kings; he spent almost thirty years justifying his claim to the title, and during his fourteen years as high-king most of his time was spent in resisting attempts to overthrow him in turn. Nevertheless, he remained strong enough to destroy the power of the Vikings permanently at Clontarf (9, 11). The only high-king to reign unchallenged after Brian was the man he had deposed, Malachy II, who died in 1022. After him, the annalists use the term co fresabra, 'with opposition' to describe the high-kings.

By this period there were five discernible major divisions of the country: Leinster, Meath, Munster, Connacht and a group of northern kingdoms. Munster was now ruled chiefly by the O'Briens (who had displaced the Eóganachta) at different times from Kincora, Killaloe and Limerick. The Eóganachta's traditional royal seat, Cashel was confirmed to the church in 1101. The O'Brien supremacy was

24a. *Ireland before the Normans: ninth century*

frequently challenged by the MacCarthys, who had several virtually independent lordships within the province.

Leinster was ruled by the MacMurroughs from Ferns and Connacht by the O'Connors. The O'Connors ruled from Tuam and later from Galway. The O'Rourkes ruled the sub-kingdom of Breffny. There were four main northern kingdoms. Tirowen was ruled from Aileach until its destruction, when the MacLochlainn kings moved to Tullahoge. Tirconnell was ruled mainly by the O'Donnells, Ulaidh by the MacDonlevys and Uriel by the O'Carrolls, who had displaced the Uí Briúin. Meath was still the territory of the southern

TIRCONNELL

TIROWEN

ULAIDH

•Aileach

•Tullahoge

URIEL

•Downpatrick

BREFENY

CONNACHT

MEATH

•Tuam

•Galway

OFFELAN

OFFALY

OMURLETHY

ORMOND

LEIX

LEINSTER

Kincora•

THOMOND

•Killaloe

Limerick•

•Cashel

OSSORY

•Ferns

M·U·N·S·T·E·R

DESMOND

DECIES

Boundaries of the
five sub-kingdoms

Boundaries of
tribal domains

Territories of the
Norsemen

W.Bromage

| Miles | 50 | 100 | Km | 80 | 160 |

24b. *Ireland before the Normans: twelfth century*

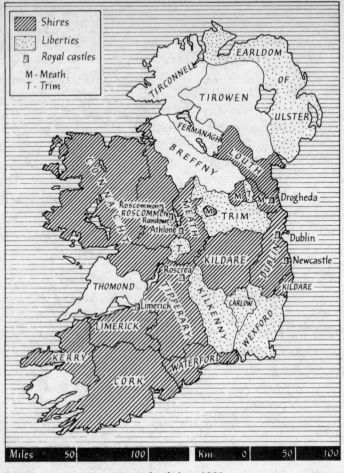

25. *Ireland* circa *1300*

Uí Néill, of whom the high-king Malachy II was a member; after his death they played no positive part in subsequent struggles for supremacy.

The high-kings with opposition during this period included Turloch O'Brien of Munster, who died in 1086, acknowledged as high-king in Leinster, Meath and Connacht. He was succeeded by his son Murcertach, who secured recognition as high-king from all the kingdoms of Ireland, although the O'Connors and MacLochlainns fought bitterly against him, and the latter ultimately defeated him

88

in 1103. Despite this, O'Brien was still able to preside at the first reforming synod (V) of the Irish church in 1110, as high-king.

Turloch O'Connor, king of Connacht, operating on the principle of 'divide and rule', conquered and politically divided Munster, Meath and Leinster, and in 1119 succeeded O'Brien as high-king, holding the position until his death in 1156. MacLochlainn, however, proved to be an indefatigable enemy, who resisted O'Connor pretensions throughout Turloch's reign, and after his death won the high-kingship from Turloch's son Rory. In 1166, however, MacLochlainn was killed after a rebellion of the sub-kings of the north in alliance with Rory O'Connor, and his ally Dermot MacMurrough was expelled from Leinster, with far-reaching consequences (12). O'Connor remained high-king in practice until the Norman invasion, and in theory until 1175, when he recognised Henry II as overlord of Ireland.

25. FOURTEENTH CENTURY IRELAND

No map can properly indicate the changing territorial divisions of Ireland during the later Middle Ages. The history of Ireland throughout the whole of this period is a story of changes in political power, a shifting kaleidoscope of Norman advance, Gaelic defeat, Gaelic resurgence and Norman retreat. This map is intended to show very generally the most important political divisions of the country at this period.

Broadly speaking, in pre-Tudor Ireland, although the country was theoretically organised according to English law and governed by a royal administration centred in Dublin, in fact the king's writ ran fully effectively only throughout a small portion of the country – the Pale – which varied dramatically in extent at different periods (27). In the territories surrounding the Pale, in Kilkenny, Carlow, Wexford and also in Waterford, Tipperary, Cork, Kerry and Limerick, which were administered by feudal lords, theoretically according to established law, the royal law was of varying effectiveness. In Galway and in the Earldom of Ulster, sporadic and usually ineffectual efforts were made to impose the law and in the rest of the country the immutable Brehon law held undisputed sway.

The map shows that part of Ireland had been shired (I) and that there were a number of liberties in existence. The concept of the liberty was borrowed from English law. During the Anglo-Saxon period many great landowners had been awarded royal dues from shire courts. The Normans extended this right by permitting feudal lords in their liberties to hold feudal courts and maintain considerable freedom from royal officialdom.

The same system pertained in Ireland. Within a liberty, the law was administered by officials of the lord and it was his writ, rather than the king's, which ran throughout his territory. Government in liberties was modelled on royal government, with seneschals acting as representatives of the lords, chancellors running the household and treasurers in charge of the exchequers. The law which was administered within the liberty was the law of the country as the lord chose to interpret it. Uniformity in the law was later to be increased by the use of charters and parliamentary statutes.

By the fourteenth century the Normans had established in Ireland basic political divisions which at least were to form the theoretical basis of those now existing. The situation shown on the map was to change, in minor ways, very rapidly. By 1350 changes included Kerry becoming a liberty under the Desmonds and Tipperary a liberty under the Ormonds (26), while Louth had been briefly a liberty under John de Bermingham. It was to take another 150 years to finish shaping the permanent political divisions of the country.

26. THE GREAT FAMILIES OF IRELAND

Despite the Normans' anxiety for territorial aggrandisement, they did not attempt to eradicate the native population. They were content to take over the good land, permitting the dispossessed Irish to remain in, or move to, poor land. Many Gaelic families therefore remained in their old territories, although keeping part of them only, while many others moved to neighbouring areas, often in turn driving out the indigenous native inhabitants.

The family names on the map are those which were most numerous or most powerful by the end of the middle ages. Despite the instability of life throughout Irish history, despite the invasions, wars, rebellions, famines, emigrations and plagues, many of these names have dominated the same areas for 500 or even 1,000 years. The O'Neills, O'Donnells, O'Connors, O'Briens and MacCarthys, for example, although their territories were progressively reduced, and although they gradually lost their political power, nevertheless

90

O'Doherty

MacDonnell

MacSweeney   O'Cahan

MacSweeney

O'DONNELL   O'NEILL

O'Neill   Earldom
Clanaboy   of
Ulster

McGuinness

Maguire

Barret   O'Dowd   O'Rourke   MacMahon
Burke   O'Connor
O'Hara

MacDonagh   O'Reilly   Plunket

O'Gara   MacDermot   O'Farrell   Preston

O'Malley

Costello   O'Connor
Don   Barnewall

O'Flaherty   O'Kelly   St.Laurence

Bermingham   O'Madden   O'Connor Earldom
Blake   O'Molloy   of
Burke   O'Dunn   Kildare   O'Toole
O'More   Fitzgerald   O'Byrne
O'Carroll

O'Brien   O'Kennedy
MacNamara   Butler   MacMurrogh
Burke   of
Ormond

Fitzmaurice   Fitzgerald
Earldom   Roche
of Desmond   Power
Fitzgerald

Mac Carthy
Mor   Barry
O'Sullivan
O'Sullivan   Mac-
Carthy
O'Driscoll

— W.Bromage —

Miles   50   100   Km   80   160

26. The great families of Ireland: late middle ages

91

appear in the histories of their various provinces throughout the whole of recorded Irish history.

By the sixteenth century, the Normans had made little progress in Ulster. The names which dominate the province are those of Gaelic chiefs; only the small territory of the Earldom of Ulster remained even nominally in Norman hands, and that had been progressively pushed back in extent by the growing territories of O'Neill Clanaboy and the O'Cahans and MacDonnells. In Connacht, mainly because of the tenacity and courage of the de Burgos, the Norman influence remained strong. Although theoretically more and more integrated with Gaelic society, the Connacht Normans maintained many of the qualities of their race. They intermarried with the Irish, adopted their customs and gaelicised their names, but they continued to consolidate their military achievements, secure their territories and capitalise on any opportunity for increasing their prosperity, from obtaining ecclesiastical appointments, of which they had locally a near monopoly, to acquiring commercial wealth. The Burkes of the fifteenth century still had much in common with their de Burgo forebears.

In Munster there were two great Norman families, the Fitzgeralds and the Butlers. The Fitzgeralds had built up the great palatine liberty of Desmond over most of the counties of Kerry, Limerick, Cork and Waterford. The Desmond earls were virtually independent of the Dublin administration, although they were defenders of the Yorkist cause. When in 1468 Thomas, Earl of Desmond was executed as a traitor for flouting the laws condemning fraternising with the Irish, by order of the lieutenant, Sir John Tiptoft, the Earls of Desmond cut themselves off completely and ruled what became virtually an independent state in the south until their downfall in 1583 (50). The great Irish families of Munster offered little resistance to the Fitzgeralds, but carved new territories for themselves from the lands of lesser chieftains. The MacCarthys and O'Sullivans moved south-west and established themselves in new territories.

In Leinster, where the Normans secured a lasting success, the great Irish families, the O'Tooles, O'Byrnes and MacMurroughs took over territory in Wicklow and Wexford, leaving Dublin and Kildare to the Normans. The liberty of Kildare was a late creation of Garret More, eighth Earl of Kildare, who brought his family to preeminence among all the families of Ireland. The territory covered land in Kildare, Meath and Wicklow. Effectively taking over the administration of the country with the virtual abdication of the Butlers and the alienation of the Desmonds, the house of Kildare kept this importance for sixty years, until its fall in 1534 after the rebellion of Silken Thomas.

The Butlers of Ormond had land extending across Tipperary and Kilkenny. Although they had been supreme among Norman lords during the thirteenth century, they were usually absentees during the fifteenth century. They made notable appearances only in aid of the fateful Lancastrian cause, and the senior line died out in 1515. In 1539, however, the head of a cadet branch of the family, Sir Piers Butler, was created Earl of Ormond. The Ormonds throughout Irish history were to show a devotion to the English monarchy which was rarely adequately appreciated. During the fifteenth century they suffered for their loyalty to the Lancastrians and during the seventeenth and eighteenth centuries they suffered for their loyalty to the Stuarts, although that loyalty was rewarded by the Restoration and the elevation of the earldom to a dukedom. Their devotion persisted despite numerous slights from monarchs who failed to see the importance of a loyalty remarkable in Britain and unique in Ireland.

27. THE PALE: 1300–1596

Until the final subjugation of Ireland in the sixteenth and seventeenth centuries, the extent of the Pale symbolised the state of English fortunes in Ireland. The limits of the Pale represented the limits of effective royal jurisdiction: outside was at best sporadic recognition of the royal authority, at worst anarchy or rebellion.

By the beginning of the fourteenth century, the limits of effective rule, in so far as they can be decisively delineated, stretched from Dundalk westwards to the Shannon, south to Athlone, east to Kildare and south to Waterford. Within that area, apart from the Leinster plateau from which it never proved possible to dislodge the main Irish families, the king's writ ran. Throughout the succeeding centuries, attempts were constantly made to maintain and consolidate and even extend the specifically English territory of the Pale. For example, one of Richard II's objectives in Ireland was to create a wholly English land, east of a line drawn from Dundalk

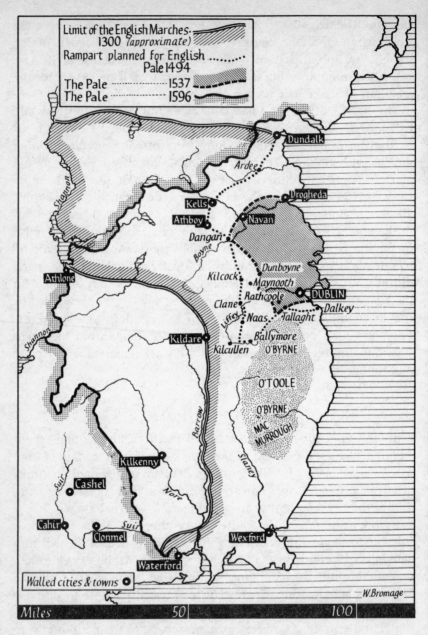

Limit of the English Marches.
1300 (approximate)
Rampart planned for English
Pale 1494
The Pale 1537
The Pale ———— 1596

Dundalk
Ardee
Kells
Athboy
Dangan
Navan
Drogheda
Boyne
Athlone
Shannon
Shannon
Dunboyne
Kilcock
Maynooth
Rathcoole
Clane
Liffey
Naas
Tallaght
DUBLIN
Dalkey
Kildare
Ballymore
Kilcullen
O'BYRNE
O'TOOLE
O'BYRNE
MAC
MURROUGH
Barrow
Kilkenny
Cashel
Nore
Suir
Cahir
Suir
Clonmel
Slaney
Wexford
Waterford

Walled cities & towns ⊙

W.Bromage

Miles 50 100

27. *The Pale*

94

to the Boyne and south to Waterford – a territory much smaller than that of the English marches of 1300, to be granted to wholly English colonists. In this he was, of course, unsuccessful. Seventy years later, in an unhappy recognition of the *status quo*, an Irish parliament of 1465, admitting that the only portion of true English land remaining consisted of the counties of Meath, Louth, Dublin and Kildare, ordered the Irish living therein 'to take English surnames, to go as English, and be sworn as lieges within a year'.

An act of 1494 provided for the construction of a ditch (never completed) around the whole area of the Pale, to prevent cattle raids; the precise area involved (see map) was delineated in the act.

By 1537 the Pale had shrunk to its smallest limits, and was described by Richard Stanihurst as 'cramperned and crouched into an odd corner of the country named Fingal, with a parcel of the King's land of Meath and the counties of Kildare and Louth'.

Despite occasional expressions of concern for the success of the Dublin administration, the interest of English kings in Ireland diminished throughout the late middle ages. From the last personal visit by an English king, that of the ill-fated Richard II in 1399, royal interest in Ireland was for the next century to be indirect. Ireland was to English kings either, at best a source of troops for the war with France, or at worst a source of danger to the crown, as, for example, when Richard of York found a secure base and widespread support in Ireland shortly after being attainted by the English parliament. During the reign of Henry VII this same adherence to the Yorkist cause showed itself in Irish support for the pretenders to the English throne, Lambert Simnel (1487) and Perkin Warbeck (1491).

The lack of English knowledge or understanding of Ireland is symbolised in the preamble of an Irish address to the English Council in 1537: 'Because the country called Leinster and the situation thereof is unknown to the King and his Council, it is to be understood that Leinster is the fifth part of Ireland.'

It is, however, from that period that the reassertion of English authority in Ireland began with the adoption of the policy of 'surrender and re-grant'. By the end of the century, confiscations had extended the boundary of the Pale to include Dublin, Wicklow, Wexford, Kilkenny, Carlow, Kildare, Leix, Offaly and Louth.

Parliaments were a thirteenth-century development throughout much of western Europe. Originally the name *parliamentum* was applied to formal sessions of courts, and probably parliament had a judicial purpose before its later financial preoccupation – taxation. The first recorded parliament in Ireland was in 1264.

The initial composition of parliament in Ireland was the council and lay and ecclesiastical magnates. By the second half of the thirteenth century, however, the pressure for representation before taxation was growing, and regularising of representation was introduced.

By the mid-fourteenth century a parliament always contained the following elements, the council, peers, bishops, clerical proctors and the commons, who were representatives of shires, liberties and towns.

A number of important acts of Irish parliaments of the middle ages included the following:

1366: The Statutes of Kilkenny were passed in 1366 to attempt to prevent any closer integration of the Norman colonists and the native Irish by forbidding the Normans to intermarry with the Irish or adopt their customs, speech and laws. These Statutes were largely unsuccessful.

1460: A parliament held at Drogheda in 1460 was summoned by Richard, duke of York, then attempting to gain the English crown from an Irish base. It declared Ireland independent of English laws, being subject only to its own parliament; it declared disloyalty to York to be treason and it ordered the striking of Ireland's own coinage.

1494: Poynings's parliament in 1494 attainted Garret More for treason, reduced the power of the Irish lords in the administration and passed a law called Poynings's Law, which stated that the Irish parliament could meet only with the permission of the king and his English council and their advance approval of the acts to be passed.

The parliaments of the Tudor period showed signs of independence and after the Reformation opposition from recusants became an increasingly important element. In 1536 the Reformation Parliament, with some disorganised opposition, passed the act which

Members of House of Commons

2 *from each County* 64
1 *from each Borough* 31
2 *from Dublin* 2
2 *from Cork* 2
1 *from Dublin University* 1

Coleraine
Londonderry
Carrickfergus
Dungannon
Belfast
Lisburn
Armagh
Downpatrick
Enniskillen
Newry
Sligo
Dundalk
Drogheda
Athlone
DUBLIN
Portarlington
Galway
Carlow
Ennis
Kilkenny
Limerick   Cashel
Clonmel   New Ross
Tralee   Wexford
Mallow   Waterford
Youghal   Dungarvan
Cork
Bandon   Kinsale

Cities & boroughs represented at WESTMINSTER

Not underlined ------ Created before 1603
Single underlining ---- Created 1603–1615
Double underlining ---- Created 1615–1692

W.Bromage

Miles   50   100   Km   80   160

28. *Irish representation at Westminster*

severed the relationship between the Irish church and the papacy. The 1541 parliament recognised Henry VIII as king of Ireland. During the sixteenth century few parliaments were held in Ireland; in the seventy years before 1613 there were only four.

From 1613–15 a parliament sat which in composition was different from its predecessors. Before 1536 no native Irish had sat in parliament. In 1613 18 of the 232 members of the commons were Irish and 100 of them Catholic. In the lords, 12 of the 36 were Catholic. This parliament demonstrated the resentment of the Old English, mostly Catholic, against the Dublin administration's handling of land titles and religious matters.

Map 28 shows the cities and boroughs which sent representatives to Westminster after the Act of Union of 1800 and indicates their parliamentary history. Of the 33 shown, 18 sent representatives to the Irish parliament during the Tudor period and 12 more during the reign of James I. Only three were later creations and even they were created during the seventeenth century. There was therefore a strong element of continuity of parliamentary representation.

29. THE IRISH PARLIAMENT: 1613–1800

Before the Stuart accession, thirty-four boroughs were in existence. Forty new boroughs were created to send representatives to the 1613 parliament, many totally unimportant and chosen solely to ensure Protestant representatives. This parliament achieved little other than the fomentation of ill-will between Catholics and Protestants.

During the Wentworth administration (16) clever use was made of the Irish parliament of 1634; many concessions were exacted without the representatives securing any compensatory measures. In the parliament of 1640, however, an alliance between the Catholics and Puritans was sufficient to contribute to the political destruction of Wentworth.

Parliament had little relevance again until after the Restoration, when it was reconvened from 1661 to 1666; in 1662 the Act of Settlement and in 1665 the Act of Explanation was passed.

Probably the most controversial parliament of the seventeenth century was the 'patriot parliament' of 1689. The Earl of Tyrconnel had succeeded in changing the representation from the boroughs

98

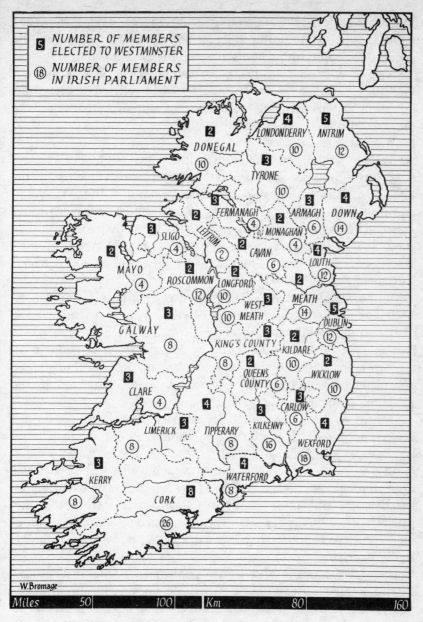

NUMBER OF MEMBERS
ELECTED TO WESTMINSTER
NUMBER OF MEMBERS
IN IRISH PARLIAMENT

29. *Irish parliamentary representation after 1613*

so that there was now a Catholic majority of 212 (17). This parliament, by means of the Bill of Attainder, confiscated the estates of over 2,000 people, although its acts were later nullified.

In 1692 William convened a parliament which was exclusively Protestant. Although scarcely enlightened in religious matters the members showed a new independence of attitude that was a forerunner of things to come and they made serious attempts to secure constitutional concessions.

In 1698 William Molyneux in his pamphlet *The case of Ireland's being bound by acts of parliament in England stated* argued that the English parliament had no right to make laws for Ireland. Simultaneously parliament was showing its resentment at English commercial pressures, culminating in the 1699 act on export of woollen goods (65). These were the two grievances which were to inspire the move of the Irish Protestants to press for an independent parliament.

The power of the Irish parliament was even further curtailed in 1720 when the 'Sixth of George I' was passed as a consequence of a constitutional dispute; this law affirmed the right of the English parliament to make laws binding on Ireland. Bitter resentment at this was symbolised in the writings of Swift (82) and his attacks on Ireland's inferior constitutional position were seminal in framing the political thought of later generations.

Pressure for electoral and constitutional reform continued to develop during the eighteenth century and in the 1770s obtained political expression from Henry Flood and his followers, who were known as the 'patriots'. The 'patriots' were not a new phenomenon; constitutional resistance from the Protestant ascendancy had manifested itself early in the eighteenth century. The setback that the patriot party experienced with the acceptance by Flood of government office was offset by the swift assumption of leadership by Henry Grattan.

The outbreak of the American War of Independence in 1775 and fear of foreign invasion from America's allies, France and Spain, led to the formation of the Volunteers (18). Their armed might although valuable to the government was resented when their influence turned to securing commercial and constitutional reforms. The trading concessions secured during 1779 and 1780 (65) were followed by a strong agitation for the repeal of Poynings's Law and the

Sixth of George I, a demand which was met by the new Whig government of 1782 which repealed the latter and considerably modified the former. This legislation, often known as 'the constitution of 1782', established the formal independence of the Irish parliament.

This independence lasted only eighteen years. It was a period of some economic prosperity. A number of religious restrictions were lifted and some half-hearted steps were taken towards parliamentary reform. But there was too much strife within parliament itself to enable it to present a united front towards those British political forces which were finally to undermine its independence. Fears that Ireland might eventually sever the connection with Britain altogether, coupled with the 1798 rising, stiffened the resolve of the British parliament to secure a union of the two countries. In 1800, largely due to the exertions of Lord Castlereagh, the Irish Chief Secretary, in persuading, bribing and intimidating, the Irish parliament voted for amalgamation.

The map shows the distribution of Irish representatives to the Irish parliament, and after the Act of Union, to Westminster. As can be seen, the Irish parliament had an enormous and uneven distribution; there were 300 members of the Irish House of Commons and only 100 Irish members at Westminster. Irish seats were most unrepresentative. A large majority of the boroughs were either rotten (virtually uninhabited) or pocket (landlord controlled).

30. O'CONNELL AND YOUNG IRELAND

Despite the modification of most of the penal laws during the 1780s and 1790s, at the beginning of the nineteenth century there were still a number of restrictions on Catholics. They could not sit in parliament, hold important state offices or obtain senior judicial, military or civil service posts. Hopes for the proposed equality known as Catholic Emancipation to follow the Act of Union proved to be misplaced.

Between the Union and 1823 all attempts to make the granting of Catholic Emancipation a political issue proved unsuccessful. It remained a middle class preoccupation until in 1823 Daniel O'Connell, an Irish lawyer, determined to make it a popular issue and with Richard Lalor Sheil democratised the Catholic Association. This organisation did not limit its aims to the securing of Catholic

1843
Estimated attendances
of over **100,000**

Sligo
Carrickmacross
Castlebar
Dundalk
Drogheda
Longford
Bellewstown
Roscommon
Clifden
Tuam
Mullingar
Trim Tara
Galway
Athlone
DUBLIN
Tullamore
Loughrea
The Curragh
Mountmellick
Baltinglass
Ennis
Nenagh
Kilkenny
Limerick
Cashel
Enniscorthy
Rathkeale
Charleville
Lismore
Mallow
Waterford
Cork
Skibbereen

W. Bromage
Miles 50 100

1848
Ballingarry
Mullinahone
Killenaule

30. *O'Connell and Young Ireland: the repeal meetings, 1843*
1848 rising

Emancipation, but also sought to represent the interests of the tenant farmers.

O'Connell set out to obtain a broadly based support, securing the active cooperation of the clergy and of Catholics of all classes. He introduced a Catholic Rent of a penny-a-month which was paid by all members, and which encouraged the active participation in the movement of even his poorest supporters; it also supplied the necessary financial backing for his organisation, at one stage bringing in several hundred pounds a week.

In 1826 the Catholic Association gave a practical demonstration of its political strength, when it intervened in the general election. In four constituencies, Monaghan, Louth, Westmeath and Waterford, the sitting members were defeated by candidates who supported Catholic Emancipation. The backing of the Association coupled with the local leadership of the clergy gave the tenant farmers the backing to flout their landlords' wishes and vote for the Association's candidates, despite the fact that voting was public and reprisals from landlords not uncommon.

An even more dramatic victory was achieved in 1828 when at a by-election in Clare, O'Connell stood for parliament and secured twice as many votes as the sitting member. Although the oath of allegiance prevented him from taking his seat, his success precipitated goverment action. The Prime Minister, Wellington, and the Home Secretary, Sir Robert Peel, were sufficiently pragmatic to see the necessity for yielding on this issue; and on 13 April 1829 the Catholic Relief Bill was passed. Although the simultaneous raising of the franchise qualification from forty shillings to ten pounds removed some of the gilt from the ginger-bread, and although the act really benefited only the middle and upper classes, it was nevertheless seen as a great popular victory.

For twelve years after the granting of emancipation O'Connell and his parliamentary followers supported the Whigs, who were in government for much of the period. A number of reforming measures were passed, including a reduction in tithes (V), extension of the franchise, the establishment of national education (75) and improvements in municipal government and the police force. With the return of a Conservative government in 1841, O'Connell decided to launch another popular agitation, this time for repeal of the union between Ireland and Britain. He followed much the same

103

strategy as that of the 1820s. He founded a National Repeal Association, collected a repeal rent and again obtained the support of local clergy. During the emancipation campaign he had held many mass meetings, but these he now vastly increased in number and scale. At the peak of the campaign in 1843 he held about forty of these meetings; the map shows the location of all those attended by over 100,000 people. It is significant that none of these was held in the area which is now Northern Ireland, and only one in the rest of Ulster.

O'Connell hoped to secure repeal by emphasising his massive popular support – but this was unrealistic. Catholic Emancipation had had the backing of many influential British politicians to whom repeal was totally unacceptable. Peel's government and the Whig opposition were united in implacable opposition to the demand. When in October 1843 the government banned a monster meeting at Clontarf, O'Connell, who was totally opposed to any risk of bloodshed, cancelled the meeting. For many supporters of the Repeal Association this was a sign of weakness and the movement gradually declined in effectiveness from then onwards, although it continued to do well in elections to parliament. Although there were thirty-nine repeal supporters in the 1847 parliament (29) – more than ever before – the writing was on the wall and popular support was fast diminishing. In 1847, with O'Connell's death the constitutional movement collapsed.

One element in the National Repeal Association which had early provided a fillip to its popularity, but was later to contribute to its destruction, was the Young Ireland movement. In 1842 a group of young men, Thomas Davis (82) Charles Gavan Duffy and John Blake Dillon founded *The Nation* newspaper to assist the repeal movement. They became disenchanted with O'Connell at an early stage, mainly due to differences over tactics, personal jealousies and their exaltation of unqualified nationalism, which O'Connell saw would inexorably lead them towards revolution. By 1844 they had split completely from O'Connell. With John Mitchel, Thomas Francis Meagher and William Smith O'Brien they became known as the Young Irelanders. Many of them made valuable contributions to Irish political thought. Davis wrote more articulately about the concept of non-sectarian Irish nationality than any of his predecessors. As a Protestant nationalist he occupied an important place in the tradition which stretched from Tone to Parnell. Gavan Duffy, who was later in his career Prime Minister of Victoria, produced valuable ideas on the tactics of parliamentary opposition, and a fringe member of the group, James Fintan Lalor, wrote trenchantly on the land question.

In practical politics, however, the Young Irelanders were incompetent. Frustration with the collapse of the repeal movement and with the wretched condition of the country after the famine led them to decide on rebellion in 1848; this was to prove more farcical even than Emmet's rising. The map shows the locations of the rebellion which petered out ineffectually due to inadequate leadership and non-existent planning.

Their rebellion was opposed by the back-bone of the repeal movement, the clergy and the middle classes and it effectively discredited the whole repeal issue. Not until Isaac Butt in 1870 began the Home Rule campaign did repeal of the union again become a respectable constitutional issue.

31. IRISH REPRESENTATION AT WESTMINSTER: 1800–1918

Until the passing of the Catholic Relief Bill in 1829 (30) there was no organised Irish party at Westminster. Most Irish members were an integral part of one of the two main parties. With O'Connell's entry into the House of Commons the nucleus of a distinctively Irish party was formed, although the drastic cut in the electorate (from over 100,000 to 16,000) resulting from the disenfranchising of the forty shilling freeholders severely restricted its support.

In his first decade in parliament, O'Connell supported the Whigs, wholeheartedly allying himself with them between 1835 and 1841. Although the Irish reforms of the government fell short of those promised, O'Connell made allowances for their weakness. His support had been sufficiently valuable to them to secure certain concessions which otherwise might not have been granted.

With the return of a Conservative government in 1841 O'Connell espoused the cause of repeal much more actively. In 1847 of the Irish members returned 39% were identifiable as being supporters of repeal, but with O'Connell's death and the collapse of the movement, the organisation of a united Irish party ceased.

The next significant development for the Irish at Westminster came with the tenant-right movement, which had as its aim the

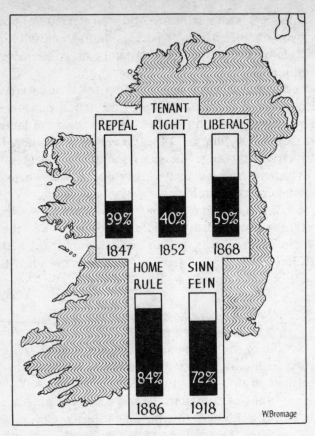

REPEAL 39% 1847

TENANT RIGHT 40% 1852

LIBERALS 59% 1868

HOME RULE 84% 1886

SINN FEIN 72% 1918

W.Bromage

31. *Irish representation at Westminster, 1800–1918*

legalising throughout Ireland of the Ulster Custom (VII). In the general election of 1852, with an electorate increased in 1850 from 61,000 to 165,000, over 40 of the Irish members elected subscribed to these principles and in alliance with the Whigs, Peelites and radicals defeated the Derby government. In the next ministry, Aberdeen's, two leading members of the party, Sadleir and Keogh, accepted office, and thus compromised the independence of the party and destroyed its unity. By the end of the decade the party was virtually no longer in existence.

There was little coherence among the Irish members at Westminster from then onwards. With improved economic circumstances, and with the Catholic clergy supporting the political *status quo*, popular enthusiasm for any movements towards independence was conspicuously lacking. It was necessary to find the right issue and the right leader. The Fenian movement (III, 47) did not believe in the virtues of constitutional agitation and worked outside parliament.

In 1870 a Protestant barrister, Isaac Butt, a Conservative who nevertheless believed that Ireland was being misgoverned, founded a Home Government Association. He saw Ireland's salvation in self-government by the middle and upper classes. This Association was non-sectarian and initially had only one aim: the establishment of an Irish parliament. When it extended its aims to include land and educational reform it began to score some successes in by-elections. In 1874 the Home Rule League, as it was now called, won 59 seats. Significantly it won only two in Ulster – both in Cavan. There was still a need to gain popular support and the need for charismatic leadership was obvious. It was answered by the emergence of Charles Stewart Parnell, who became leader in 1880. In 1879 he had become president of the Land League (47, 56) and this gave him a solid base of popular support with which to ally his parliamentary party. Parnell's party had supported the Conservatives in the 1885 election, but Gladstone's conversion to Home Rule caused him to combine with the Liberals to defeat the Conservative government and in 1886 allow Gladstone to form a government. Gladstone's first Home Rule bill was narrowly defeated in 1886 and at the ensuing general election the Liberals lost power. Liberal Unionists won 78 seats and supported the Conservatives.

The alliance between the Home Rule party and the Gladstonian Liberals continued until the O'Shea divorce action in 1890, in which Parnell was named as co-respondent, split the Irish party. By 1891 Parnell was dead and the party which his skill and leadership had built up over a decade to form a disciplined and effective unit had become permanently divided. Although the party continued to be a major force in Irish politics for the next 27 years, it never recovered its former importance, although it continued to win an impressive number of seats. In the 1892 election the Irish party lent its support to Gladstone to enable him to form a ministry and in 1893 he introduced the second Home Rule bill. It passed the Commons but was defeated in the Lords. With Gladstone's resignation in 1894 and Rosebery's assumption of the prime ministership, the alliance began to falter. In 1895 the government resigned and the ensuing election proved a triumph for the Unionists who remained in office until 1906.

The split which had occurred over Parnell's leadership after the divorce case did not end with his death. During the 1890s the Irish party was concerned with its own battles and many of its supporters turned from party politics to cultural movements like the Gaelic League (76) or more extreme movements like Sinn Féin or the Irish Republican Brotherhood. When the Liberals returned to power in 1906 the prospects for home rule looked brighter, and after the 1910 election the Irish party under John Redmond held the balance of power. In 1914, Asquith's Home Rule Bill was passed, although it was suspended for the duration of the war.

The Irish party under Parnell had been the focal point of Irish political action. Despite Redmond's achievements in the House of Commons, his activities were becoming almost incidental to the main area of Irish political activity. The I.R.B., which had developed from the Fenian movement, was gaining strength and the Gaelic Athletic Association, founded in 1884, came more and more under I.R.B. influence in the late nineteenth and early twentieth centuries. The Gaelic League, although solely committed to cultural nationalism, was also to prove to be an influence on revolutionary separatist movements. Political expression was given by Sinn Féin, founded in 1905 by Arthur Griffith, which was committed to political independence and economic prosperity. Although Griffith did not support revolution he capitalised on the public sympathy arising from the 1916 rebellion and in the 1918 general election the reconstructed Sinn Féin party under de Valera crushed the Irish Parliamentary Party.

Although Ireland did not secure independence officially until 1921, 1918 saw the end of effective Irish representation at Westminster since the Sinn Féin members refused to take their seats.

32. TWENTIETH-CENTURY POLITICAL AFFILIATIONS

Sinn Féin won 73 seats in the December 1918 Westminster elections, the Irish Party 6 and the Unionists 26. All 105 were invited to take their seats in an independent national assembly, Dáil Éireann, on 21 January 1919. Only Sinn Féin members accepted, and of them only 28 were free to attend. This group declared a republic, agreed a constitution and a programme of social and economic reform and appointed delegates to the Peace Conference (they were never allowed to participate). Coincidentally, on the same day, the Anglo-Irish war began (21).

In April 1919 de Valera, on the run from prison, was elected President, with Griffith his deputy and Minister for Home Affairs and Collins at Finance. The new executive set out to establish a republican infrastructure throughout the country, with alternative courts, police and other institutions, a task that was carried out with considerable success. The British hold over Irish institutions was further weakened by Sinn Féin's success in the 1920 local elections. Lloyd George's Government of Ireland Act (1920), which gave very limited powers to parliaments representing the six north-eastern and 26 other counties, was rejected by Sinn Féin and accepted by the Unionists. Elections under this Act were held in May 1921; Sinn Féin was returned unopposed throughout the south and formed the second Dáil. In July 1921 de Valera agreed to a truce.

From October to December 1921 treaty negotiations were held in London. The leading members of the British delegation were Lloyd George, Austen Chamberlain and Lord Birkenhead. Arthur Griffith led the Irish delegation, among whom were Michael Collins and Erskine Childers. The treaty was signed on December 6 and it approved the setting up of an Irish Free State with dominion status. It stipulated, however, that an oath of allegiance to the crown should remain obligatory on Irish legislators. It was mainly this that led to the split which led to civil war.

The Dáil debated the treaty until January 7 when it was approved by only 64 votes to 57. Those in favour of it argued that it offered, in Collins's words, the 'freedom to achieve freedom'. De Valera led the anti-treaty side and when he lost the deciding vote resigned as President of the Dáil. Griffith succeeded him and Collins was appointed Chairman of the Provisional Government set up under the Government of Ireland Act of 1920. The Provisional Government went to the electorate in the 26 counties of southern Ireland and won a decisive victory over the anti-treaty party, then known as the Republicans. Concurrently with the split in the Dáil had come a split in the Irish Volunteers, the anti-treaty party of which broke away from Dáil control (22).

The general election of 16 June 1922 showed a clear majority for

ELECTION	JUNE 1922	SEPT 1923	JUNE 1927	SEPT 1927	MARCH 1932	JAN 1933	JULY 1937	JUNE 1938	JUN 194
DÁIL	3RD	4TH	5TH	6TH	7TH	8TH	9TH	10TH	11T
No OF SEATS	128	153	153	153	153	153	138	138	138
GOVERN-MENT	PRO-TREATY	C na nG	C na nG	C na nG	FF	FF	FF	FF	FF

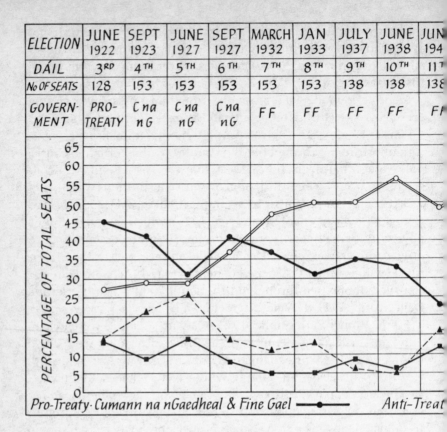

32a. Dáil Éireann general elections, 1922–77

the treaty; 12 days later the civil war broke out. Within two months the Free State government had lost two outstanding leaders, with the death of Griffith from a cerebral haemorrhage on August 12 and of Collins in an ambush ten days later. The new head of government was W. T. Cosgrave, with Kevin O'Higgins at Home Affairs and Richard Mulcahy at Defence; they proved to be as effective and ruthless as their predecessors in crushing their opponents. By April 1923 the Republicans were defeated. De Valera, who had not taken an active role in the war, although he had supported and encouraged the Republicans, ordered a cease-fire in May.

The bitterness engendered by the events of the civil war have coloured Irish politics for half a century. It caused a polarisation of attitudes which has determined the choice of political affiliations.

MAY 1944	FEB 1948	MAY 1951	MAY 1954	MARCH 1957	OCT 1961	APRIL 1965	JUNE 1969	FEB 1973	JUNE 1977
12TH	13TH	14TH	15TH	16TH	17TH	18TH	19TH	20TH	21ST
138	147	147	147	147	144	144	144	144	148
FF	FG INTER-PARTY	FF	FG INTER PARTY	FF	FF	FF	FF	NATL. COALITION	FF

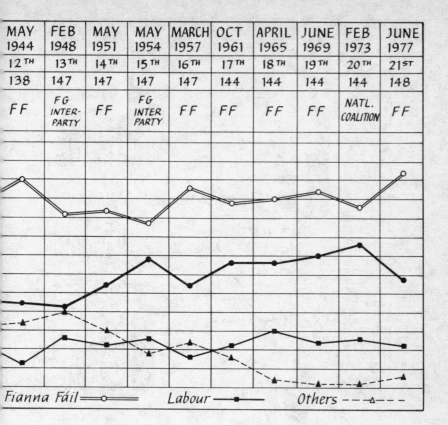

Fianna Fáil ═══○═══   Labour ──■──   Others ──△──

The main differences between the two main parties have been historical, not founded on policy, although there has been a discernible difference between them in their attitudes to foreign policy. The followers of de Valera, including Fianna Fáil, have consistently followed a more anti-British line than those of Cosgrave, including Fine Gael.

The Free Staters first set up a political party called Cumann na nGaedheal in 1923, which from 1933 was called Fine Gael. The Republicans were not represented in the Dáil until 1927; although 44 members of a new Sinn Féin party had been elected in 1923, they did not take their seats. In 1926 de Valera split from Sinn Féin and founded the Fianna Fáil party. Having won 44 seats in the fifth Dáil the members agreed to take the oath of allegiance.

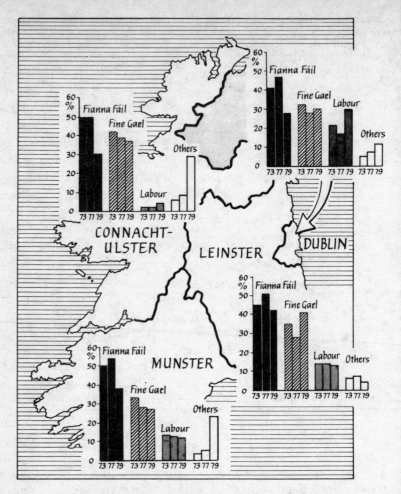

32b. *Distribution of first preference votes, 1973–9*

By 1932 they had formed a government. The Cumann na nGaed-heal government had ruled for a decade and had succeeded in establishing the credibility of Ireland as an independent country under a responsible government. De Valera soon proved himself to be a pragmatist. He had come to power pledged to economic self-sufficiency. During the early 1930s he waged an economic war with Britain, which was initiated by the Irish government's refusal to pay the land annuities still owing from the land acts (56). This proved very expensive for Ireland, being especially disastrous for agriculture, and in 1938 de Valera was obliged to compromise by making a trade agreement with Britain. On the other hand the trade war enabled him to protect infant industries which gave some employment and perhaps checked emigration.

A feature of Irish politics during the 1930s was the problem which both major parties had with extremist groups. When Fine Gael was formed in 1933 it included Cumann na nGaedheal, the Farmers' Party and General Eoin O'Duffy's Fascist Blue Shirt movement. O'Duffy was elected president of Fine Gael but was later asked to resign and was succeeded by Cosgrave. The Blue Shirts had a brief period of notoriety before O'Duffy disappeared to Spain with a small force to aid General Franco in the Spanish Civil War.

Simultaneously Fianna Fáil was being embarrassed by its erstwhile allies in the I.R.A. During the 1920s the I.R.A. had become a military organisation and during the early 30s assassinations and sporadic fighting increased. De Valera dealt with this situation, again pragmatically, by setting up a military tribunal and declaring the I.R.A. an illegal organisation.

From first taking office in 1932 until 1973, Fianna Fáil were out of office for only six years, and appeared to have established themselves as the natural governing party. The only other large party, Fine Gael, had failed to make the required breakthrough, and the Labour party had not succeeded in increasing their level of electoral support. However, long-discussed plans for coalition came to fruition early in 1973, when Fine Gael and Labour formed a National Coalition party which successfully fought a snap general election in February.

An interesting feature emphasised by the graph is the decline of the smaller parties, of which there have been a large number over the period of independence. Important among these was Clann na Talmhan, the Farmers' Party, which won fourteen seats in 1943, eleven in 1944, and a handful in succeeding elections until it went out of existence in the early 1960s. Clann na Poblachta was a new Republican party founded in 1947 with a policy of ending partition and creating a separate Irish currency. After initial success in 1948, when it won ten seats, it secured only two in 1951. Since 1965 the system has become three- rather than multi-party.

The success of the National Coalition of Fine Gael and Labour in 1973 was largely due to its emphasis on social and economic policies, an emphasis which ironically was probably mainly responsible for Fianna Fáil's landslide victory in 1977. Despite the importance of the Northern Ireland crisis there was evidence that the electorate seemed at last to be sloughing off the legacy of the civil war. Ireland's increasingly youthful electorate may intensify this trend, as should the supra-national demands of E.E.C. membership (49). Whether the hold of the two major parties will be weakened in consequence, enabling other parties to seize the electoral initiative, remains to be seen.

33. GOVERNMENT IN IRELAND

The Irish Republic, *de facto* since 1937, has a president as head of state, elected for seven years by the whole electorate. The president is empowered (on the recommendation of the house of representatives, the Dáil) to appoint the prime minister (taoiseach), sign laws, and invoke the judgement of the supreme court on the legality of bills: he is also supreme commander of the armed forces.

The Irish parliament (oireachtas) consists of the president and two houses, the Dáil, comprising 148 members elected by adult suffrage according to a system of proportional representation, and the Senate (Seanad Éireann) comprising 60 members, 11 nominated by the taoiseach and 49 elected to represent the universities, culture and education, labour, industry and public administration, and the social services. The Senate can delay legislation passed by the Dáil for a maximum of ninety days.

Since the foundation of the Irish Free State there have been a number of electoral acts which have served to increase the number of constituencies and decrease the number of members per constituency. In 1923 the majority of constituencies had between five and nine members; under the Electoral Acts of 1969 and 1974, the majority have only three members, each representing about 14,000 electors. This change was brought about largely because smaller parties have tended to be more successful in constituencies with more members. Under the present system of proportional representation, using the single transferable vote, it is difficult for any party to secure an absolute majority; governments have usually had to rely on the support of smaller parties or independents. For this reason Fianna Fáil attempted unsuccessfully in a referendum in

114

DONEGAL
5

NORTHERN
IRELAND

SLIGO-
LEITRIM
3

CAVAN-
MONAGHAN
5

LOUTH
3

EAST
MAYO

WEST-
MAYO

ROSCOMMON
-LEITRIM
3

LONGFORD-
WESTMEATH
4

MEATH
4

A

CMAYO
3

WEST
GALWAY
4

EAST
GALWAY
4

LAOIS-
OFFALY
5

KILDARE
3

B
C
F
D
E

WICKLOW
3

CLARE
3

NORTH
TIPPERARY
3

CARLOW-
KILKENNY
5

EAST
LIMERICK
4

WEST 3

SOUTH
TIPPERARY
4

WEXFORD
4

NORTH
KERRY
3

NORTH-EAST
CORK
4

WATERFORD
4

SOUTH-
KERRY
3

MID-
CORK
5

SOUTH WEST
CORK 3

CORK CITY 5

W.Bromage

DUBLIN			
A North County	3	D South County	3
B West County	3	E Dun Laoghaire	4
C Mid County	3	F Dublin City	27

Miles 50   100   Km   80   160

33. *Government in Ireland: electoral boundaries*

1959 to replace proportional representation by the simple majority vote. A similar attempt, partly supported by Fine Gael, was made in 1968, again unsuccessfully.

As a percentage of the total population, electors have increased from 1% in 1832 to 14% in 1885, 58% in 1923 and 63% in 1977. First-time voters in 1977, when 18-year-olds first voted, constituted 25% of the electorate.

The average duration of Irish governments is three years, which is comparable with the United Kingdom. This suggests that the failure of governments to obtain absolute majorities is less of a hindrance to effective government than might be expected. This insecurity does, however, appear to encourage a conservative approach towards the conduct of government.

V Religion

There is little precise information about the pre-Christian religions in Ireland, although the massive burial tombs built by the Neolithic inhabitants almost certainly testify to a widespread devotion to their gods (IV). Unquestionably, sites such as Brú na Bóinne, the concentration of tombs on the Boyne, were centres of worship, burial sites of kings and temples to gods.

When the Celts came to Ireland they brought with them their own gods, many of whom survive by name in Irish mythology. The Tuatha Dé Danann were Celtic gods who were later recorded in the oral tradition as one of a series of pre-historic invaders. The Celtic priests, the druids, had a privileged place in the Irish community, and they put up a stout resistance to Christianity. Nevertheless Christianity was successfully introduced to Ireland, the missionaries showing considerable skill in reconciling pagan traditions with Christian ritual.

With Christianity writing was introduced to Ireland, which hitherto had relied almost entirely on oral communication, the only exception being ogam writing (40). The Irish monasteries provided a great service in educating the people, and gradually the druids adapted to the new religion and became either professional men of learning or monks.

The early Irish Christians were a very fervent group and they took to the monastic life with tremendous dedication. They were less enthusiastic about the episcopal structure that was introduced, along the lines of the Roman model. Ireland was politically too diversified to conform to a centralised administration, and it was not for several centuries that bishops became really powerful in the Irish church. The expansion of monasticism within the country continued until the seventh century, when the impetus slackened somewhat. The monastic life was strict by Continental standards, and there was a tendency towards extreme austerity in many individual monasteries, particularly in those following the rule of Columbanus (41). From the sixth century onwards, much of the missionary spirit of the Irish monks was directed outwards to the Continent (41) and for several centuries they had a widespread and respected reputation for sanctity and scholarship. Even abroad, however, the Irish were slow to accept the Roman system of episcopal jurisdiction.

The Viking wars (11) brought disruption to the Irish church; by the early eleventh century, there was less spiritual fervour, and most monasteries had become more hibernicised and worldly. The Irish church took little effective action against infringements of some aspects of reformed Christianity, including concubinage, and from late in the century Rome began to take an active interest in the moral and jurisdictional well-being of Ireland. During this period a series of reforming popes were successfully tightening up discipline throughout the Christian church, and it was only a matter of time before Ireland came under close scrutiny. At the same time Lanfranc, the reforming Norman archbishop of Canterbury, began to take an interest in Ireland and wrote to the high-king urging him to summon a reforming synod. Three important synods were held during the twelfth century, Cashel in 1101, Rathbreasail in 1111 and Kells in 1152. These synods set out to reconcile the Irish law with Roman canon law, restrict the power of the great monastic foundations by making the country orientated to episcopal authority, and set up an episcopal if not a diocesan organisation. This was largely accomplished within the century. The synod of Kells set up a structure which is very close to that still in existence. Ireland was divided into four ecclesiastical provinces; Armagh, Dublin, Cashel and Tuam (IV). The synod also conformed to Roman church law in its legislation on Christian marriage.

The most important names in the Irish reform movement are those of two prelates of Armagh, Celsus and St Malachy, Gilbert, bishop of Limerick, and St Laurence O'Toole, archbishop of Dublin. As a result of the work of these and many other reforming clergy and laymen, and specifically the achievement of St Malachy in bringing the Cistercians to Ireland, the church in Ireland at the time

118

of the Norman invasion was spiritually and administratively very healthy. Nevertheless, Pope Adrian IV in his bull *Laudabiliter* authorised the invasion of Ireland in the interests of ecclesiastical and moral reform, and the Irish church quickly accepted Norman rule.

The Normans were enthusiastic patrons of the church and they gave financial aid to old and new religious orders and throughout Ireland built many magnificent monasteries and churches (33). Many of them joined the church, one of whom, Archbishop Richard FitzRalph of Armagh was the most distinguished theologian and churchman of medieval Ireland.

During the later middle ages the Irish church once again entered a period of spiritual decline although reformed orders of friars during the fifteenth century had considerable success in restoring some moral prestige to the clergy. Paradoxically it was the Reformation which was to re-kindle the spiritual imagination of the people, and by the end of the Counter-Reformation (37), despite the poverty of the church and the persecution to which it was exposed, it commanded great devotion from the Irish people. The Reformation, however, established episcopalian Protestantism as the officially recognised form of Christianity, though most of the people continued to be Roman Catholic.

By 1829 most anti-Catholic legislation was removed from the statute-book but Catholics were still required to pay tithes to the established church. This cause of resentment was not removed until Gladstone's disestablishment of the Church of Ireland in 1869. Throughout the modern period the history of the Irish church is mainly concerned with the Catholic church's emergence from a state of persecution to that of being not only tolerated but given special privileges under the law. Under Article 44 of the constitution of the Irish Republic the Catholic church was recognised as having a special position, and it was not until 1972 that as a result of constitutional change it was placed on a footing of equality with, not superiority to, other religions. Throughout the last four hundred years, religion in Ireland has been both a unifying and a divisive force. It served to unite the Irish and Old English against a common enemy, and to give all social classes a common bond. On the other hand, religious divisions have served to polarise attitudes in Northern Ireland where a Presbyterian colonisation in the seventeenth century led to a situation where a man's religion normally determines his social and financial status and his political and moral attitudes.

34. THE COMING OF CHRISTIANITY

'Ad Scottos in Christum credentes ordinatus a papa Caelestino Palladius primus episcopus mittitur.' Thus Prosper of Aquitaine tells of Pope Celestine's consecration of Palladius in 431 as the first bishop of the Irish who believed in Christ. This and other evidence shows that there were Christian settlements in Ireland before the arrival of St Patrick. Little information is, however, available on the widespread conversion of the Irish. The efforts of Palladius and other missionaries were ignored by contemporary and later chroniclers, who chose to attribute to Patrick credit for the conversion of the whole island. This belief persisted perhaps because Patrick seems to have been concerned with the pagan Irish while other missionaries were more involved with the believing Irish. Nevertheless, conversion was not fully complete even by the sixth century.

As a result of popular legend and Patrick's own writings, especially *The Confession*, his reputation as the Apostle of Ireland has obscured those of his contemporaries. It is still not clear whether he worked in Ireland from the 430s to the 460s or from the 460s to the 490s. However, even if exaggerated, his impact was considerable. His main achievement seems to have been to inspire a great many fervent disciples, who with their successors were to complete the conversion of Ireland and extend their influence throughout Britain and Europe (41).

The Irish church was theoretically episcopal, and dioceses were formed to correspond with the petty kingdoms (I), but monastic ideals quickly took root, and by the end of the sixth century abbots were more powerful than bishops, and over 800 monasteries had been founded. Some of the more important of these are shown on the map. The monasteries had an international reputation for piety and many of them also for learning. The copying of manuscripts became an important part of the monastic traditions, producing such masterpieces of illuminated manuscripts as the *Book of Kells* and the *Book of Durrow*. Irish monastic scholarship was characterised more by dedication to the highest artistic standards in the transcription of

120

Tory I. + Fahan
Raphoe + Derry
Connor +
Ardstraw + Antrim +
Moville + Bangor
Nendrum +
Armagh + Dromore
Drumcliff + Clones Downpatrick
Fenagh + Louth +
Elphin + LannLeire + Clogher
Ardagh + Monasterboice
Slane + Lusk
Inishbofin Tuam + Clonard + Duleek
Durrow Finglas +
Clonmacnois + Rahan
Clonfert + Lynally
Aran + Terryglass + Kildare
Kilfenora + Roscrea + Glendalough

Ferns +
Scattery Is Emly + Begerin +
Taghmon

Lismore +
Cork + Ardmore +
Ross Carbery +
Skellig Michael +

W. Bromage

Miles 50 100 Km 80 160

34. *The coming of Christianity: ecclesiastical foundations c. 5th–8th centuries*

manuscripts than by originality, but above all it displayed a deep veneration of learning.

Over fifty large churches were also founded during this period, many of them allegedly by St Patrick. Some of the more famous Irish saints of the period were St Colmcille (Derry, Durrow), St Finnian (Clonard, Moville), St Ciaran (Clonmacnois), St Kevin (Glendalough), St Brigid (Kildare), St Brendan (Clonfert), and St Enda of Aran.

35. MEDIEVAL ECCLESIASTICAL IRELAND

After the early fervour of the monastic movement in Ireland the church began to decline. Fewer monasteries were founded, and with the attacks of the Vikings, many existing monasteries were destroyed or abandoned.

By the time of the Norman invasion, there were few monasteries still surviving; these conformed to the early Celtic kind and showed little sign of foreign influence. The reform movement of the twelfth century set up a territorial diocesan hierarchy like those common in the Western Church, which with minor modifications, such as Tuam's absorption of Mayo and Annaghdown, has remained in existence until now. The synod of Kells, held in 1152, determined this hierarchy, setting up four metropolitan archbishoprics, Armagh, Dublin, Cashel and Tuam, with Armagh retaining the primacy of Ireland.

Following on the revival of religious enthusiasm manifested in the reform movement came a monastic revival. This was inspired first by Malachy of Armagh, who introduced Augustinians of Arrouaise and Cistercian monks to Ireland, and then by the Normans, who were responsible for many foundations, especially of Knights Hospitallers and Templars. There was less and less mixing of the two races in monasteries, strict segregation being encouraged.

Religious fervour was re-ignited in the thirteenth century with the arrival of the mendicant orders, but the economic and social disasters of the Black Death (1348–9) and other famines and pestilences of the fourteenth century had a serious effect on existing foundations. Between the mid-fourteenth century and the Reformation no more monasteries of monks or regular canons were founded, although there were over 100 new houses of friars.

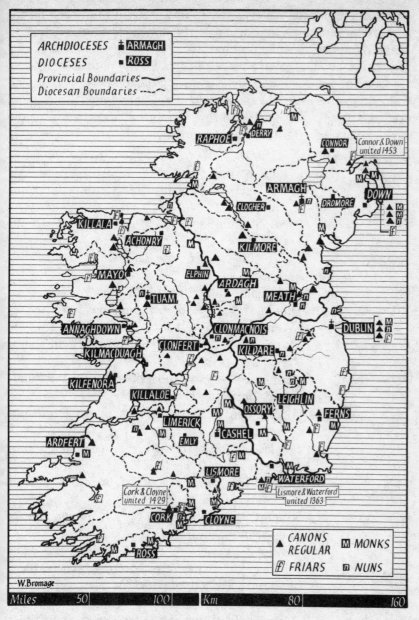

Legend items in image:
ARCHDIOCESES ✚ ARMAGH
DIOCESES ■ ROSS
Provincial Boundaries —
Diocesan Boundaries ----

CANONS REGULAR ▲   M MONKS
F FRIARS   n NUNS

35. *Medieval ecclesiastical Ireland*

The monastic life degenerated considerably during the fifteenth century, succumbing through poverty and paucity of recruits to indiscipline and spiritual decline.

It is not possible to give precise figures for the number of monastic foundations existing in Ireland during the medieval period. The map notes the major foundations and indicates their distribution. An estimate is given below of the number of foundations of the major religious orders during this period.

Canons Regular: Augustinians of Arrouaise – 181 foundations, mostly twelfth century.

Crutched Friars – 19 foundations, mostly thirteenth century.

Premonstratensians – 19, mostly thirteenth century.

Monks: Benedictines – 16 foundations, mostly twelfth century.

Cistercians – 52, mostly twelfth century.

Friars: Dominicans – 41 foundations, mostly thirteenth century.

Franciscans – 62 foundations, mostly thirteenth century.

Carmelites – 65 foundations, mostly thirteenth and fourteenth centuries.

Augustinians – 22 foundations, mostly fourteenth century.

Franciscan Third Order Regular – 48 foundations, mostly fifteenth century.

Military Orders: Knights Templars – 16 foundations, mostly twelfth century.

Knights Hospitallers – 21 foundations, mostly thirteenth century.

Nuns: Records for many convents are often poor or non-existent, so figures are uncertain. There were about 90 recorded, of which over 40 were under the rule of Augustinians of Arrouaise.

Hospitals and Hospices: During most of this period these were maintained by the regular orders, notably the Crutched Friars, Augustinian canons and Benedictines. They numbered over 200.

The other important foundations of this period were the secular colleges which were founded mainly in the thirteenth century and were about 35 in number.

36. POST-REFORMATION IRELAND

In 1534 King Henry VIII became 'Supreme Head on Earth of the Church of England' and in 1536 'Supreme Head on Earth of the Church of Ireland'. He set out to reform the Irish church at a time when it was temporally prosperous and spiritually poor. Despite the efforts of the friars, and especially the Franciscan Third Order Regular, to bring about a spiritual revival in the early sixteenth century, the need for reform was still very obvious. Consequently, there was less opposition to Henry's proposed reforms than might have been expected, there being in his favour the positive need for reform and some anti-clericalism.

Outside the monasteries in the rest of the Irish church the position was no better. In the Gaelic areas parishes and dioceses went to scions of the powerful local families. Within the English areas, royal support was a necessary prerequisite for ecclesiastical office. The clergy were often poor, greedy and uneducated.

The main responsibility for introducing the Reformation to Ireland was given to George Browne, Archbishop of Dublin from 1536 to 1554, who began by participating in a parliament in 1536, which unwillingly declared Henry 'Supreme Head on Earth of the Church of Ireland'. It passed a number of other acts. The Act of Slander declared that the penalty for calling Henry a heretic, schismatic or usurper would be conviction of high treason. The act against the authority of the Bishop of Rome provided for the effective outlawry of any person supporting 'the advancement and continuance of the [pope's] . . . fained and pretended authority'. Under the act declaring the King, his heirs and successors, to be Supreme Head of the Church of Ireland it was laid down that any subject could be required to take an oath of allegiance to Henry as head of the church; anyone refusing was guilty of high treason. Contemporaneously, provision was made for the suppression of the monasteries (37).

The reformation had little success initially, except in the Pale and in the towns: in the Gaelic areas there was a passive resistance

Legend:

Diocesan boundaries- c.1570

Under royal control—

Independent of royal control—

Nominally under royal control but maintaining Catholic rites-

RAPHOE · DERRY · CONNOR & DOWN · ARMAGH · DROMORE · CLOGHER · KILMORE · KILLALA · ACHONRY · ELPHIN · ARDAGH · MEATH · MAYO · TUAM · CLONMACNOISE · KILDARE · DUBLIN · ANNAGHDOWN · KILMACDUAGH · CLONFERT · KILFENORA · KILLALOE · LEIGHLIN · OSSORY · FERNS · CASHEL · EMLY · LIMERICK · ARDFERT & AGHADOE · CLOYNE & CORK · WATERFORD & LISMORE · ROSS

W. Bromage

Miles 50 100 Km 80 160

36. *Post-Reformation Ireland*

to it. Edward VI's (1547–53) attempts to introduce doctrinal innovations were strongly resisted in Ireland. Mary (1553–8), although she theoretically restored Roman Catholicism, did little in practice and failed to restore more than a few monasteries.

Elizabeth (1558–1603) set out to extend the Reformation throughout Ireland. A parliament of 1560 reaffirmed the provisions of the 1536 parliament, and added the Act of Uniformity, which enforced, on pain of a fine, attendance on Sundays at a service performed according to the Book of Common Prayer. Ultimately, her religious policy was no more successful in Ireland than that of her predecessors. The Jesuits had considerable success in countering attempts at proselytising, and by the end of Elizabeth's reign Roman Catholicism was as strong, despite persecution and deprivation, as it had been for generations. Additionally, opposition to the new religion had proved to be a force for unity between the Gaelic Irish and Old English.

37. THE DISSOLUTION OF THE MONASTERIES

Over 400 monasteries were suppressed during the reigns of Henry VIII and Elizabeth, the majority during the reign of Henry VIII in areas where the king's writ ran. However, in many cases, suppression was more apparent than real. Local officials often reported the suppression of a monastery, while in fact allowing it to remain in existence. It was not easy for monasteries to survive for long, since they relied on endowments which could not continue after confiscation, but the friars, who traditionally relied on the generosity of the local people, could continue in many areas indefinitely.

During Elizabeth's reign she tried to ensure the suppression of religious houses in practice by granting them to towns, Anglo-Irish or Gaelic lords, or English settlers. However, some of these grantees were themselves Catholic in sympathy, and did not expel the monks. Despite this occasional tolerance, the persecution of religious became increasingly severe, resulting in the imprisonment and execution of many. Between 1570 and 1603, seventy-six identifiable individuals were put to death in reality on religious grounds, and twenty died in prison. Of these, seven were prelates, eighteen secular priests, seven Cistercians, two Dominicans, thirty-six Franciscans, two Jesuits, twenty-three laymen and one a laywoman.

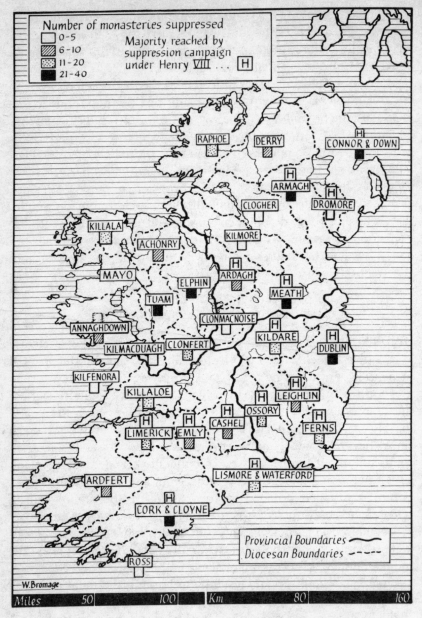

Number of monasteries suppressed

- □ 0–5
- ▨ 6–10
- ▒ 11–20
- ■ 21–40

Majority reached by suppression campaign under Henry VIII ... H

RAPHOE
DERRY
CONNOR & DOWN H
ARMAGH H
CLOGHER
DROMORE H
KILLALA
KILMORE
ACHONRY
MAYO
ARDAGH H
ELPHIN
MEATH H
TUAM
CLONMACNOISE
ANNAGHDOWN
KILMACDUAGH
CLONFERT
KILDARE H
DUBLIN H
KILFENORA
KILLALOE
LEIGHLIN H
OSSORY H
FERNS H
LIMERICK H
EMLY
CASHEL H
LISMORE & WATERFORD H
ARDFERT
CORK & CLOYNE H
ROSS

Provincial Boundaries ‿‿
Diocesan Boundaries – – –

W. Bromage

Miles 50 100 Km 80 160

37. *The dissolution of the monasteries*

Persecution was at its height during the early 1580s; between 1579 and 1584 forty-six of the deaths occurred.

During Elizabeth's reign few Catholic bishops remained in Ireland. Most of the dioceses were ruled by absentees, and few parochial clergy remained; only the friars performed services. Nevertheless, the courage of the Catholic clergy remaining in Ireland during the period of persecution proved a fine example to the people for whom they were working, and helped to keep Catholicism strong throughout the country. By the end of the century, although few religious houses remained in existence, even the Pale and the towns were still Catholic.

Early in the seventeenth century, there was a religious revival. The Jesuits, who, with a number of isolated friars had been working in Ireland from the middle of the sixteenth century, were joined by new recruits and by members of the mendicant orders, who had trained abroad at Continental colleges (42). In 1615 large numbers of Capuchin Franciscans arrived and in 1625 many Discalced Carmelites. Gradually many of the old foundations were rebuilt and reoccupied, and new ones built. It is estimated that during this period the number of religious in Ireland equalled the number in the country at the zenith of the medieval period.

38. DISSENTERS IN IRELAND

Although Ireland was always numerically dominated by Roman Catholics she had a large and varied Protestant population. Those Protestant groups which refused to conform to the Church of Ireland suffered at various times, like the Catholics, from discriminatory laws and the requirement to pay tithes to the established church. This discrimination persisted until disestablishment of the Church of Ireland in 1869.

A brief summary of the history of the main groups of dissenters follows. The map shows the distribution of some of the less numerous groups whose location by the early eighteenth century can be demonstrated with some certainty.

Huguenots: French Protestants were known as Huguenots; they became disciples of Calvin and were basically Presbyterian. Their intensive persecution began in France, and during the sixteenth

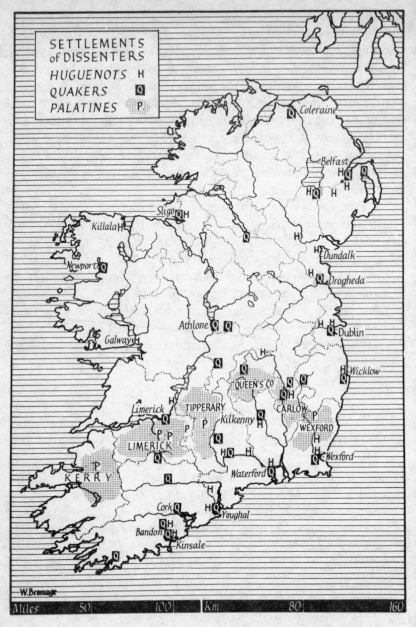

38. *Dissenters in Ireland: some eighteenth-century settlements*

century many emigrated to England and there were some small and unsuccessful settlements in Ireland in Cork and Swords. After the Edict of Nantes in 1598 gave them protection, most returned to France. The recommencing of persecution in the seventeenth century led to mass emigration to England, Scotland and Ireland. The main exodus to Ireland came from the 1620s to 1641, in 1649 with Cromwell and from 1662, when the Duke of Ormond introduced into Parliament 'An Act for Encouraging Protestant Strangers and Others to Inhabit Ireland'. He established a number of colonies throughout the country. More came to Ireland with William of Orange from Holland and Switzerland and established new settlements in Lisburn, Kilkenny, Dundalk and Lurgan. They were celebrated for their textile expertise, specialising in weaving, lace making, glove making and manufacturing of linen and cloth. They were easily absorbed through intermarriage.

Presbyterians: Presbyterians were numerically by far the most numerous group of dissenters. Most Irish Presbyterians were Scots in origin and settled in Ulster. The Presbyterian Church under John Knox was strong in Scotland when James VI and I began his persecution. He later encouraged them to emigrate to Ireland. The vast majority of them settled in Ulster during the seventeenth century, but during the eighteenth century large numbers emigrated to America to avoid the Penal Laws (43).

Some English Calvinists settled in Dublin and the south of Ireland; a less severe sect than other Calvinists, they united with the Presbyterians in 1696.

Quakers: Quakers were an extreme section of the Puritan movement of the mid-seventeenth century. Their first Irish group was established in Lurgan in 1654 and they spread throughout Ulster, Leinster and Munster before the Restoration. They also specialised in textiles, but were additionally merchants and farmers.

Palatines: To escape persecution, about 3,000 German-speaking Protestants from the Palatinate of the Rhine fled to Ireland, arriving in Dublin in 1709. They settled in substantial numbers throughout Limerick, and scattered throughout several counties. Many of them became Methodists at a later date.

Baptists: Baptists, Congregationalists and Independents came to Ireland during the Commonwealth and Protectorate; they formed a large part of the Cromwellian army and were very powerful politically. After the Restoration many of them emigrated to America. In the eighteenth century Congregationalists and Independents ceased to be distinct sects. Most of those who did not emigrate after the Restoration suffered persecution and became absorbed into other churches.

Methodists: John Wesley founded Methodism to encourage a more personal religion; he did not intend the break from the established church which happened later. Methodism in Ireland originated in the 1730s and by the early nineteenth century had over 30,000 members.

The numbers of dissenters have been declining over the last two centuries as a result of emigration and conversion. By 1834 as a body they comprised less than 9% of the whole population, and by 1971, although they now represented 13% of the population as a result of the massive drop in the population of Catholics in Ireland, their numbers had declined by 12%.

39. RELIGIOUS AFFILIATIONS

When Sir William Petty in 1672 made an estimate of the population of Ireland as 1,100,000 he judged that more than 72% of these were Catholic. By 1834 when a Royal Commission looked at religion in Ireland it established the following figures:

Religion	Number of Members	Percentage of the Population
Roman Catholic	6,436,060	81%
Established Church	853,160	11%
Presbyterians	643,058	8%
Other Protestant Dissenters	21,822	·3%

The 1861 Census found that Roman Catholics had an absolute majority over all other religions except in Counties Antrim, Armagh, Down and Londonderry and in the towns of Carrickfergus and Belfast. This census examined religious affiliations in detail and produced the following figures for each province:

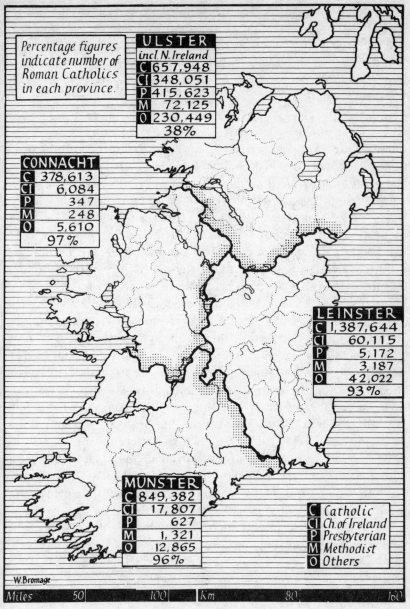

Percentage figures indicate number of Roman Catholics in each province.

ULSTER
incl. N. Ireland

C	657,948
CI	348,051
P	415,623
M	72,125
O	230,449
	38%

CONNACHT

C	378,613
CI	6,084
P	347
M	248
O	5,610
	97%

LEINSTER

C	1,387,644
CI	60,115
P	5,172
M	3,187
O	42,022
	93%

MUNSTER

C	849,382
CI	17,807
P	627
M	1,321
O	12,865
	96%

C	Catholic
CI	Ch. of Ireland
P	Presbyterian
M	Methodist
O	Others

W. Bromage

Miles	50	100	Km	80	160

39. *Religious affiliations, 1971*

Province	R.C.	Total Prots.	C. of I.	Pres.	Meth.	Ind.	Bap.	Jews	Quaker	Others
Ulster	50·5%	49·47%	20·4%	26·3%	1·7%	·1%	·2%	—	·1%	·67%
Leinster	85·9%	14·01%	12·4%	·85%	·4%	·1%	·03%	·02%	·1%	·13%
Munster	93·8%	6·07%	5·3%	3%	·3%	·03%	·02%	—	·05%	·07%
Connacht	94·84%	5·13%	4·45%	·34%	·29%	·03%	·01%	—	—	·01%

These figures are easy to interpret. The fundamental problem of Ulster is shown in the evenness of the division between Catholic and Protestant, while throughout the rest of Ireland only in Leinster were there any significant number of Protestants – over 20,000.

The trend continued steadily towards an increasing Catholic majority in the Republic – from 89·5% in 1881 to 95·4% in 1971. Connacht has achieved a Catholic majority of 96·9%. All Protestant groups are declining steadily in the Republic. The Church of Ireland has dropped from 8·2% of the population in 1881 to 3·3%, the Presbyterians from 1·5% to ·6% and Methodists from ·5% to ·2%. The only groups increasing in size apart from the Catholics are the Jews, and those classified as others. In 1881 there were 394 Jews in Ireland but since 1901 there has been a steady population of slightly over 3,000. 'Others' having dropped from over 11,000 in 1881 to 7,290 in 1936 are rising steadily. This classification comprehends a number of small sects including Quakers and Unitarians and the ·2% who either have no religion or decline to state it.

In Northern Ireland the trend is little different. Since 1926 the percentage of Catholics has dropped from 33·5% to 31·1% while the Church of Ireland has dropped from 27·0% to 21·8%. Presbyterians have dropped from 31·3% to 26·4%. there have been marginal increases among Methodists, Plymouth Brethren, Baptists and Congregationalists. The largest increase has been among those who refuse to state their religion – from ·2% to 9·3%.

VI The Irish Abroad

Over a period of fifteen hundred years the Irish have left Ireland for two main reasons, either to evangelise or to escape poverty or persecution at home. Not since the fifth century has territorial aggrandisement been a reason for emigration, and only a few Irishmen have ever been explorers.

There are obvious reasons why a warlike and predatory people such as the Irish of the fourth and fifth centuries proved themselves to be, should have ceased to indulge in external military aggression. With the advent of Christianity in the fifth century their main drive became religious in character, and many of the military aristocracy became noted monastic or episcopal leaders.

The Irish monks who went abroad from the sixth century to the early part of the ninth left in a spirit of self-sacrifice and mortification, seeking exile. Wherever they settled they became missionaries. From the mid-ninth century onwards the emigration of religious was for self-preservation, to escape the depredations of the Viking invaders.

Throughout the medieval period the Irish church was inward rather than outward looking. Although many Irishmen, both religious and lay, went on pilgrimages, especially to Italy and Spain, and although many of them went to Rome in search of jobs or benefices at home, contact with the Continent was essentially one-way, and involved the importation into Ireland of Roman ideas on church uniformity and of foreign religious orders.

From the ninth century onwards there was never to be an opportunity again for Irish military activity abroad, except as members of foreign armies, since Irish political leaders were to be preoccupied with warfare either against each other or against the Vikings, and later, the Normans. The main foreign contacts came through Irish and foreign traders (X).

Emigration did not again become a significant element in Irish life until after the Reformation, when persecution drove many religious to seek sanctuary on the Continent (42). From the early seventeenth century also began the phenomenon of large-scale emigration of Irish soldiers, who were to serve in large numbers in Continental armies throughout the seventeenth and eighteenth centuries. This exodus reached its height between 1690 and 1745, during which time the military and the religious were joined on the Continent by students, farmers, merchants and others whose way of life in Ireland was being seriously affected by persecution.

Simultaneously, persecution of the dissenters was initiating emigration to the United States. The mass emigration which began after the Napoleonic wars, and increased to enormous proportions during the mid-nineteenth century was to be the most important element in the social history of Ireland. Famine and emigration were to reduce the population by 29% in only twenty years – from 1841 to 1861. Those Irish who went abroad were to have an important influence on the development of a number of countries. They caused a serious social problem in Britain, especially in Scotland, and for a long time proved to be primarily a disruptive force within the community. In America they were also a disruptive force for a considerable period, until the majority of immigrants began to identify more with America than with Ireland.

This question of identification has been the crucial problem of Irish abroad. The insistence of many Irish on being Irish first, and on putting the interests of their homeland and compatriots before those of the country in which they had chosen to make their permanent home, was to be a bone of contention for a long period. This self-conscious 'Irishness' was to be a divisive force in Australian religion and politics until very recently (44). The insistence of the Catholic church on sectarian education was an isolating force in countries such as Australia, New Zealand and America where the majority of Catholics were Irish.

The Irish in America have succeeded in integrating far more thoroughly than those in Britain, for a number of reasons. Firstly, emigrants to America have no historical antipathy to the country, and their isolation from their homeland forces them to accept the permanence of the move and consequently to make the best of it. Irish political success in America has also been a major reconciling factor. It is significant in studying the Irish Americans involved in Clan na Gael (47), to see how quickly the majority of them began to see themselves as Americans first and Irish second. De Valera's refusal to realise and accept the commitment of the successful Irish Americans to the country which had given them social and financial security and status was the main reason for his split with Clan na Gael. Ultimately the Irishman abroad retains an interest in his native country, but commitment to his new country eventually comes with acceptance by the indigenous community. Even in Britain the Irish are emerging as part of the general community rather than as a race apart. This, however, has primarily been due to their acceptance by a society which is now affected more by colour than by sectarian or other prejudices.

40. FOURTH-CENTURY EXPANSION

By the end of the third century A.D., the Goidels of Ireland (or *Scotti* as they are generally described) had begun to carry out sporadic raids on the western coasts of Britain. During the course of the fourth century they established a number of settlements in Britain, and became politically powerful, especially in south-western Wales and western Scotland.

Evidence for the extent of Irish expansion is largely archaeological, although some literary evidence exists in Welsh sagas and Irish legend. Some remains of Roman forts suggest that they were built to hinder Irish attacks across the Pennines.

The main evidence is, however, in the distribution of ogam stones, which were stone monuments with ogam inscriptions. Ogam writing was a method of representation of Latin letters by groups of lines set at different angles. With the exception of a few ogam stones which are of Pictish origin, all those found in the British Isles are of Irish origin, and testify to the spread of the Irish settlers. As map 40 shows, the vast majority of ogam stones are found in Ireland; there are over 200 in Cork and Kerry alone. However, as indicated, others have been found in north and south Wales, in Cornwall, Devon, Hampshire, and some in Scotland, as

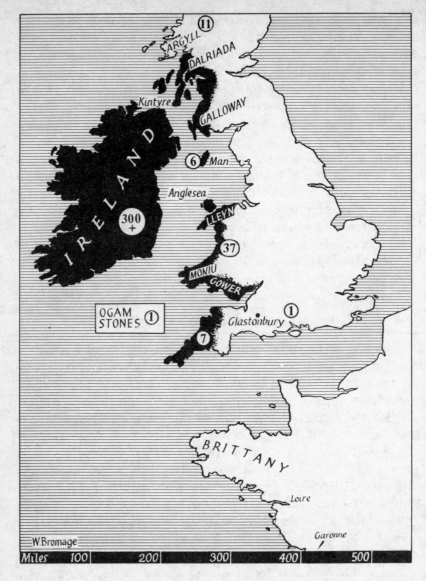

40. *Fourth-century expansion*

138

far north as Orkney and Shetland. It is the absence of these stones from Brittany which suggests that the traditional stories about Niall of the Nine Hostages's attacks on Brittany may not be founded in fact, or at least that no settlement occurred.

The decline of the Roman Empire made Irish attacks on Britain possible, while her wealth made it profitable. By the mid-fifth century the Irish seem to have ceased their plundering expeditions and to have become more peaceful. By then the Irish tribes of the east coast, the Laigin, the Déisi and the Uí Liatháin had set up kingdoms in Wales, while the Dál Riada, who dwelt in the far north-east of Ireland set up a kingdom in Scotland, which, unlike the Welsh kingdoms, survived. The Isle of Man was named after an Irish deity, Manannan and remained an Irish dependency for several centuries.

One important result of this extensive contact with Britain was to aid the early introduction of Christianity which came to Ireland initially from Gaul via the British settlements and through trading associations.

41. IRISH INFLUENCE ABROAD: 500–800

It is paradoxical that the prime determining factor in encouraging Irish monks to leave home and travel abroad was the security, prosperity and veneration which the Irish church enjoyed. Asceticism, not missionary fervour, was the driving force. The impulse was towards what was to an Irishman the ultimate sacrifice – permanent exile. Columcille left Ireland in 563 for Iona in this spirit of mortification. However, once established there, like so many later travellers from Ireland, the need which he found locally for missionary activity led him to spend his life not in solitary prayer but in dedicated labour to convert the Picts.

Among the most famous of Irish monks abroad were Fursey of East Anglia and north-east Gaul, the patron saint of Péronne, who died in 650; Killian who was martyred at Würtzburg in 689; Fergal, who had become Bishop of Salzburg by the time of his death in 784; Aidan of Lindisfarne, who with Finan and Colman converted Northumbria in the mid and late seventh century; Gall of Switzerland, a disciple of Columbanus, who died in 650, a monastery called after him being founded in 720 where he had lived;

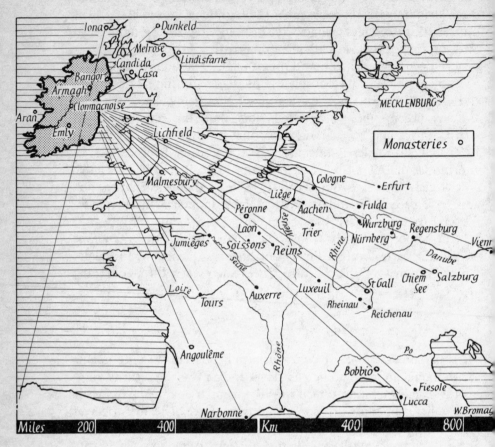

41. Irish influences abroad, 500–800

and greatest of them all, Columbanus (540–615), who is symbolic of the Irish Church abroad. Driven by a combination of political difficulties and unwelcome success in attracting to his monasteries multitudes of disciples and rich endowments, he travelled extensively in Europe, founding monasteries – notably Luxeuil and Bobbio. Hundreds of later foundations are said to be descended from his foundations. A distinctive feature of his monasteries was his harsh rule, which included penalties of fasting, corporal punishment and exile. He enjoined upon his followers discomfort of body and submission of will.

140

Columbanus in his correspondence with political and ecclesiastical leaders showed a magnificence of rhetoric and an intransigence of attitude. He challenged Pope Gregory the Great on the method of calculating the date of Easter – a controversy in which the Irish had been liturgically out of step with the rest of the church for a considerable period. Honorius I in 634 demonstrated papal irritation with Irish obstinacy on this question when, according to the Venerable Bede, he wrote to the Irish 'earnestly exhorting them not to think their small number, placed in the utmost borders of the earth, wiser than all the ancient and modern churches of Christ, throughout the world'.

Although the Irish abroad learned much about Continental art and scholarship from their travels, they maintained much of their institutional individuality, for example, their distinctive tonsure and monastic independence of episcopal rule. However, despite their peculiarities, the fervour, dedication and zeal of the Irish monks abroad achieved great missionary success and made them great monastic and episcopal leaders. Their reputation as religious pioneers and leaders was secure in Europe by the seventh century, and by the ninth Irish scholars also had a widespread European reputation. Charlemagne had appointed Irish masters to his Palace schools, and during the ninth century Irish scholars, many fleeing from the Viking invasions, had an important role in the establishment of France as a centre of learning. Notable among these scholars were the geographer Dicuil and the philosopher and theologian Sedulius Scotus, both of whom taught at Liège, and most important of all, the greatest scholar and philosopher of the age, John Scotus Eriugena, who taught at Laon and was the author of *De Naturae Divisione* and was described as 'the last representative of the Greek spirit in the West'.

The scholars were an interesting contrast to their monastic predecessors; renowned more for their conviviality than for their asceticism – many ninth-century drinking songs are attributed to them. Stories of Irish piety told about the monks are counterbalanced by stories of Irish wit told about the laymen. Colonies of Irish scholars existed at Liège, Cologne, Reims, Reichenau, Fulden and Tours.

42. *Irish colleges in Europe*

42. IRISH COLLEGES IN EUROPE

There was widespread emigration from Ireland by the end of the
Tudor period and this continued throughout much of the seventeenth century. There were three main streams of emigrants:
soldiers, religious and students. The first group were Irishmen going
abroad to join foreign armies; the second were religious forced to
go abroad to avoid persecution and the third were those who were
unable to gain an education at home. These latter included both
religious and laymen, and they left – many of them never to return
to Ireland – to study at the Irish colleges on the Continent.

Most of the Irish colleges had in fact been established early in
the seventeenth century: the life-span of most of them was between
100 and 150 years. By the end of the eighteenth century most of
them had closed or been closed. But they do not all follow the

142

same pattern. The Capuchin college at Charleville was abandoned as early as 1684, while the Augustinian Irish College at Rome continues to operate today.

Broadly speaking, however, the Irish colleges were at their zenith during the early part of the eighteenth century, when religious persecution in Ireland was at its height and the influence and generosity of the exiled Stuarts was a powerful aid to their success. The presence of the Stuart monarchy on the Continent gave an enhanced status to exiled Irishmen.

The colleges differed greatly in size. The largest were at Paris and Nantes, where the numbers of students could exceed one hundred, and the smallest were Santiago, Seville, Tournai and Toulouse, which always had fewer than a dozen.

The finances of the colleges were precarious; they depended largely on Irish patrons, although many Catholics throughout the Continent made generous contributions. Benefactors included Anne of Austria, the kings of France and the Stuarts, particularly Mary of Modena, James II's wife. Students at the colleges were supported either by private money, burses or the funds of the individual colleges. Students who were priests could supplement their income by saying masses or undertaking other religious functions.

One of the most interesting features of the history of these colleges is the spread of Jesuit influence. Although only Poitiers was nominally a Jesuit college, many of the secular colleges had Jesuit rectors including, at different times, Rome, Tournai, Lisbon, Salamanca, Santiago and Seville. With the papal suppression of the Jesuits in 1773 the colleges suffered a severe blow to their prestige and this, coupled with economic difficulties and the large-scale confiscations following on the French Revolution, brought to an end the career of most of the Irish colleges. By the end of the century only Madrid, Lisbon and Salamanca continued to operate, although some of the others reopened in the nineteenth century.

A significant number of Irish priests settled on the Continent permanently and pursued their pastoral work there. These are to be distinguished from the large body of Irish clerics, particularly bishops, who were exiles on the Continent until the easing of the Penal Laws permitted their return to Ireland, some of them proving very reluctant ever to return. Many of these lived in extreme poverty, depending on the charity of the Vatican, the Stuarts or

43. *destinations of the emigrants, 1845–55*

other benefactors. A few of them received some benefices while abroad, sometimes assisting the local bishops.

A number of Irish girls went abroad to join foreign convents. Ypres was the only wholly Irish convent, although Irish girls joined convents at Lisbon and elsewhere on the Continent.

43. DESTINATIONS OF THE EMIGRANTS

Emigration became a fact of life for the Irish in the seventeenth century. After the defeat of the Stuarts thousands of Irish Jacobites and Catholics emigrated to avoid persecution and to find a new way of life on the Continent. This flow began to ease off by the middle of the eighteenth century.

More sporadic emigration had been going on for a long period. Irish vagrants were a familiar phenomenon in Britain in the

fifteenth and sixteenth centuries and seasonal migration to help in harvesting was becoming a regular event by the seventeenth century.

Serious permanent emigration really began with the Ulster Scots. Bad harvests, religious discrimination against Presbyterians and high rents set the pattern of a steady exodus. Throughout the eighteenth century an average of about 4,000 a year emigrated. Many of these went to Britain, but more to America. Catholic emigration to America was not as high as might be expected, since there were laws to restrict Catholic immigration and public worship was forbidden to them until 1780.

Emigration figures increased dramatically at the end of the Napoleonic wars. Ireland had enjoyed considerable economic prosperity during the war, but peace brought an agricultural slump. In 1818 20,000 people emigrated. Important factors in encouraging

145

increased emigration were the liberalising of attitudes to Catholics in America and the rise of the North Atlantic timber trade. The cargo ships carrying timber to Britain returned to North America carrying emigrants at low fares. By 1832 fares to America from Liverpool were only £3 10s. Simultaneously, Canada was opening its doors to emigrants.

Precise figures for emigration cannot easily be given – especially for emigration to Britain. However, records of emigrants were kept at British ports, from which most Irish emigrants left. Even before the famine the figures were high. It is estimated that between 1831–41 the following numbers of emigrants left for these destinations:

British America (many of these went on to America):	189,225
America:	19,775
Australia:	4,554
West Indies:	494

An analysis of the British Colonies in 1861 showed the proportion of Irish in the relevant populations:

Country	Irish as percentage of the population
Western Australia	21·3%
Queensland	18·4%
Victoria	16·1%
New South Wales	15·6%
Upper Canada	13·7%
South Australia	10·0%
Prince Edward Island	6·1%
Lower Canada	4·5%
Nova Scotia	2·8%
Jamaica	0·1%
Tobago	0·04%

The map shows the numbers and the main destinations of those emigrating between 1845 and 1855 – the heaviest years of post-famine emigration. The towns marked bore the brunt. The same pattern of emigration continued as time went on, with the United States being the Mecca for the Irish poor. The years immediately following the famine were appalling for travel, with overcrowding

146

and disease rampant. It took six to eight weeks to reach the United States and months to reach Australia. Not until the introduction of the steam ships later in the century did travel become moderately comfortable. Nevertheless, many of the Irish found the hardships of travel to unknown destinations preferable to the grinding poverty that faced them at home.

44. IRISH CATHOLICISM ABROAD

The mass emigration from Ireland during the nineteenth century posed a serious problem for the Catholic church. Many of these emigrants were Catholics who were settling in countries which had few, if any, Catholic churches or pastors. It was therefore necessary for Irish priests to solve the problem by travelling with their people and founding churches wherever they were required.

The map shows how far the tentacles of the Irish Catholic church had reached by 1900. Those places named are locations of the earliest recorded activity by Irish clergy, and the date given for each country is that of the first record of an Irish religious arriving either to minister to an immigrant Irish community or to convert the local population. Their early activities are outlined below.

Africa: Irish missionary activity in Africa began in Liberia in 1842 when at the request of Pope Gregory XVI three Irish priests were sent there. In spite of the dangers comparatively large numbers of Irish priests, brothers, and nuns have devoted themselves to missionary work there. The Irish were part of an effort which included French, Belgians, Dutch, Italians and Germans. The major strides were, however, made during the twentieth century when missionary effort in Africa became intensive and widespread; the most effective work of Irish missionaries was in the sphere of education.

Australia: Transportation of Irish convicts to Australia began in 1791. By 1803 there were 2,086 Irish convicts in Australia. Despite the popular belief that these were largely political prisoners, in fact over 60% of them had been sentenced for criminal offences. An Irish priest, James Dixon, transported for political offences, celebrated the first mass in Australia in 1803. With the increase in transportation and emigration to Australia the need for Catholic priests increased. By 1836 there were 21,898 Catholics in the country, mostly Irish and almost half of these were convicts. They were

147

44. *Irish catholicism abroad*

severely discriminated against within the colony. The prejudice was anti-Catholic and anti-convict rather than anti-Irish. With the appointment of the first bishop in 1835 began the really serious organisation of the Australian Catholic church. There were inner disputes within the church between those who urged Catholics to be Australians first and those who urged them to identify with their Irish origins. With the appointment of a large number of Irish bishops during the 1860s the ultra-Irishness of Australian Catholicism was exaggerated, to the detriment of successful integration. Cardinal Moran, who arrived in Australia in 1883 moderated this view to some extent, refusing to adopt an ultra-Irish position. Nevertheless the Irishness of his episcopacy and clergy continued to foster the image of the Australian Catholic church as Irish and it is only in recent years that the church has become more Australian than Irish.

The Orient: There is evidence of missionary work in China as far back as the seventeenth century, but the Irish were not involved

148

until much later. Throughout the nineteenth century Irish priests were concentrating their efforts mainly on ministering to their own people in Australia and in North America and there were few available for missionary activity. It is for that reason that most of the work done there was accomplished by nuns and Christian Brothers. By 1900 there were sixteen Irish convents in India. Missionary activity during the twentieth century has been much more intensive. There has been conspicuous success in the Philippines and steady progress throughout the Orient, although China has proved unconquerable.

Canada: Both Irish and French clergy have borne the responsibility for ministering to the Catholics of Canada. The Irish were dominant throughout the nineteenth century in Newfoundland, Nova Scotia, and New Brunswick and made important contributions in Prince Edward Island, Quebec and Ontario. In west and north Canada, and latterly in Quebec and New Brunswick, the French dominate.

149

South Africa: Substantial emigration to South Africa began with about 5,000 British settlers in 1820. The Irish among them, and later arrivals, tended to congregate around Grahamstown. Irish immigration was very limited, so that Irish priests sent to South Africa were less concerned with ministering to an Irish community than with serving a whole community and undertaking missionary work. Growth was slow; by 1879 there were only 5,500 Catholics throughout South Africa, although there are now nearer a million. After this period there was a considerable amount of missionary activity, with schools and hospitals also being provided. The Irish contribution was substantial.

South America: By 1832 there were about 2,000 Irish living in Buenos Aires and this had risen to 4,500 by 1848. In the second half of the century immigrants moved to other parts of the country and the Irish priests followed. Throughout the country Irish immigration increased until in 1900 it is estimated that there were about 75,000 Irish; since then, however, immigration has been virtually non-existent. On the whole the Irish contribution to South American Catholicism has been marginal.

New Zealand: Irish emigration to New Zealand was quite substantial and in the nineteenth century most priests and nuns throughout the country were Irish. The Catholic population was mainly Irish and the Irish clerical contribution has continued during this century.

U.S.A.: The story of the Irish church in America is the story of the Irish people there. Irish priests are strong where Irish settlements are substantial, and during the nineteenth century the priests were mainly ethnic in outlook and greatly involved in Irish patriotic movements (46, 47). The shading on the map indicates how widespread was Irish Catholic clerical effort during the century.

45. THE IRISH IN BRITAIN

The history of the Irish in Britain as vagrants, wanderers and seasonal workers dates back to long before the eighteenth century. Many Irish joined the British army and navy during the eighteenth century, including the celebrated Gaelic poet Eoghan Ruadh Ó Súilleabháin (82), who joined both services, travelling with the navy as far as the West Indies. In the Napoleonic wars there were large numbers of Irish on both sides.

Mass emigration to Britain began in the early nineteenth century and Irish immigrants tended to congregate in areas of heavy industry or mining, where their labour was welcome. The great mass of the Irish were in the big towns. In England they were to be found in large numbers in the north-east and the midlands, and also of course in London. By 1841 1·9% of the population of England were Irish-born. Only 0·6% of the Welsh population were Irish-born, but over 60% of these were concentrated in Glamorgan, in Swansea and Cardiff. In Scotland they made up 4·8% of the population, a large percentage of these being in Glasgow and Edinburgh.

Politically they were active. Many of them joined the Chartists and became involved in a class struggle, while many others supported the Irish movement for repeal of the union (30).

The 1841 Census showed 419, 256 Irish-born in Great Britain; by 1851 this had risen to 733,866 and was still rising. There was still a strong tendency of Irish immigrants to congregate in the same areas. The map shows their main areas of concentration. Overall, by 1851 they represented 3% of the population of England and Wales and nearly 7% of Scotland. Like so many later generations of immigrants they caused resentment and opposition by forming ghettos in large cities. In 1855 Karl Marx wrote 'Ireland has revenged herself socially upon England by bestowing an Irish quarter on every English industrial, maritime or commercial town of any size'. There were numerous conflicts between Irish and English navvies working on the railways since the Irish also formed a high proportion of mobile workforces. While the British worker aimed at having a trade, Irish workers were prepared to continue as labourers and unskilled factory workers.

Much of the fear of Irish immigration was justified. Shiploads of diseased and starving Irish landed throughout the second half of the 1840s and the early 1850s. In 1848 more than 60% of the Poor Law funds of Glasgow were spent on Irish immigrants. Discrimination against Catholics also affected them since most Irish immigrants were Catholic. Unlike those emigrating to America the Irish were unwilling to be assimilated in Britain, and their church leaders did not encourage it either. Irish patriotism and religion were inter-twined. Consequently, they were seen as enemies by

151

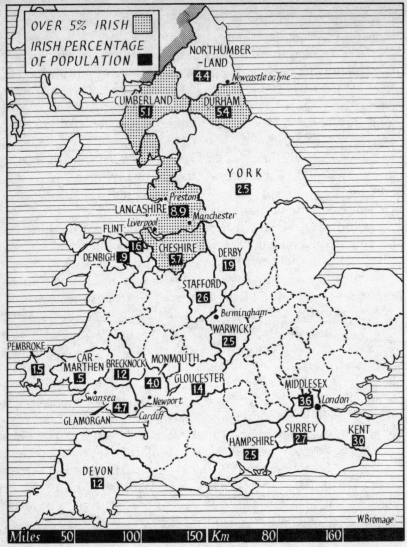

Inside the map:

OVER 5% IRISH

IRISH PERCENTAGE OF POPULATION

NORTHUMBER -LAND 4.4 · Newcastle on Tyne

CUMBERLAND 5.1   DURHAM 5.4

YORK 2.5

Preston

LANCASHIRE 8.9 · Manchester

FLINT 1.6   Liverpool

DENBIGH .9   CHESHIRE 5.7   DERBY 1.9

STAFFORD 2.6

· Birmingham

WARWICK 2.5

PEMBROKE   CAR-MARTHEN .5   BRECKNOCK 1.2   MONMOUTH 4.0   GLOUCESTER 1.4   MIDDLESEX 3.6 · London

1.5

Swansea   GLAMORGAN 4.7   · Newport   Cardiff

SURREY 2.7   KENT 3.0

HAMPSHIRE 2.5

DEVON 1.2

W. Bromage

Miles   50   100   150   Km   80   160

45a and b (opposite). *The Irish in Britain, 1851*

many of the British, and there were many popular anti-Catholic
demonstrations, culminating in the Stockport riot of 1852 in which
an anti-Catholic mob destroyed Catholic property and injured a
number of Irish Catholics.

With the ending of discrimination against Catholics and with the
abandonment by most Irish-born in Britain of support for revolutionary movements, assimilation has become easier. Emigration has

152

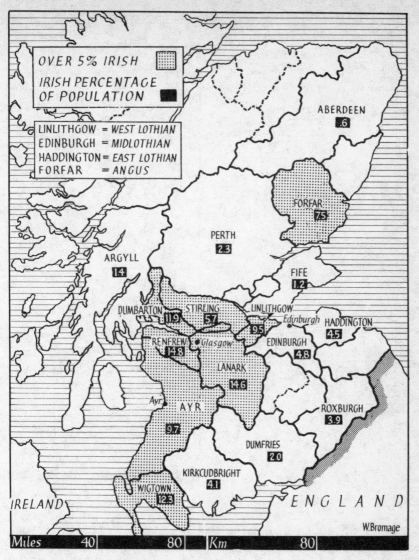

OVER 5% IRISH

IRISH PERCENTAGE
OF POPULATION

LINLITHGOW = WEST LOTHIAN
EDINBURGH = MIDLOTHIAN
HADDINGTON = EAST LOTHIAN
FORFAR = ANGUS

ABERDEEN
.6

FORFAR
7.5

PERTH
2.3

ARGYLL
1.4

FIFE
1.2

DUMBARTON
11.9

STIRLING
5.7

LINLITHGOW
Edinburgh
9.5

HADDINGTON
4.5

RENFREW
14.8

Glasgow

EDINBURGH
4.8

LANARK
14.6

Ayr

AYR
9.7

ROXBURGH
3.9

DUMFRIES
2.0

KIRKCUDBRIGHT
4.1

WIGTOWN
12.3

IRELAND

ENGLAND

W. Bromage

Miles   40   80   Km   80

lessened. There are fewer Irish-born in Britain now than there were
a century ago; the 1971 figure was 720,985, which is only 1·34%
of the whole population. Popular anti-immigrant prejudice has been
diverted towards the coloured population, and with the Irish no
longer representing an economic threat their integration has
become easier. A century ago the Irish were almost exclusively in
labouring jobs; they now contribute a proportionately high number
of nurses, doctors, teachers and civil servants.

153

46. *The Irish in America*

Politically the Irish in Britain tend to identify with the Labour Party, although their loyalty to the Liberal Party, which dated from Gladstone's conversion to Home Rule in the 1880s (31), continued until the 1930s. This political stance conflicts oddly with the comparative lack of success of the Irish Labour Party and also with the middle-class aspirations of most of the Irish community in Britain, but it is mainly a consequence of a long-standing antipathy to the Conservative Party, which has in part been returned.

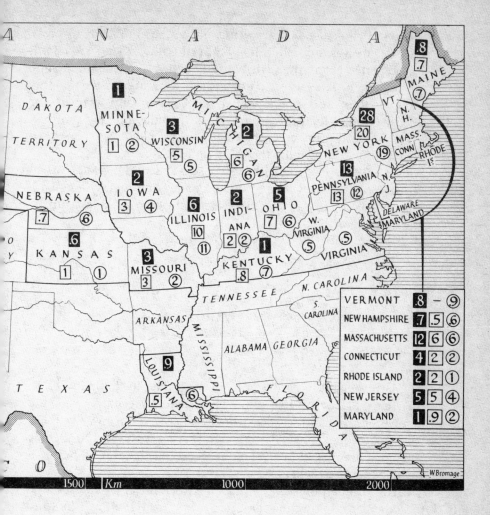

VERMONT	.8	–	9
NEW HAMPSHIRE	.7	.5	.6
MASSACHUSETTS	12	6	6
CONNECTICUT	4	2	2
RHODE ISLAND	2	2	1
NEW JERSEY	5	5	4
MARYLAND	1	.9	2

W.Bromage

46. THE IRISH IN AMERICA

In the eighteenth century, when there was a high level of Irish Presbyterian emigration to the United States, there was a welcome for them there. There was a need for labour. Massachusetts and Pennsylvania, for example, wanted white labour to help repel the Indians on the frontiers. South Carolina wanted white labour because of a fear of being overwhelmed by a coloured population.

But a steady immigration rate of a few thousand Presbyterians was one thing; an influx of poverty-stricken, disease-ridden Catholics was another, and there were initially serious problems of prejudice. There was great ill-feeling between Catholics and Protestants in the period before the Civil War and anti-Catholic discrimination was common. The Irish had established themselves as the majority group within the Catholic church in America, and were on the offensive rather than the defensive. By the time the Civil War was over they had won acceptance, and Irish churchmen played an important part in helping the assimilation of the immigrants.

By 1870 therefore the Irish were a settled and important element in American life. It is interesting to see the pattern of Irish emigration to the country during the nineteenth century, shown in the following figures:

Year	Number of Irish immigrants
1820	3,614
1830	2,721
1840	39,430
1850	164,004
1860	48,637
1870	56,996

Not surprisingly the period of main opposition to the Irish within the United States was that of the mid-nineteenth century, when the number of immigrants had grown enormously. From 1847–54 there were more than 100,000 immigrants every year. As the figures slackened and began to level off at an acceptable level, so the Irish became more integrated.

Useful comparisons can be made between the Irish and some of the other principal ethnic groups in America – the English, Scots and Germans. In 1870 it was estimated that the numbers of native-born of these groups in the country were as follows:

Irish	1,855,827	English	550,688
Germans	1,690,410	Scots	140,809

Their distribution is interesting: the variations between the Irish, English and Scots can be seen in the map. The Germans congregated mainly in Illinois (12%), Indiana (4·6%), Michigan (3·8%), Minnesota (2·4%), Missouri (6·7%), New Jersey (3·2%), New York (18·7%), Ohio (10·8%), Pennsylvania (9·5%) and Wisconsin (9·6%).

In their choice of occupations, a useful contrast can be made between the Irish immigrants and the other major Catholic group – the Germans. The Germans were on the whole in better jobs and economically superior to the Irish; it is surprising to see that the Irish, coming from a predominantly agricultural economy, should have tended to avoid agriculture – perhaps because of fear of a repetition of the famine, and also because of an innate conservatism which kept them from venturing out of the cities.

The percentages of the communities in various occupations were as follows:

Occupation	Irish	German
Agriculture	7·5%	13·3%
Personal and professional services	23·0%	11·3%
Trade and transportation	6·4%	6·7%
Manufacturing and mining industries	14·3%	18·0%

The Irish progressed quickly economically, politically and socially in America. From the early and middle nineteenth century, when they competed with blacks for the worst jobs, they advanced to better jobs through improved education and greater financial security. They showed an early interest in American politics and quickly gained a reputation for ruthlessness and corruption in politics; part of the Irish support for the Kennedys was a burning ambition to achieve political respectability, and to get rid of the Tammany Hall image.

47. AMERICA AND IRISH POLITICS

Many of the emigrants who left Ireland for America during and after the famine brought with them a legacy of bitterness, which soon became transformed into political activity. This bitterness was harnessed by John O'Mahony, a Young Irelander, who with James Stephens had fled to Paris after the failure of the 1848 rising. In America he later founded a political group called the Emmet Monument Association, which by 1858 had been renamed the Fenian Brotherhood. Stephens founded a sister movement in Ireland, also known as the Irish Republican Brotherhood (I.R.B.) or 'the Organization', and branches of it spread throughout Britain and America. The movement was dedicated to the principle of republicanism. The out-break of the American Civil War in 1861 put paid to plans for a rising, since American political and financial support was

47. *American and Irish politics:*
    De Valera's American tour

no longer forthcoming. However, it was hoped that following the Civil War trained Irish soldiers from both sides would be available to fight for independence, possibly with support from the American government. At the end of the Civil War several hundred Irish soldiers arrived in Ireland from America. The government moved before the Fenians could rise, and crippled the movement to such an extent that its final effort, in March 1867, was a total failure.

Fenianism nevertheless remained a potent force in Britain, Ireland and America. In 1879 under the leadership of the American Fenial John Devoy, head of the political organisation Clan-na-Gael, which cloaked Fenianism, the movement joined in a tripartite agreement between Parnell and Michael Davitt in the joint struggle for constitutional and land reform; this alliance, referred to as the New

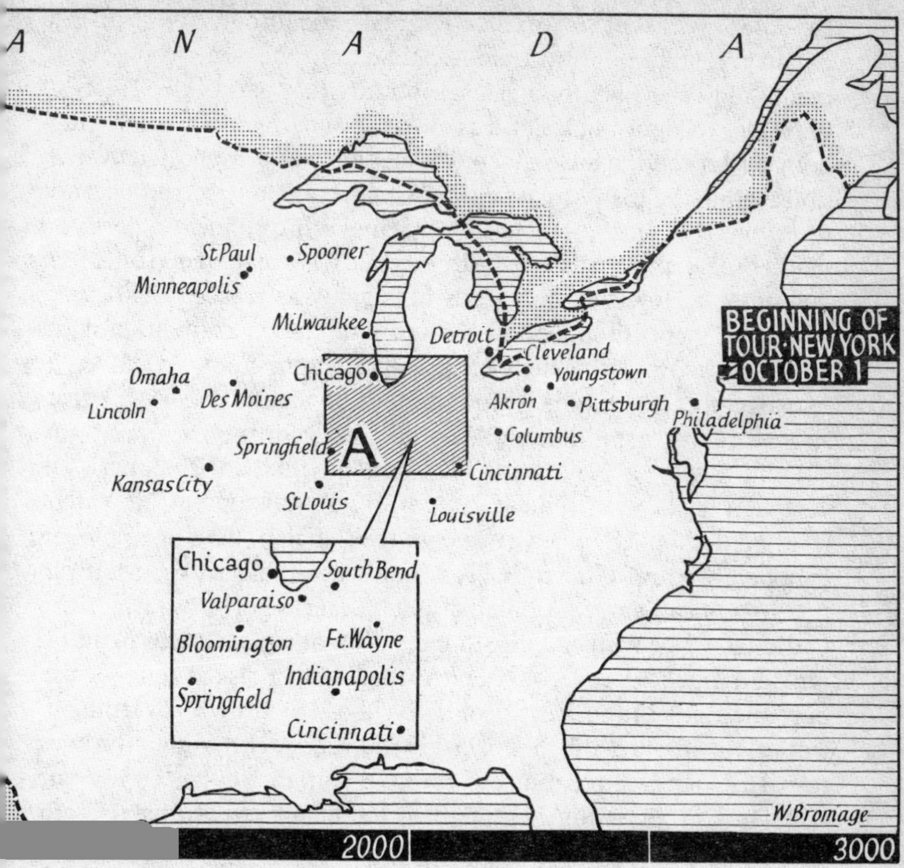

A   N   A   D   A

St Paul • Spooner
Minneapolis•

Milwaukee• Detroit
Cleveland
Youngstown
Omaha Chicago•
Lincoln Des Moines Akron • Pittsburgh
• Columbus Philadelphia
Springfield• A
Cincinnati
Kansas City
St Louis
Louisville

BEGINNING OF
TOUR·NEW YORK
OCTOBER 1

Chicago• • South Bend
Valparaiso •
Bloomington• Ft.Wayne
• Indianapolis
Springfield•
Cincinnati •

W.Bromage
2000   3000

Departure, provided political and financial support. On Parnell's
American visit in 1880 he collected $200,000.

Although this alliance did not last, the Irish-Americans kept a
voice in Irish affairs. It was Clan-na-Gael which organised Douglas
Hyde's tour of America in 1906 on behalf of the Gaelic League, when
he collected £12,500. It was Devoy who was largely responsible
for encouraging Thomas Clarke to return to Ireland from America
in order to work for revolution. During the time leading up to the
1916 rising, negotiations between the I.R.B. and the German
government on arms were conducted through Devoy.

When, therefore, during the war of independence which lasted
from January 1919 to July 1921 Dáil Eireann needed financial and
political support, it was natural to turn to Clan-na-Gael and Devoy.

De Valera was sent to America with two major objectives: first, to obtain recognition for an Irish Republic from the American government, and consequently a refusal to ratify that part of the Treaty of Versailles recognising Ireland as an integral part of the United Kingdom, and second to raise a loan. His mission was complicated by divisions within the Irish Americans, some of whom preferred propaganda to revolution. De Valera failed to achieve his political objectives; neither the Republicans nor the Democrats were prepared to offer him any support. However, financially his stay was a great success. Everywhere he went throughout the country he drew enormous crowds. The map shows the extent of his official tour, from 1 October to 29 November 1919, which took in the main areas of Irish-American strength. Over 5 million dollars were raised for the External Loan.

Politically, he achieved little. Dissension with the Irish-Americans centred over how to achieve American political support; de Valera rejected the advice of Devoy and Judge Cohalan, who having been snubbed by the Democratic President Wilson, placed their faith in the Republican party. Cohalan also felt that support from American parties could be won only by stopping short at requesting recognition for the republic, but recommended that they be asked to recognise only the right of the Irish people to choose their own government. De Valera insisted on taking a hard line, and his resolution was rejected by the Conventions of the two parties. Neither Devoy nor Cohalan had given much support to the de Valera campaign, both because of personality differences and their clash of interests; and de Valera claimed that they were Americans first and Irish second. His dispute with the Irish-Americans came into the open in the columns of the *Gaelic American*. By February 1920 there was an open breach.

De Valera left the United States in December 1920. The breach with Devoy and Cohalan had not been healed; indeed de Valera had founded a rival Irish-American organisation called the American Association for the Recognition of the Irish Republic (A.A.R.I.R.). During the Irish Civil War which was to follow, the Republicans received support from the A.A.R.I.R. while the Free Staters were supported by the older Irish-American movement. The leading spirit of the A.A.R.I.R. was Joseph McGarrity, who later broke with de Valera when he began to act against the I.R.A. (32). His group and their successors continued to give some measure of financial support to the I.R.A.

When violence erupted in Northern Ireland in 1969 (79) there were many within the Irish-American community who foresaw a civil war and wanted to help the Catholics. Of all the official and unofficial groups collecting American money for Irish Republicans during the 1970s, the most effective and notorious was the Irish Northern Aid Committee (NORAID), which collected well over $1 million. Ostensibly intended for the families of 'political prisoners', NORAID funds are widely believed to have been channelled mainly towards arming and otherwise assisting the Provisional I.R.A. It and other such groups have been denounced by leaders of the major Irish political parties and – with possibly more effect – by the four most influential Irish-American politicians, Senators Edward Kennedy, Patrick Moynihan and Tip O'Neill and Governor Hugh Carey of New York.

The condemnations have had their effect on the majority of Irish-Americans, who have no wish to see their money go to buy bombs or guns; but, as always, a hard core of I.R.A. supporters have remained loyal. During the 1970s the Provisional I.R.A. received from Irish-America not just large sums of money but also shipments of dynamite stolen by construction workers and rifles (particularly the M-1, Enfield and Armalite) purchased easily and legally in the American gun-stores. By the late 1970s the Provisional I.R.A. carried weapons more modern than those of the Loyalist paramilitary forces or the British army.

48. INTERNATIONAL RELATIONS

Under the Cosgrave governments (1922–32) the Irish Free State played an important role in changing the nature of the British Commonwealth. In 1931 the Statute of Westminster formally acknowledged that in future the dominions would have equality with Britain and would not without their consent be bound by Westminster legislation. Although Fianna Fáil had consistently denounced Cumann na nGaedheal as pro-British, it was this change in dominion status which gave the de Valera governments of the next 16 years the basis on which to build in securing independence from Britain (32).

On 11 December 1936, the day of Edward VIII's abdication, the Dáil passed the External Relations Act which made Ireland a republic

48. *International relations: dates of diplomatic exchanges*

in practice, although the British monarch still had a role for the purposes of accreditation of Irish diplomats. In 1937 de Valera introduced a new constitution which affirmed Ireland's independence and made no mention of king or commonwealth. It was approved by the Dáil in June 1937 and by 57% of voters in July. In May 1938 Ireland's first President, Dr Douglas Hyde, was elected. The following year there was an Anglo-Irish agreement which ended the economic war (32) and removed from Britain all military and naval facilities in southern Ireland; this latter concession made it possible for Ireland to remain neutral during the Second World War (23).

The 1948 inter-party government decided to clarify Ireland's con-

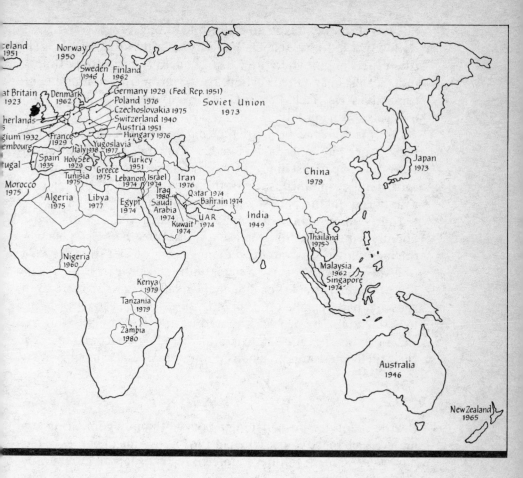

Iceland 1951
Norway 1950
Sweden 1946
Finland 1962
Germany 1929 (Fed. Rep. 1951)
Great Britain 1923
Denmark 1962
Poland 1976
Czechoslovakia 1975
Soviet Union 1973
Netherlands
Switzerland 1940
Austria 1951
Belgium 1932
France 1929
Hungary 1976
Luxembourg
Italy 1938
Yugoslavia 1977
Portugal
Spain 1935
Holy See 1929
Turkey 1951
Japan 1973
Morocco 1975
Tunisia 1975
Greece 1975
Lebanon 1974
Israel 1974
Iran 1976
China 1979
Algeria 1975
Libya 1977
Egypt 1974
Iraq 1980
Qatar 1974
Bahrain 1974
Saudi Arabia 1974
Kuwait 1974
UAR 1974
India 1949
Nigeria 1960
Thailand 1975
Malaysia 1962
Singapore 1974
Kenya 1979
Tanzania 1979
Zambia 1980
Australia 1946
New Zealand 1965

stitutional position which was that of a *de jure* but not *de facto* member of the commonwealth and a *de facto* but not *de jure* republic. In November 1938 the External Relations Act was repealed and the state declared a republic. This final step marked the end of Ireland's almost total preoccupation in foreign affairs with Anglo-Irish relations. Although Ireland had joined the League of Nations in 1923 and had been elected to its council in 1930, and although de Valera was a respected president of the council in 1932, Ireland showed very limited interest or faith in the League. Not until 1955 when Ireland was elected to the United Nations did she begin seriously to consider herself to have a worthwhile international role.

163

She has since then taken an active role in U.N. peace-keeping missions. By 1980 Irish soldiers had served in the Middle East, Zaire (then the Congo, where they lost 26 men), Cyprus, New Guinea, India, Pakistan and the Lebanon. The government's commitment to this activity was such that, in 1964, one-sixth of Ireland's army was on peace-keeping duty.

Disarmament has been another major objective of Irish foreign policy since joining the U.N. She has also tended to take a consistently anti-imperialist line, and latterly has been showing some concern about economic justice for the Third World. Development aid rose twelve-fold to almost £10 million between 1973 and 1978.

The 1970s brought Irish membership of the E.E.C. (49) and consequently required her to establish new priorities in foreign policy. As the map shows, she continued to move ever further from the isolationism of her early days as a state. Within seven years of joining the E.E.C. she had established diplomatic relations with 28 more countries and had upgraded several other postings from non-residential to residential. The problems caused in the 1970s by the Northern Ireland crisis did not detract from Ireland's new commitment to constructiveness and pragmatism in international relations.

49. IRELAND IN THE E.E.C.

Having spent decades pursuing a policy of non-alignment, Ireland implicitly changed course when in 1961 its two major parties (which have very similar priorities in foreign policy) supported the unsuccessful application to join the European Economic Community. During the 1960s, economic necessity obliged Ireland nevertheless to abandon its traditional wide-ranging protectionism by gradual but extensive measures of trade liberalisation. Therefore, when in 1970 she once again applied to join the E.C.C., she was in a much stronger position to face up to intensive international competition.

On 10 May 1972 a referendum on E.E.C. membership yielded an 83% vote in favour despite opposition from the Labour Party, trade unions and extreme nationalist groups. The vote reflected an enthusiasm for the E.E.C. that has helped to make Ireland a more significant figure in the community than her size would warrant. The Department of Foreign Affairs has been significantly expanded and strengthened, and in all relevant government departments there has

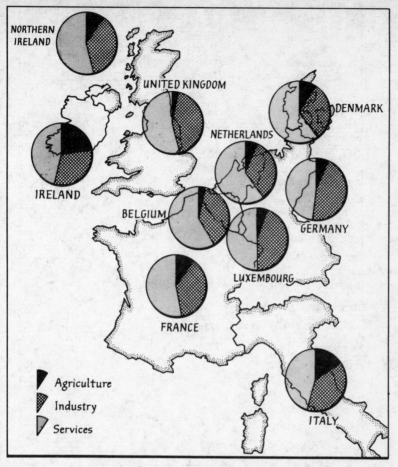

NORTHERN IRELAND

UNITED KINGDOM

DENMARK

NETHERLANDS

IRELAND

BELGIUM

GERMANY

LUXEMBOURG

FRANCE

Agriculture

Industry

Services

ITALY

49a. *Civilian employment in the E.E.C., 1977*

been a policy of selecting high calibre civil servants for E.E.C. related work.

Although membership has posed some problems of adjustment, the overall benefits have been considerable. Programmes such as the Common Agricultural Policy (C.A.P.) and the Regional and Social Fund made Ireland a net beneficiary from the E.E.C. in financial terms of £1,357 million for the period 1973 to 1979. Growing resentment within the community about the inefficiency and wastefulness of C.A.P. is likely to lead to reforms that will reduce Ireland's share of the cake, but meanwhile E.E.C. subsidies have helped to accelerate

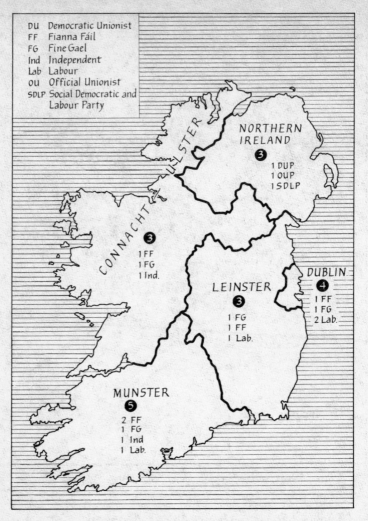

DU Democratic Unionist
FF Fianna Fáil
FG Fine Gael
Ind Independent
Lab Labour
OU Official Unionist
SDLP Social Democratic and
       Labour Party

ULSTER

NORTHERN
IRELAND
3
1 DUP
1 OUP
1 SDLP

CONNACHT
3
1 FF
1 FG
1 Ind.

LEINSTER
3
1 FG
1 FF
1 Lab.

DUBLIN
4
1 FF
1 FG
2 Lab.

MUNSTER
5
2 FF
1 FG
1 Ind
1 Lab.

49b. *Ireland in the E.E.C.: European elections, 1979*

the urgent industrialisation programme. Map 49a shows how heavily dependent on agriculture is Ireland still, compared to the other E.E.C. members.

The benefits have not been purely financial, E.E.C. membership has done a great deal to enhance Ireland's self confidence as a nation, reduce her parochialism and make her look to the future more than to the past (which helps to explain the distaste for the E.E.C. shown by extremist nationalist groups). It was an expression of that self-confidence that led Ireland in March 1979 to break the link with sterling and join the European Monetary System (E.M.S.). Northern Ireland, like the rest of the United Kingdom, has considerably less reason to be enthusiastic about the benefits of membership.

Map 49b shows the results of the June 1979 elections to the European Parliament. In both Northern Ireland and the Republic the electorate voted for personalities rather than parties or policies; hence winning candidates included controversial figures like Síle de Valera of Fianna Fáil, Ian Paisley of the Democratic Unionists and two independents. One consequence of this has been a fragmentation of Irish political alignment within Europe. The 18 Euro-M.P.s are aligned as follows:

Fianna Fáil:	European Progressive Democratic Group
Fine Gael:	European People's Party (Christian Democrats)
Labour *S.D.L.P.*	Socialist Group
O.U.P.:	European Democratic Group (European Conservatives)
D.U.P.:	Non-aligned
Thomas Maher (Ind.):	Liberal and Democratic Group
Neil Blaney (Ind.):	Group for the Technical Coordination and Defence of Independent Groups and members

VII Land

The land question has dominated Irish politics for four centuries since the first plantations were attempted under the Tudors. Previously, although the Viking and Norman invasions resulted in the dispossession of many native Irish from their lands, the settlers were insufficient in number to expel the Irish from occupation of at least a part of their old lands. The main victims were the Gaelic leaders, who lost their power to the invaders, rather than the mass of the population, whose way of life did not alter radically.

Mary Tudor was the first monarch to pursue actively the possibilities of plantation. She recognised the necessity for importing settlers in substantial numbers in order to change the composition of the population. She did not succeed because she failed to provide the necessary incentives for prospective settlers, and although she made a number of grants of estates, the newcomers could not expel the native Irish. Similarly Elizabeth made a large number of grants, and although in the case of the Desmond lands the grantees met little opposition from the natives, this was a direct result of the catastrophic effects of the Desmond rebellion on the lives of the natives rather than any acceptance of the newcomers. In fact, the result was similar to that which obtained in Leix and Offaly. The grantees obtained nominal control, but eventually the natives resumed their old lands and their old way of life.

James I was the first ruler to consider the problem of plantation systematically. He saw that no plantation could succeed without the importation of enough settlers to re-people the land in large numbers. He was fortunate in that the long-standing associations of the Scots and northern Irish (XII) had given the Scots a familiarity with Ireland which encouraged them to accept the challenge of emigrating there. Poverty at home was another powerful incentive, as was later the persecution which the Scots Presbyterians were to experience at the hands of James I in his capacity as King James VI of Scotland.

The Plantation of Ulster therefore succeeded in changing the character of the population, in that those native Irish who remained in planted areas were forced to work as labourers for an alien people or to content themselves with land vastly inferior to their earlier possessions.

The confiscations which followed the Cromwellian invasion and the defeat of the Stuarts continued this process. Both the middle and lower classes, as well as the aristocrats, suffered directly from the confiscations and were forced to move away from their traditional homes or to work as labourers.

The Penal Laws of the eighteenth century continued the movement in the ownership of land from Catholics to Protestants and intensified the trend towards absentee landlords, letting land through middle men to a multitude of tenants. Even resident landlords encouraged the development of the small farm, since from 1793 with the enfranchisement of the forty shilling freeholder (30) political power could be extended by the increase of the number of small holders of land. Other landlords did not attempt to increase the size of holdings, realising that ultimately unchecked sub-letting would lead to economic disaster, but such reforms could be achieved only by the imposition of great misery on the existing inhabitants through evictions. Since there was virtually no way of making a living except through occupation of a piece of land, any landlord expelling tenants was probably condemning them to death.

The greatest hardship was experienced in Connacht, western Munster and western Ulster, since those were the areas with the poorest land and the highest populations. Other parts of the country, like Leinster and the midlands, had lower populations and better land, and some industries. Ulster was more prosperous both because of her widespread domestic industry which was usually combined with farming and because her tenants had better conditions. Not until the land acts of the late nineteenth century was any serious attempt made to give by law to all Irish tenants those protections which were available in Ulster by custom. Tenant-right, or the Ulster Custom, gave tenants security of tenure and some compensations for improvements made on their land. The granting of these concessions, even though they alleviated the situation in the short-term, failed to attack the root of the problem which was that the country was farmed by tenants rather than owners. Once this was recognised by the government the land question was on its way to being answered, and the transference of the land to those who worked it was accomplished with speed (56).

50. TUDOR PLANTATIONS

After Henry VIII had broken the power of the house of Kildare (26) in 1534, he set out to become King of Ireland *de facto* as well as *de jure*. He accomplished the latter in 1541, when his title was changed by an Irish parliament from Lord of Ireland to King of Ireland.

He set out to achieve the former by a steady process of establishing his claim to the whole of Ireland. He already commanded the Pale and he had confiscated the Kildare lands, although he had permitted the Irish occupiers to remain. He believed that it would be possible to persuade the semi-independent Gaelic and Anglo-Irish lords outside the Pale to accept his authority, if in exchange he offered them greater security in their territories by giving them legal title to their lands. The principle by which rulers of various territories surrendered their lands to the Crown and received them back *in capite* by re-grant under certain conditions is usually known as 'Surrender and Re-grant'. Forty of the most important lords accepted this principle, some of them receiving English titles, for example O'Neill became Earl of Tyrone, O'Brien Earl of Thomond, MacWilliam Burke of Galway became Earl of Clanrickard, and MacGillapatrick Baron of Upper Ossory.

The apparent success of his policy caused Henry to leave these grantees undisturbed. He was prepared to rule indirectly through them, although he managed during the course of his reign to extend his immediate rule throughout Leinster and into Munster. With the succession of Edward VI, a more aggressive policy was pursued by the English government. In reprisal for insurrection, O'Connor of Offaly and O'More of Leix were imprisoned and their lands

170

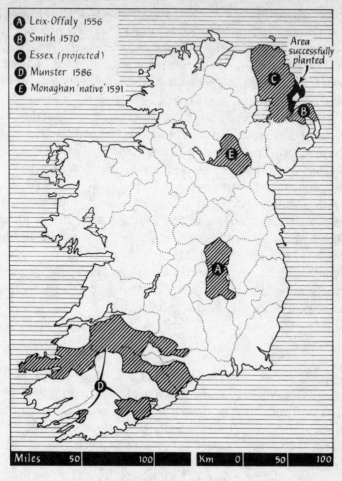

50. *Tudor plantations*

declared forfeit. In 1556, under Mary, a plantation scheme for most of Leix and Offaly was declared, the countries being renamed Queen's County and King's County. One hundred and sixty families, mostly from England and the Pale, were granted estates. The natives resisted, and there were many risings of varying degrees of seriousness during the rest of the century.

Under Elizabeth determined encroachments upon independent territories caused suspicion leading to insurrection. The Fitzgeralds of Desmond, for both religious and territorial reasons, rebelled twice between 1569 and 1573, and 1579 and 1583. In 1583 the Earl of

171

Desmond was killed and in 1586 his whole territory – 574,628 acres in counties Cork, Limerick, Kerry and Waterford – was formally confiscated, with a view to a plantation. Ultimately, however, only 210,000 acres were actually settled, being divided mainly into estates of 12,000, 8,000, 6,000 and 4,000 acres, although Sir Walter Raleigh received about 40,000 acres. Although there was little resistance from the native population, many of them having died during the Desmond wars and many more having fled to safer parts of the country, the plantation did not prove sufficiently rewarding financially to Elizabeth to encourage its repetition. When MacMahon of Monaghan was attainted in 1591, and his land confiscated, rather than attempt another plantation she divided the territory between the MacMahons and MacKennas. After the death of the rebellious Shane O'Neill Elizabeth confiscated his land. Although over the next decade she made a number of abortive grants to Englishmen, including the Earl of Essex and Thomas Smith, she was ultimately obliged to permit Turloch Luineach O'Neill to rule the whole territory formerly held by Shane.

51. PLANTATIONS OF JAMES I

After the submission of O'Neill and O'Donnell in 1603 (15), James restored them to their lands. However, his imposition of English law and government upon Ulster proved unacceptable to the proud northern chiefs who left for exile in Italy in September 1607, accompanied by over ninety other Irish leaders. This afforded an opportunity for confiscation of their lands, and the six counties of Armagh, Coleraine (later Londonderry), Donegal, Tyrone, Fermanagh and Cavan were duly escheated to the crown. Monaghan, which had been subject to surrender and regrant in 1591, was exempt from this confiscation.

This land comprised about 3,800,000 acres, of which 1,500,000 acres were either partly or wholly infertile – this portion being restored to the native Irish. Of the remaining land, substantial grants were made to the Established church, Royal Schools, military forts and towns. An agreement was made between James and the city of London according to the terms of which the county of Coleraine – renamed Londonderry and slightly extended in size – was to be granted to the city in exchange for financial backing for the plantation. In consequence of this a number of

Areas included in the
plantations of JAMES I

Private plantations

DONEGAL
LONDON-
DERRY
ANTRIM
TYRONE
DOWN
FERMANAGH
ARMAGH
LEITRIM
CAVAN
LONGFORD
WESTMEATH
KING'S COUNTY
QUEEN'S COUNTY
WEXFORD

W. Bromage

Miles 50 100 Km 80 160

51. *Plantations of James I*

English planters settled in the county. The city's failure to observe regulations concerning Irish tenants was to result in the confiscation of the counties by Wentworth (16). The 'Articles of Plantation' of Ulster, issued in May 1609, appointed the remaining 500,000 acres of fertile land for colonisation.

There were three divisions of settlers:

Undertakers:	Scots and English of high rank who were to receive estates of 2,000, 1,500 or 1,000 acres at a rent of £5 6s. 8d. per acre and who could have English or Scots tenants only.
Servitors:	Mainly administrators or military men who were granted estates of similar size at a rent of £8 per 1,000 acres – Irish tenants were permitted in certain cases.
Native Irish:	These paid £10 13s. 4d. per acre and were allowed Irish tenants – their estates were usually between 100 and 300 acres.

The undertakers and servitors receiving 2,000 acres were required to bring in a minimum of 48 Scots or English tenants to settle on their estates.

This plantation was successful. Although it proved impossible to persuade the planned number of English and Scots to emigrate to Ireland, nevertheless a substantial number arrived. By 1618 it is estimated that there were about 40,000 Scots in Ulster, who had emigrated to obtain land and escape religious persecution.

A simultaneous plantation was taking place in Antrim and Down. In 1605 the north-east of Down was granted to Hugh Montgomery and the north-west to James Hamilton. Sir Arthur Chichester was granted a large stretch of land in Antrim. Hamilton and Montgomery brought in Scottish immigrants; about 10,000 were settled in Down by 1614. Although Chichester established an English colony, many Scots also settled in the south of Antrim. These private plantations proved very successful. Nevertheless, throughout Ulster, the natives usually managed to remain, often surreptitiously, frequently as virtual serfs to the new owners.

Emboldened by the success of the Ulster Plantation, the government followed it up by a series of minor plantations in distinctively Irish areas, where a legal quibble could prove the Crown's title to

174

the land. During the remainder of James's reign, plantations were carried out in Irish-held territories in Leitrim, Westmeath, King's County, Queen's County and Longford. Although there was some success in establishing a strong Protestant element in Wexford and Ely O'Carroll (the baronies of Clonlisk and Ballybrit [3] in King's County), these plantations achieved only a very limited success.

52. CROMWELLIAN LAND CONFISCATIONS

After 1650 the Cromwellian parliament saw Ireland mainly as a vehicle for paying its debts. These debts were primarily to soldiers and adventurers, who had subscribed money between 1642 and 1646 for the conduct of the war. An extensive land survey was undertaken, twenty-two counties being surveyed under the supervision of Petty (II). This survey enabled the government to dispose of the land with some degree of accuracy.

The Irish population were dealt with decisively. Many of the soldiers went to serve in European armies; beggars were sent to the West Indies. A series of Acts of 1653 decreed that Irish landowners were to be transplanted to Connacht and Clare and their lands in the rest of the country confiscated for the creditors of Parliament. This of course involved massive confiscations throughout Connacht and Clare also, in order to cater for the transplantees. The map shows the percentage of land confiscated in each county and also shows the class of assignee to whom the land was given.

Of the eleven million acres of land confiscated in Leinster, Munster and Ulster nearly eight million were considered profitable land. Additionally, north-east Mayo and all of county Sligo were later taken. Precise figures of the number of planters are not available. There were over 1,000 adventurers and it was originally intended that 35,000 soldiers should be granted land in Ireland. The vast majority of these, however, sold their entitlements. It is thought that less than a quarter of them actually settled in Ireland.

There was a logical plan for the dispersal of adventurers and soldiers. Soldiers were concentrated in areas where military security was important – for example in the land surrounding Connacht. The plan did not, however, work as well as had been expected. The numbers of planters were much fewer than had been planned

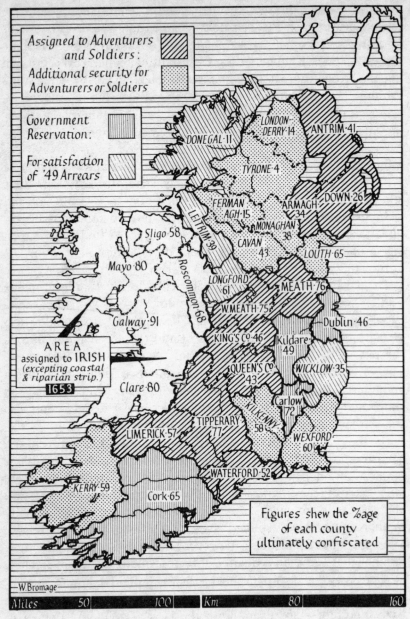

Legend

- **Assigned to Adventurers and Soldiers:**
- **Additional security for Adventurers or Soldiers**
- **Government Reservation:**
- **For satisfaction of '49 Arrears**

DONEGAL·11
LONDON-DERRY·14
ANTRIM·41
TYRONE·4
DOWN·26
FERMANAGH·15
ARMAGH·34
LEITRIM·39
Sligo·58
MONAGHAN·38
CAVAN·43
LOUTH·65
Mayo·80
Roscommon·68
LONGFORD·61
MEATH·76
W.MEATH·75
Galway·91
Dublin·46
KING'S Cº·46
Kildare·49
AREA assigned to IRISH (excepting coastal & riparian strip.) 1653
QUEEN'S Cº·43
WICKLOW·35
Clare·80
KILKENNY·58
Carlow·72
TIPPERARY·77
WEXFORD·60
LIMERICK·57
WATERFORD·52
KERRY·59
Cork·65

Figures shew the %age of each county ultimately confiscated

W.Bromage

Miles 50 100 Km 80 160

52. *Cromwellian and Restoration land confiscations, 1653–65*

for, and they showed an early tendency to intermarriage with the Irish. Nevertheless, it was overall a remarkable operation. By the Restoration the whole character of the ownership of land throughout Ireland had changed. Charles II did little to alter the position. Ownership was now largely in Protestant hands – and the ensuing development of a country owned by an ever decreasing number of Protestant owners with an ever increasing number of Catholic tenants was to dominate the later history of Ireland.

Another important development came from the confiscation of property in all the cities and towns which had been held by the Confederate forces (16). City government was henceforth to be a Protestant monopoly, except for a brief period under James II. This also set a pattern which was to store up problems for the future.

53. THE TRANSFER OF LAND OWNERSHIP: 1603–1778

At the end of the Tudor monarchy, in 1603, despite the Tudor confiscations and plantations, 90% of Irish land was still in Catholic hands. By 1641, mainly due to the success of the Ulster Plantations, this proportion had been reduced to 59%, a figure which was further reduced by the Cromwellian Plantation. By the accession of James II in 1685, only 22% of land was left in Catholic hands. After the Treaty of Limerick had been implemented, with yet more changes in land ownership, Catholics held only 14%. The Penal Laws reduced this proportion even more by a series of restrictive acts.

An act of 1704 dictated that no Catholic could purchase any interest in land other than a lease of thirty-one years or under. No Catholic could acquire land from a Protestant by marriage or inheritance. A Catholic could not dispose of his estate by will; it was automatically divisible on his death among all his sons. However, if the eldest son became a member of the established church he would receive the whole estate. If during his father's lifetime he conformed, his father could not dispose of the property, since he became a life tenant only.

This act was vigorously enforced and had a profound effect on the disposition of land. Failure to conform to the Church of Ireland brought economic ruin to Catholic families. By the 1770s, when

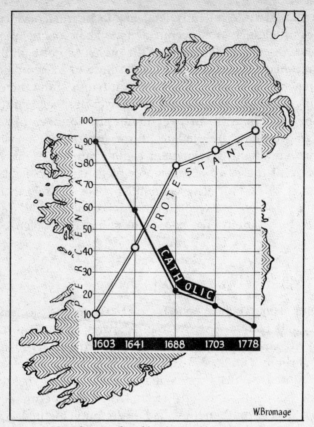

53. *The transfer of land ownership, 1603–1778*

the relaxation of the Penal Laws began, only 5% of land was left to the Catholics.

In addition to losing their land, economic recessions forced the majority of the Irish people to make their living from agriculture. Absentee landlords became more common. Their estates were let to one or several middle-men who usually divided and let the land, which was often then sub-let again. Proportionately, the highest rent was paid by the farmer at the bottom of the pyramid. The pattern of too many tenants paying inflated rents for inadequate land was to have disastrous consequences in the nineteenth century.

Concessions to Catholics on land ownership began in 1771, when the 'Bogland Act' was passed, allowing Catholics to acquire leases of up to sixty-one years on fifty acres or under of unprofitable land.

Gardiner's Relief Act of 1778 permitted Catholics to acquired leases of land for indefinite tenure if they took an oath of allegiance. They could also inherit land in the normal way. In 1782 Catholics were finally allowed to buy, hold or inherit freehold land and leases on the same terms as Protestants. As a safe-guard against Catholics now asking for the re-examination of earlier claims to land, 'Yelverton's Act' confirmed earlier land settlements.

The graph shows the stages of change in land-ownership over 175 years between the Stuart accession and the Relief Act of 1778.

54. PRE-FAMINE AGRICULTURE

Famines were not uncommon in Ireland in the nineteenth century. Potato famines occurred in 1800, 1816, 1817, 1822 and 1836. Usually, failure of the potato crop was partial and was for one season only. In the Great Famine of 1845–8, however, the blight, which was selective in 1845, was general in 1846. There was an unblighted though small crop in 1847 and a partial failure again in 1848.

Agricultural and economic conditions throughout most of the country were such that a crop failure of this magnitude was bound to end in disaster. Because of untrammelled sub-letting, combined with a massive growth in population, more and more people came to depend on less and less land for the means of survival. As map 54a demonstrates, in 1841 the areas with the worst overcrowding also had the poorest land. The proportions of arable land in each county are illustrated, that is, the amount of land suitable for the growth of crops and the pasturing of cattle. Throughout the country there was a very uneven distribution of such land; most of the east and south-east had rich land and a manageable population, while in the west there was appalling over-crowding and poor soil. In Kildare for example, over 85% of the land was arable, supporting 187 people per square mile, while Mayo, with 36% arable land, was supporting 475 people per square mile.

In the north-east of Ireland, though agricultural conditions were poor, the textile industry continued to give employment to a large proportion of the population. The textile industry which had existed in other parts of Ireland had declined during the early nineteenth century, so that while Ulster peasants had an extra source of

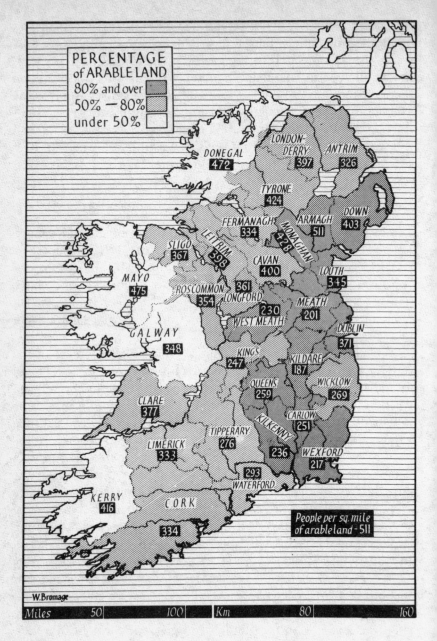

DONEGAL 472

LONDON-DERRY 397

ANTRIM 326

TYRONE 424

DOWN 403

FERMANAGH 334

ARMAGH 511

MONAGHAN 428

SLIGO 367

LEITRIM 398

CAVAN 400

LOUTH 345

MAYO 475

ROSCOMMON 354

LONGFORD 361

MEATH 201

GALWAY 348

WEST MEATH 230

DUBLIN 371

KINGS 247

KILDARE 187

WICKLOW 269

QUEENS 259

CLARE 377

CARLOW 251

KILKENNY 236

TIPPERARY 276

WEXFORD 217

LIMERICK 333

WATERFORD 293

KERRY 416

CORK 334

People per sq. mile
of arable land - 511

W. Bromage

Miles 50 100 Km 80 160

54a. *Pre-famine agriculture, 1841*

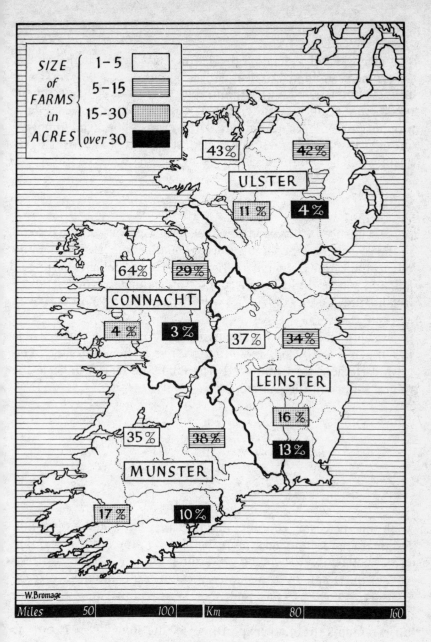

54b. *Farm sizes, 1841*

income, for most peasants in the rest of Ireland agriculture was the only means of survival.

When the full extent of the famine was realised, the British government attempted to deal with it by means of relief works and also by public food distribution centres. Although government reports and studies by independent observers had for years been prophesying an agricultural and social catastrophe, contemporary attitudes to state intervention made it impossible to avert or significantly ameliorate the disaster.

55. POST-FAMINE AGRICULTURE

A consequence of the practice of sub-letting was a continual trend in the years before the famine towards uneconomic farm sizes. Early nineteenth-century observers believed that it was possible to support a family on as little as seven acres of reasonably good land. In Ireland, the majority of families were living on farms of under seven acres in 1841.

The famine, by reducing the population, brought a rapid change in farm sizes in Ireland, and during the rest of the century the trend towards larger farms continued. The following figures indicate the radical nature of the change:

Farm Size	1841	1851	1871	1901
1–5 acres	44·9%	15·5%	13·7%	12·2%
5–15 acres	36·6%	33·6%	31·5%	29·9%
15–30 acres	11·5%	24·8%	25·5%	26·0%
30 plus acres	7·0%	26·1%	29·3%	31·9%

With this increasing concentration on larger farms and a more professional approach to agriculture, has come a drop in the proportion of the population depending on farming for a way of life. In 1841, 66% of those employed were in agriculture; this dropped to 52·6% in 1851, 42·6% in 1861 and in 1977 was down to 23% in the Republic and 10% in Northern Ireland. However, agricultural produce remains the main export item of the Republic (67) and an important export from Northern Ireland.

There is a marked difference in agricultural organisation in the two parts of Ireland. In Northern Ireland there are a large number

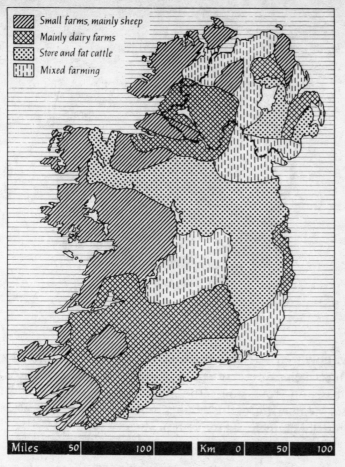

Small farms, mainly sheep
Mainly dairy farms
Store and fat cattle
Mixed farming

Miles 50 100   Km 0 50 100

55a. *Modern agriculture: main farming types*

of small farms which are intensively cultivated for commercial purposes, with crops like cereals and potatoes. In the Republic only the west still has many small farms, and there what has been described as 'cottage farming' is prevalent, that is, the holders can do little more than garner a bare living from the soil.

Overall, the majority of Irish farming is mixed, with a bias towards the raising of cattle. Most farms produce arable crops and also raise livestock on pasture land. Flexibility is possible with mixed farming, and therefore Irish farmers have in general learned to change their products according to the demands of the market. Basi-

183

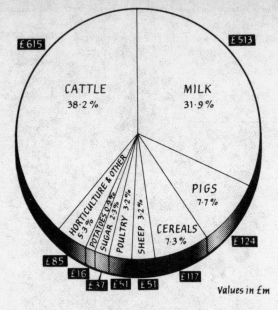

CATTLE
38·2%

MILK
31·9%

£615

£513

HORTICULTURE & OTHER
5·3%

POTATOES 0·3%

SUGAR 2·3%

POULTRY 3·2%

SHEEP 3·2%

PIGS
7·7%

CEREALS
7·3%

£124

£85

£16

£37 £51 £51

£117

Values in £m

55b. *Agricultural output (Republic), 1978*

cally, however, Irish farming is grass farming with cattle and dairy products being pre-eminent. In Northern Ireland there is more emphasis on crops, and cattle are of less importance than in the south. Membership of the EEC has brought to the Republic's farmers an initially dramatic increase in prosperity (49).

56. THE TRANSFER OF LAND OWNERSHIP: 1870–1916

In 1870, after the passing of the first Land Act, only 3% of Irish householders owned any land. By the time of the 1916 rebellion that figure had grown to 63·9% and the battle for land ownership was won. That this happened in so short a time was a tribute to a number of radical and far-seeing measures passed by successive British governments. It was also due to a change of government economic thinking.

The finances of the Union put the stress upon Irish and British mutual contributions to the Exchequer; after 1817 amalgamation of the exchequers took place and it was decided that the Irish contribution should be in the ration of 2:15. For decades a rigid view

184

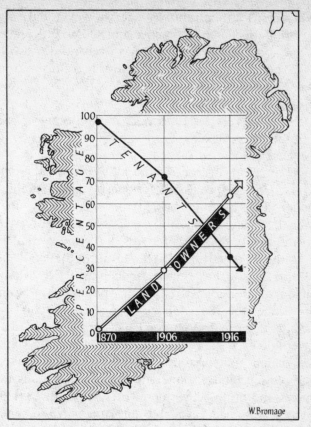

56. *The transfer of land ownership 1870–1916*

prevailed which dictated that all Ireland's economic needs should be met from her own contributions. The inflexibility of the whig government's interpretation of this view was to frustrate the attempts to introduce adequate relief measures to cope with the famine. In the 1890s there was a radical change in this attitude which was to facilitate the transfer of land ownership by making adequate funds available for land purchase. Without this development, the land acts would have been ineffective.

Deasy's act of 1860 converted feudal relations into a contractual agreement and was intended as a protection for tenants. Gladstone's Landlord and Tenant (Ireland) Act (1870) attempted to implement this in a practical way by requiring landlords to pay some compensation for improvements and giving tenants theoretical security of tenure if they paid their rents. The act, however, did not have the teeth to bring this about in practice and so had little effect. At this period, about 80% of profitable land in Ireland was owned by less than 4,000 people. Nearly 10% of the whole country was owned by 20 people. To deal effectively with landowners of such power, more sweeping laws were required.

The Irish Land Act (1881) was much more effective. It extended the Ulster Custom to the whole country and gave the 'Three F's' – fair rent, fixity of tenure and free sale. It set up a Land Court and a Land Commission, among whose responsibilities were the establishment of fair rents, and the provision of money to tenants to buy land.

Although these measures helped, they did not solve the problem of the tenants who had no capital whatsoever, and these could not avail themselves of the offer of 2/3rds of the money under the 1870 Act or 3/4ths under the 1881 Act. Not until the land acts of 1885 and 1891 made all the purchase money available to tenants was it possible really to see the transfer of land on a large scale become a reality. Under the 1885 Ashbourne Act five million pounds was made available for loans from the Land Commission. The Conservative governments of Salisbury and Balfour became committed to the idea of land purchase and made substantial sums of money available and encouraged landlords to sell their lands by offering good prices and using active moral persuasion. In 1891 thirty million pounds was made available for land purchase, and in 1903 the Wyndham Act allocated one hundred million pounds to the same purpose. These acts brought about a major breakthrough. As a consequence of the Wyndham Act, 252,400 tenants purchased their holdings and after the Birrell Act of 1909 a further 66,500 became landowners.

In 1891 the Congested Districts Boards were set up to deal with the poorest parts of rural Ireland: their initial terms of reference confined them only to areas in Donegal, Leitrim, Sligo, Roscommon, Mayo, Galway, Kerry and West Cork, but they were later permitted to extend their sphere of influence. Although many of their experiments with new industries were not particularly successful, they improved economic conditions considerably in many parts of the country, helped 59,510 tenants to buy their land, and gave assistance with improving land and setting up fishing centres and light industries.

Since 1922, the processs of distributing land for purchase by the tenants has continued. During the 1930s de Valera refused to continue paying the annuities (the annual payments by which the tenants repaid their loans) still owing to the British government and an economic war commenced (32). De Valera's main argument was that the Northern Ireland government were no longer required to pay them. A major problem of the Land Commission in the Republic has been the uneconomic holdings which still persist. The Commission has had the responsibility of organising scattered and uneconomic holdings into viable farming units. This they have dealt with successfully.

VIII Communications

The physical difficulties of travel in Ireland were daunting to the traveller, until comparatively recently. The combination of mountains, drumlins, rivers, lakes, bogs and extensive woods (8) made progress difficult and although there were roads they were inadequate in their coverage of the country and badly maintained. The roadways which were constructed in early Ireland were not improved upon substantially until the Norman invasion, and even then the woods continued to bar effective progress until their virtual eradication during the seventeenth century.

The most common method of travel throughout the early and medieval period was by water, especially for trade. Treacherous though the coasts undoubtedly were in many parts of the country, on the south and east they were easier for the transportation of goods than were the inadequate roads. Inland waterways were often used also (63). During this period the Irish were fine sailors.

As the medieval period progressed, improvements in roads were marginal. The Pale usually kept in touch with Waterford, Cork, Limerick and Galway by sea. During the Tudor period a good deal of attention was paid to the improvement of communications. Legislation tried to free main rivers of weirs which blocked transport. Military considerations accelerated the progress of road and bridge building; methods were, however, somewhat unscientific and plans haphazard. In the early seventeenth century, however, in 1614, a Highways Act initiated a more systematic approach to communications. It outlined schemes for linking the principal towns of the plantations, which were taken up enthusiastically in some parts of the country, especially in Ulster, where the planters were hardworking and very conscious of the need for good communications. Since, however, control of communications rested locally, standards throughout the country were very variable. Additionally, however good the roads might be, normal transport was limited to horseback and was therefore slow, and for long journeys, very uncomfortable.

The eighteenth and nineteenth centuries saw a series of transformations in transport, with a new road network and the introduction of jaunting-cars for passenger transport, and first canal and then railway construction (58). With the twentieth century came the upheavals in the transport system caused by the introduction of the motor car and the aeroplane and a revolution in communications in general through the development of radio, television and the telephone (59).

57. EARLY COMMUNICATIONS

The exact routes followed by roads in early Ireland cannot be delineated with certainty; the map, however, reflects the most likely routes of the major roads having regard to contemporary evidence. Certainly there can be no doubt of the existence of wide, soundly-constructed roads (the Irish word being 'slighe'). Where the Irish learned their expertise in road construction is unclear. The Celts used wheeled vehicles which would have required paved roads. It is also likely that contact with Roman Britain taught the Irish to appreciate the skills of road building and their strategic importance.

That early Irish roads were of military importance is unquestionable. They were good enough to make possible the movement of soldiers about the country, and the comparative speed of progress of the Norman invaders was to a considerable extent the result of the road system.

The locations of roads obviously depended to a considerable extent on the location of places of importance, for example royal seats such as Rathcroghan, Ailech, Tara and Cashel, and monasteries hospitable to visitors, such as Derry, Clogher, Fore, Durrow and Roscrea. In addition to the roads shown on the accompanying map, there were of course many lesser roads, such as that from Limerick to Cork, which were of great importance.

The early roads appear to have been paved with stone, wooden

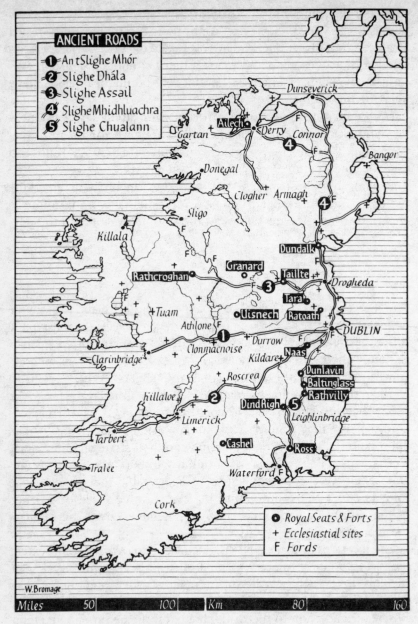

ANCIENT ROADS

❶ An tSlighe Mhór
❷ Slighe Dhála
❸ Slighe Assail
❹ Slighe Mhidhluachra
❺ Slighe Chualann

Dunseverick
Ailech
Gartan
Derry
Connor
Bangor
Donegal
Clogher
Armagh
Sligo
Killala
Dundalk
Granard
Rathcroghan
Tailtte
Drogheda
Tara
Tuam
Uisnech
Ratoath
Athlone
DUBLIN
Clonmacnoise
Durrow
Clarinbridge
Kildare
Naas
Roscrea
Dunlavin
Baltinglass
Killaloe
DindRigh
Rathvilly
Leighlinbridge
Limerick
Tarbert
Cashel
Ross
Tralee
Waterford
Cork

● Royal Seats & Forts
+ Ecclesiastial sites
F Fords

W. Bromage

Miles 50 · 100 · Km · 80 · 160

57. *Early communications*

190

causeways being constructed over bogland. The routes are as follows:

An tSlighe Mhór: The Great Road. A low ridge of eskar (postglacial gravel) known as *Eiscir Riada* marked a dividing line between north and south and enabled journeys to be made across the bogland of the centre of Ireland. This route seems to have formed a basis for the construction of an tSlighe Mhór, stretching from Dublin to the west coast.

Slighe Dhála Meic Umhóir: The Road of Dála, son of Umhóir. This road was designed mainly to link Tara with the south-west coast: it followed a route to the south of the Kildare bog-lands, through the Curragh, across the Barrow and by Slieve Bloom.

Slighe Assail: The Road of Assal. This was considered to be the route connecting Tara with Rathcroghan, the capital of Connacht at a very early period, and dividing Meath into north and south. It diverged from the Slighe Mhidhluachra north of Drogheda, travelled through the gap of Mullingar, between Loughs Owel and Ennell, and across marshy land to Rathcroghan.

Slighe Mhidhluachra: The Road of Mid-luachair. This was the main northern road, from Tara to Armagh. The road led across the plain of Louth to Dundalk, whence it branched off to Armagh, the main-road continuing via the Moyry Pass up to the north-eastern coast, with branches off.

Slighe Chualann: The Road of Cuala. This was the great road linking Dublin with Waterford, passing by the foot of the Wicklow Mountains across the Liffey to the Barrow, crossing it at Dind Righ and thence to Waterford.

58. LATER COMMUNICATIONS

In the eighteenth century there was a significant improvement in communications with the introduction of turnpike roads, which were built as a commercial venture. During the 1730s and 1740s there was an intensive period of road-building throughout most of the country. It did not, however, prove sufficiently profitable for the Grand Jury of each county to plan roads and finance them from the rates.

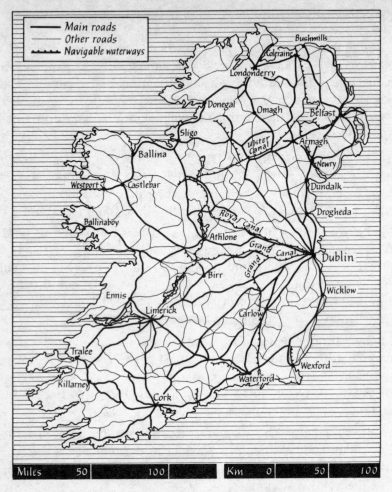

Main roads
Other roads
Navigable waterways

Bushmills
Coleraine
Londonderry
Donegal
Omagh
Belfast
Sligo
Ulster Canal
Armagh
Ballina
Newry
Westport
Castlebar
Dundalk
Ballinaboy
Drogheda
Royal Canal
Athlone
Grand Canal
Grand Canal
Dublin
Birr
Ennis
Wicklow
Limerick
Carlow
Tralee
Wexford
Killarney
Waterford
Cork

Miles 50 100   Km 0 50 100

58. Communications: early nineteenth century

By 1800 it was considered that Irish roads were comparable with those of Britain. The eighteenth century had also seen the beginning of canal building. The Newry Canal, the Lagan Navigation (Belfast to Lough Neagh), the Tyrone Navigation and the Strabane Canal were all completed by 1796. The first half of the nineteenth century saw the completion among others of the Grand Canal, the Royal Canal, the Ulster Canal and navigation works on the Boyne, Barrow, Nore, Suir, Slaney and Shannon Rivers. With the advent of the railway in the next century enthusiasm for canal building waned rapidly. At

192

this period methods of passenger transport were still slow and expensive. Canals were suitable for freight rather than passengers, and few people could afford the mail coach. A dramatic improvement in transport was made in 1815, when Charles Bianconi introduced to Clonmel jaunting-cars for public transport. By 1845 his cars were operating over 3,000 miles of road, covering Munster, Connacht and much of Leinster. With the arrival of the railways he was astute enough to adapt his road services to complement rather than to compete.

Railways operated in Ireland from 1834, when the Dublin-Kingstown route was opened, but their development was comparatively slow. In 1839 the Ulster Railway Company opened the Belfast-Lisburn line, and in 1842 extended it to Portadown. By 1844 the Dublin-Drogheda line was in operation. During the 1840s and 1850s there was a boom in railway ᐧconstruction and by the early 'fifties lines were open from Dublin to Belfast, Galway, Limerick, Cork and Waterford. Although there was little railway construction in the poorer areas, by 1866 there were 1,909 miles of railway, a figure which by 1978 had been reduced to 1,250. In the late nineteenth century light railways were set up to more remote rural districts, but these did not have a very long life. By the 1920s railway services had begun to decline. The development of the motor car forced their contraction.

59. MODERN COMMUNICATIONS

Corus Iompair Eireann was set up in 1944 and it took over by degrees the Great Southern Railway, the Dublin United Transport Company, and the Grand Canal Company. In 1948 the Ulster Transport Authority was set up, and it now performs the functions of the Belfast and County Down Railway, the Northern Ireland Road Transport Board and other earlier boards. C.I.E. and the U.T.A. together took over the Great Northern Railway in 1958.

These two organisations have worked well both together and separately to integrate and rationalise transport services. On the railways, however, only the main trunk routes now survive although efforts have been made to compensate for the lack of railway transport by providing bus and lorry services even in remote

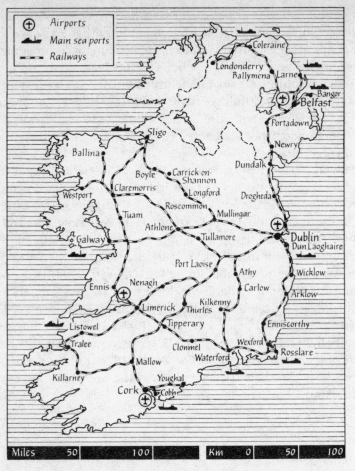

59. *Communications, 1978*

areas. On the western coast, only Tralee, Limerick, Ennis, Galway, Westport, Ballina and Sligo have rail service.

In 1978 passenger journeys on C.I.E. railways were almost 16 million and on road services almost 200 million, while rail freight amounted to almost 4 million tons. It is interesting to note that the number of passengers carried on the railway is increasing, while the number carried on road public transport is decreasing. This is largely because of improved roads which with increased affluence have resulted in a rapid rise in the numbers of private cars in use.

While bus and rail services consistently operate at a loss, international transport by sea and air is flourishing. In recent years the Republic's larger ports have been modernised, notably through containerisation and increased mechanisation. Air transport is expanding quickly and profitably: passenger traffic in 1978 at the Republic's three commercial airports was over 3,500,000.

Northern Ireland's pattern of transport use has been distorted by the events of the 1970s which saw a vast increase in military traffic and a corresponding decrease in tourist traffic; nevertheless, modernisation of Aldergrove airport and the main commercial ports has continued apace.

Considerable progress is also being made in other communications. Despite competition from other news media and from the British press, Irish newspapers are still very numerous north and south proportionate to the population. Seven daily newspapers are published in the Republic and three in Northern Ireland. Broadcasting in the Republic is the responsibility of Radio Telefís Éireann, which is expanding both its radio and television services to match competition from Britain. Northern Ireland's broadcasting services are integrated with those in the rest of the United Kingdom and are run respectively by the British Broadcasting Corporation and the Independent Broadcasting Authority.

Owing mainly to under-capitalisation, the Republic's telecommunications services have lagged in efficiency and market penetration behind those of most of Europe. In 1976 there were only 14 telephones per 100 of the population compared with 38 in the United Kingdom. Membership of the E.E.C., coupled with an export drive that is spearheaded by multinational companies (67), has made it imperative to improve services; a massive modernisation and expansion programme is under way.

IX Industry

The origins of Irish industries were in domestic manufacture and agriculture. By the seventeenth century, cottage industries were widespread, weaving and spinning being a supplementary income in many parts of the country. The influence of the Huguenots and the Quakers on the development of textile industries was significant, especially in the north-east, where they settled in comparatively large numbers and concentrated on linen manufacture.

Throughout the eighteenth century brewing and glass industries grew steadily and despite British protectionism, the domestic market was large enough to encourage the growth of the woollen industry.

The development of the linen industry was encouraged by the government to meet the demands of the English market. They invested money in the industry and set up a Linen Board in 1711 to assist its growth. Dublin merchants, however, provided most of the capital for the industry during the eighteenth century, despite its increasing concentration in the north-east. Initially the industry was mainly in north-east Ulster, in Antrim, Armagh, Down and Derry, but it spread south gradually, first into Tyrone, Monaghan, Cavan and later in Leinster – to Louth, Meath, Westmeath and Longford. Auxiliary industries, such as the spinning of the yarn, were more widespread, extending as far as Roscommon, Mayo, Sligo, Galway, Kerry and King's and Queen's counties.

Unlike the linen industry, the woollen industry was more urban in emphasis, although for a period there was some domestic weaving rurally, especially in the midlands and the south-west.

Other industries were operating with some success by the beginning of the eighteenth century – catering mainly for the domestic market. Many of these had of necessity to be concentrated in the ports, or nearby towns, because of their dependence on imported coal. Distilling, brewing, sugar-refining, glass-making and iron-working were particularly dependent on coal, while milling of grain, paper, wool and flour tended to be concentrated along rivers. There was, however, increasingly a tendency towards the centralisation of industry to take advantage of technological innovations and economies of scale.

There was ample capital available in Ireland to finance industrial expansion. Banking increased in extent greatly during the first half of the eighteenth century, and although later economic crises brought about a number of bankruptcies, nevertheless by the early nineteenth century banks were widespread throughout the country. Apart from banking investments, financial banking was available from landowners, merchants and the government, the latter making substantial grants for industrial development.

The introduction of power-spinning to the Irish linen industry in the 1820s spelled the end of domestic spinning, and concentrated the industry more narrowly in the north-east. By this time the woollen industry was dying; the superiority of cheaper English wool had finally had its effect. This was to impoverish the west of Ireland further as milling and weaving ceased. In 1838 Ireland had to import 86% of her woollen cloth. Cotton, which had also begun as a domestic industry had been industrialised in the 1770s when machines for spinning were introduced, mainly in Belfast, Dublin and Cork. The industry did not have a long period of success, however. By the 1820s the Lancashire cotton industry, like the Yorkshire woollen industry, was gradually strangling all opposition in the British Isles.

The concentration around Belfast of the linen industry which resulted from the investment in power spinning was in Ireland the most dramatic result of the Industrial Revolution, for mechanisation changed the whole industry from a widespread domestic industry to a purely urban industry.

The same kind of concentration was to be seen in brewing and distilling. Within fifty years of 1785, malt houses in Ireland dropped in number by 83% while increasing productivity by 100%. Milling was expanding also, and agricultural industries, like bacon production, maintained their importance up to the famine.

By the middle of the nineteenth century, after the famine, a number of smaller industries were expanding steadily, for example paper, glassworks, ironworks, tanning and shipbuilding. The improvements in communications resulting from the advent of the railways was to be another force for centralisation, since local industry was faced with stiffer competition. They brought compensatory local benefits, however, by vastly extending the range and variety of the retail and wholesale trades. During the second half of the century this centralisation adversely affected such industries as glassmaking, tanning, sugar refining, paper making and milling. By 1885 Parliament found it necessary to appoint a committee to enquire into Irish industry. The work of organisations like the Congested Districts Board (VII) helped to some extent, but industrial recovery was a result more of improvement on the agricultural side, particularly in the dairy industry, than of any overall recovery. There was, however, a gradual improvement in industry. There was even more centralisation in industries like milling, baking, wool and clothing. Greater efficiency of production resulted, and distilling and brewing continued to grow. Linen kept its pre-eminence, and shipbuilding continued to grow, as did engineering, in the north-east.

By the time partition came, industry was still distributed as it had been from the seventeenth century. The only significantly industrialised part of the country was the north-east – a fact which was to be of considerable future significance (81).

When Arthur Griffith died in August 1922 his economic policy of promoting rapid industrialisation with the help of protective tariffs virtually died with him; it was de Valera's government in the 1930s that revived it. Greater industrialisation followed, as did the creation of publicly owned services like Aer Lingus and Bord na Móna (the Peat Board). In the 1950s state intervention was stepped up as part of an effort to expand the economy by encouraging exports, and there was a marked improvement in the range and quality of economic planning. During this period began the highly successful policy of attracting foreign investment by means of incentives (67).

Despite inevitable problems with, for instance, balance of payments deficits, inflation and unemployment, most years in the 1960s and 1970s have seen a growth in output in the Republic that has

198

exceeded those of most European nations; it has created in the country, at least for the time being, an optimism that is reflected in the rising population figures and the halt to emigration (XI).

60. PRE-FAMINE INDUSTRY

The 1841 Census calculated the whole population of Ireland as being over eight million, of whom about 40% were classified as having an occupation. Of these just over one million were classified as working in industry, fishing or transport. Over half of these were in Ulster. Textiles was by far the greatest industry and there were more textile workers in Ulster than in the rest of Ireland put together. More people worked in the clothing industry in Ulster than in any other province.

The figures show that about 80% of the population relied on agriculture or textiles for employment and many of those depending on the latter were experiencing economic disaster as a result of the mechanising of industry.

Agricultural industries were based mainly in the south, where indeed, like the west, there was very little else in the way of industry. Milling continued to grow, both in the eastern and western coastal towns, with small mills being scattered throughout the country. During the 1830s there were almost 2,000 mills in Ireland. It is possible that with more enterprise from local landlords enough small industries could have been initiated or kept going to mitigate the universal poverty. The hitherto widespread textile industry had contracted. Cotton, wool, muslin and silk, which in earlier times had been prosperous were now in decline, and linen was concentrated in the north-east of the country.

Although brewing and distilling had prospered before the 1840s and were to do so again, they suffered a serious setback with the campaign in Ireland in the 1830s of Father Theobald Mathew, a Tipperary-born Capuchin friar, who led a remarkably successful temperance campaign. Drunkenness was certainly a problem in Ireland and was greatly reduced by his Total Abstinence Societies, but the slump in the home market was a serious blow to the industry, although it had partially recovered by the mid-1850s. Concentration in these industries led to increasing prosperity for a few big firms like Guinness and Beamish and Crawford.

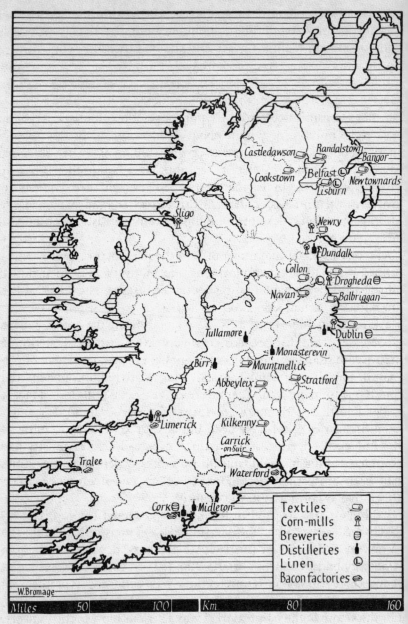

Castledawson
Randalstown
Bangor
Cookstown
Belfast
Newtownards
Lisburn
Newry
Sligo
Dundalk
Collon
Drogheda
Navan
Balbriggan
Tullamore
Dublin
Monasterevin
Burr
Mountmellick
Abbeyleix
Stratford
Limerick
Kilkenny
Carrick
-on-Suir
Tralee
Waterford
Cork
Midleton

Textiles
Corn-mills
Breweries
Distilleries
Linen
Bacon factories

W.Bromage

Miles 50 100 Km 80 160

60. *Pre-famine industry*

One of the remarkable lacunae in Irish industrial development lay in fishing. Fish in earlier centuries was an important export, but by the nineteenth century the industry was barely in existence. Although fish was plentiful, both cheap fish like herrings and exotic fish like salmon, oysters and lobster, the lack of a proper industry seems to have been due to a simple reluctance on the part of an erstwhile maritime people to venture onto their dangerous coastal waters.

Sir Robert Kane, in 1844, produced a book called *Industrial Resources of Ireland* in which he surveyed, among other aspects of industry, the mineral potential of the country. He charted the mineral wealth of Ireland, which is widely distributed though very limited in quality. Although extensive coalfields could be found in the south and south-west, they were made up of seams too narrow to be economically mined and of a poor quality. Iron mines existed mainly in the east, lead in the east and west, copper in the south and east. Unfortunately, minerals mined in Ireland proved uncompetitive by foreign standards, because of expense of production and lack of quality.

Overall therefore, pre-famine Ireland was seriously under-industrialised outside the north-east. The most prosperous industry in the south was the agricultural industry which was to suffer seriously with the approach of the famine.

61. MODERN INDUSTRY

A major factor in making it possible to widen the distribution of industry in the Republic and extend its efficiency and scope has been the rapid extending of electrification. The Electricity Supply Board (E.S.B.) was set up to operate a central electrical network in 1927, and at the same time the first hydro-electric station was built on the Shannon. Later more hydro-electric plants were built on the Liffey, the Lee and the Erne. Peat and the very limited coal supplies have been used to power industry and it has proved possible to limit fuel imports to less than 50% of the Republic's requirements.

Government intervention in industrial development has been mixed in its success, but it has managed to encourage some dispersal of industry. The industries which flourish in modern Ireland include traditional ones like food-processing, tobacco, drink

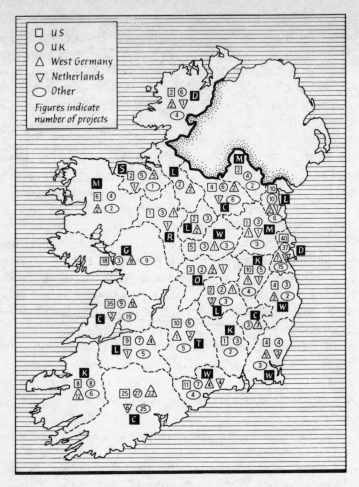

61a. *Foreign investment, January 1979*

(Guinness has in Dublin the largest brewery in Europe and is the greatest beer exporter in the world) and clothing. Of the more modern industries, the fastest growing include engineering, metals, chemicals, clay, cement and glass. (For Northern Ireland, see 81.)

Ireland's industrial revolution of the 1960s and 1970s has to a significant extent been financed by foreign investors attracted in large numbers by incentives which include substantial investment grants and tax relief on export profits. Between 1960 and 1978, 656 manufacturing companies from overseas were assisted by the Industrial Development Authority to begin production in Ireland. The

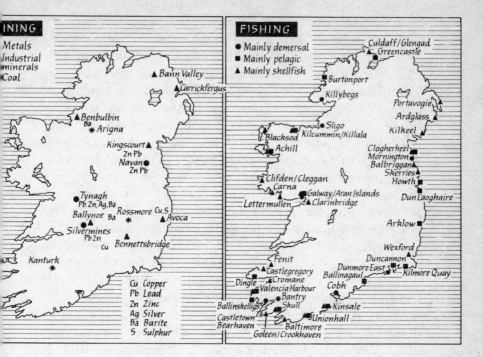

MINING

Metals
Industrial minerals
Coal

▲ Bann Valley
▲ Carrickfergus

▲ Benbulbin
Ba
✳ Arigna

Kingscourt ▲
Zn Pb
Navan ●
Zn Pb

● Tynagh
Pb Zn, Ag, Ba
Ballynoe Ba   Rossmore Cu. S
✳   ▲ Avoca
Silvermines
Pb Zn
Cu   ▲ Bennettsbridge

Kanturk
✳

Cu Copper
Pb Lead
Zn Zinc
Ag Silver
Ba Barite
S   Sulphur

FISHING

● Mainly demersal
■ Mainly pelagic
▲ Mainly shellfish

Culdaff/Glengad
▲ Greencastle
● Burtonport
Killybegs ●
Portavogie
Ardglass ▲
● Sligo   Kilkeel ▲
Blacksod Kilcummin/Killala
Achill   Clogherheel ■
                            Mornington
                            Balbriggan ▲
                            Skerries ▲
                            Howth ■
Clifden/Cleggan
Carna
● Galway/Aran Islands   Dun Laoghaire
Lettermullen ▲ Clarinbridge
                            Arklow ■
                            Wexford ●
Fenit   Duncannon ▲
▲ Castlegregory Dunmore East ● ▲
Dingle ▲ Cromane Ballinagaul ● ■ Kilmore Quay
Valencia Harbour Cobh
● Bantry
Ballinskelligs Skull
Castletown   Kinsale
Bearhaven   ▲ Unionhall
Goleen/Crookhaven Baltimore

61b. *Two important industries*

map shows those in operation in January 1979. Of the 656 companies, the United States accounted for 215, the United Kingdom 176, West Germany 99, the Netherlands 37, Switzerland 21, Sweden 18 and France 17. The remainder come mainly from other European countries, Canada and Japan. New industries attracted include producers of engineering goods, electronics and electrical equipment, chemicals and pharmaceuticals, synthetic textiles and foodstuffs.

Although foreign-owned companies by the late 1970s provided a quarter of all jobs in Irish manufacturing industries, the importance to the economy of Irish-owned firms must not be overlooked. In 1979 four Irish firms, Jefferson Smurfit, Cement-Roadstone, Waterford Glass and Carroll's, had each a turnover in excess of £100 million. A substantial number of indigenous Irish firms already have significant operations in the United Kingdom, Europe and further afield.

Two success stories in recent decades are mining and fishing. The 1960s saw a revival in mineral exploration that showed the Republic to be relatively rich in base metals. Tynagh mine, opened in 1965, is now the biggest lead-zinc-silver mine in Europe; Silvermines, opened in 1968, is one of the biggest lead mines in Europe; Navan mine, opened in 1977, has a lead-zinc deposit estimated at a massive 51 million tonnes. The Republic is fast becoming a leading world producer of zinc ores; she is also well supplied with cement, building stones, and aggregates. Her energy requirements can be met in part from extensive peat resources and some natural gas. So far, Northern Ireland's mineral resources seem limited to salt and diatomite.

Fishing has also seen considerable expansion in recent years. In the Republic, Bord Iascaigh Mhara (the Sea Fisheries Board) have provided assistance towards modernising the fishing fleet and developing new markets. In Northern Ireland similar work is undertaken by the Fishery Harbour Authority. The map shows the important sea fisheries for the three main types of sea fish. Pelagic fish are those that usually swim at or near the surface of the water; demersal fish usually stay near the sea bottom; shellfish are crustacea and molluscs. Those commercially important to Ireland include herrings, mackeral and sprats (pelagic); sole, brill, turbot, plaice, cod, haddock, hake and whiting (demersal) and lobsters, crawfish, crabs, Dublin Bay prawns, oysters, mussels and cockles (shellfish).

Inland fisheries are also extensive, with salmon, trout and eels being of most commercial importance. Trout and oyster farms have been set up north and south. In addition to providing several thousand jobs (full-time, part-time and seasonal), partially satisfying the home market and yielding several million pounds worth of exports (£32 million from the Republic in 1979), Irish fisheries are an important tourist attraction.

X Trade

Like most island people, the Irish were for many centuries a maritime race whose warriors (40) and merchants had close contacts with Britain and Europe, and whose fishermen fished not only for the domestic market but also for export. This was to alter to some extent with the coming of Christianity, in that military expeditions abroad ceased, although commercial intercourse continued.

Although initially the Vikings (11) disrupted Irish life, their contribution to the growth of organised trade was to be crucial. They introduced Irish goods to Viking settlements in Britain and on the Continent. Trading was a way of life for the Vikings, for their familiarity with the seas and their scattered settlements, extending as far as Russia, gave them security from which to operate. For their commerce, the east coast of Ireland was ideally placed geographically, since Dublin had easy access to their settlements in Scandinavia, Britain and the Continent.

Although the Viking settlers initially resisted the Norman invaders (12) they soon made peace with them and took advantage of the founding of new towns and the new opportunities for a more widespread trade with Britain. Despite the many disruptions which occurred during the medieval period, the coastal towns suffered less than many other parts of the country, and Dublin in particular was a haven of commercial peace. Reinforced by merchants from the Continent (63), the Viking and Norman inhabitants of the coastal towns continued to trade profitably, despite the fact that domestic markets were severely limited by poor communications and political and military upheavals.

It was not until the English government began to look critically at Irish trade during the mid-sixteenth century, with a view to hiving off some of the profits for the benefit of the administration, that trade began to face real obstacles. Until then trading was most lucrative, both for the merchants and for the towns in which they operated. Even widespread piracy could not greatly affect the prosperity of their enterprises.

By the early seventeenth century Irish trade was suffering from government intervention which imposed heavy customs duties and from the effects of the political and military instability which had affected many of the towns during the Nine Years War. Northern ports began to achieve a new significance through the work of the Ulster Scots in improving them and increasing exports. A period of stability before the middle of the century, combined with Wentworth's encouragement of certain industries and his success in ridding the seas of piracy helped to stage a recovery, which was, however, frustrated by the political upheavals of the rest of the century. The late seventeenth and early eighteenth centuries were to see British protectionism at its height succeed in limiting the nature and extent of Irish trade.

Although free trade was a reality by the end of the eighteenth century, Irish trade had already become so restricted in its scope that its prosperity was to prove to be built on sand. By the early nineteenth century Irish exports were very narrowly based. The only really significant manufactured export was linen, and as a result of the Industrial Revolution that was now being produced in one small part of the country. The other main export was provisions, which was the only important product of Connacht and Munster and much of Leinster.

The effects of the famine were to prove the need for diversity in industry and trade although the problem continued for a considerable time. It was necessary to learn the lesson that disproportionate dependence on any one product could mean disproportionate hardship should markets change rapidly. It is only in recent years that the Irish Republic has really begun to find answers to this problem. Although agricultural produce is still the major export, it is much more varied than before, and Irish farmers are flexible enough to meet changing market demands. Northern Ireland has until recently had a lesser problem since by the time of partition the province was heavily industrialised and its exports relatively broadly based. Northern Irish trade has been more extensive than that of the Republic despite its small size.

62. MEDIEVAL TRADE

The lack of adequate documentary evidence makes any account of medieval Irish trade somewhat conjectural, but there is ample proof of significant trading contacts with Britain and the Continent; the most important of the known contacts are shown on the map. We know the main goods which were exchanged, although we cannot gauge the extent or profitability of the trade.

Although there was some foreign trade before the Vikings established coastal towns, it was sporadic and ill-organised. From the first century A.D. there are references in history and legend to foreign merchants attending the great fairs and there exchanging their wines, spices and cloth of gold for hides and cloth.

The Vikings introduced an organised trade to Ireland. The development of their towns, and later the widespread Norman foundations, helped this trade and encouraged contacts with Britain and France. Gerald of Wales testifies to the flourishing nature of Irish trade with France at the time of the Norman invasion. Apart from the conjectural sea-routes indicated on the map, Irish goods travelled throughout the Continent by means of well-established inland trading routes, although there were direct links between Ireland and a number of major trading towns.

Broadly speaking, the Irish exported necessities and imported luxuries. Their staple exports were hides, wool and grain, although salmon, hake, herring, linen cloth, timber, butter, gold, gold vessels and ornaments are frequently mentioned as subsidiary exports. By the thirteenth century Irish linen and serge were popular abroad. Important imports were spices from Lisbon, Florence and Lucca, corn and English cloth, and salt, coal, silks and metals. The major import was however wine, which came mainly from France. Brian Ború is alleged to have exacted as a tribute from the Vikings of Dublin 150 vats of wine and from the Limerick Vikings a daily barrel. Dublin's main trade was with Bristol and Chester, and it had a highly profitable slave trade during the twelfth century. Bristol was given Dublin by Henry II in the twelfth century, so even

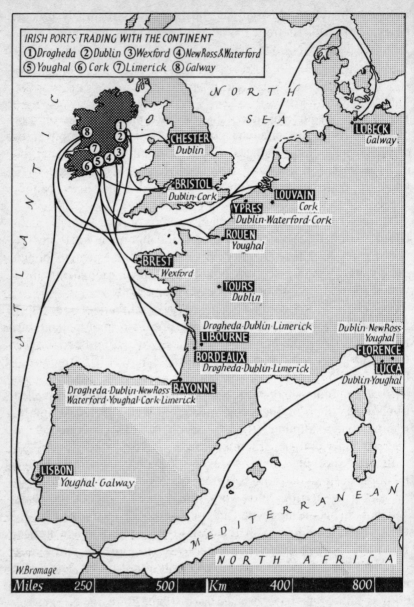

62. Medieval trade

when Dublin secured its independence there were very close ties between the two ports.

Economic considerations made the towns bastions of conservatism and loyalty to the established order. The citizens were of many races: Irish, Vikings and Normans formed the majority, with a substantial minority of Welsh, and some Flemish and French merchants and Italian bankers and financiers. The Florentine banking family of Frescobaldi stationed members of the family in Dublin, Waterford, Youghal and Cork in the thirteenth century. The Ricardi, a family of money-lenders, were active in both eastern and western coastal towns at the same period.

63. TUDOR TRADE

In 1436, the anonymous author of the polemic called the *Libelle of English Polycye* urged upon the English government the patriotic necessity of maintaining a strong navy in order to protect and expand English trade. In the course of his tract the author drew attention to the economic possibilities of Ireland and urged that England take an active interest in the trade of a land 'so large, so gode, so plenteouse, so riche'. That the English government was successively too weak and too preoccupied with other concerns to interest itself effectively in Ireland's trade until the middle of the sixteenth century was a matter of good fortune for Ireland, which had continued its Continental trade undisturbed.

The eastern ports, particularly Dublin and Wexford, traded mainly with Britain, although Dublin maintained trading contact with the French wine-growing areas. The eastern ports also had a widespread internal trade. Dublin was an important port, despite having a bad harbour, because of her political importance. Her traffic was not especially profitable, being mainly imports of luxury goods bought in England. The southern and western ports had far more widespread trade. Galway had an extensive foreign trade, mainly with Spain and Flanders, and supplied most of Ireland with wine. She benefited from a considerable degree of fiscal autonomy, being free for much of this period from the necessity of paying any customs duties to the king. The removal of this privilege in 1584, in addition to increasing political instability, was to herald the steady decline of Galway from the mid-sixteen century onwards. Her main

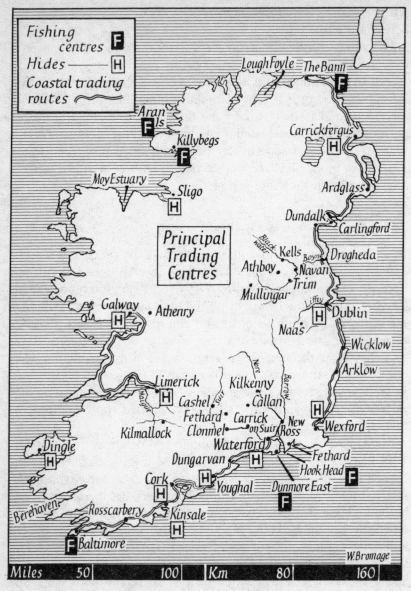

Fishing centres F
Hides H
Coastal trading routes

LoughFoyle · The Bann F
Aran Is F
Killybegs F
Carrickfergus H
Ardglass
Moy Estuary · Sligo H
Dundalk
Carlingford
Principal Trading Centres
Blackwater · Kells · Drogheda
Boyne
Athboy · Navan
Trim
Mullingar
Liffey
Galway H · Athenry · Dublin H
Naas
Wicklow
Arklow
Nore
Barrow
Limerick H · Kilkenny
Cashel · Callan
Fethard · Carrick on Suir · New Ross · Wexford H
Kilmallock · Clonmel · Waterford H · Fethard · Hook Head F
Dingle H · Dungarvan · Youghal · Dunmore East F
Cork H
Berehaven · Rosscarbery · Kinsale H
Baltimore F

W. Bromage

Miles 50 100 Km 80 160

63a and b (opposite). *Tudor trade*

210

ICELAND

CANADA

NEWFOUNDLAND
Fishing centre

SCOTLAND
• Glasgow
• Carlisle
Beau- • Liverpool
maris
• Chester
IRELAND ENGLAND
Bristol Antwerp
Calais Ghent NETHER
Bruges LANDS
Rouen
Brest St Malo
FRANCE
Bordeaux
Bayonne
Santander
PORTUGAL SPAIN Barcelona
Valencia
Lisbon
Cadiz

W. Bromage

211

commercial contacts were with Castile, Andalusia, Gascony, and Iceland; she was a port of call for Bristol ships sailing to Iceland. She also controlled coastal commerce between the Shannon and Donegal. Her great commercial rival in the wine trade was Limerick, a port which suffered similarly at the end of the century. Limerick's main contacts were with the Iberian peninsula.

Cork also depended largely on her foreign trade, which began to suffer after the Desmond rebellions. Her privileges were fewer than those of Waterford. Her main contacts were with Flanders, western France and the Iberian peninsula. Waterford had an extensive interior trade, especially along the Barrow, Nore and Suir. It had an excellent harbour, and although it never had quite the independence of Galway, it had extensive privileges. It was the pre-eminent Irish port, having connections with France, Portugal, Spain and the fishing lands of Newfoundland. Wexford had a rivalry with Waterford akin to that of Limerick with Galway, from a similar position of inferiority. Her harbour was so poor that few foreign ships could enter it, and she was obliged to build her own ships for foreign trade, which was mainly with Bristol.

Of the smaller ports, New Ross, Dungarvan, Youghal, Kinsale and Dingle were important until the mid-sixteenth century. All of them traded with England and the Continent, mainly with France. Other small ports, such as Carrickfergus and Ardglass, and the more important Drogheda, traded mainly with Scotland, although they had some contacts with Brittany. Carrickfergus was the main centre of northern trade.

Internal trade was mainly conducted around the coast or by means of inland waterways. The map shows the main internal trading contacts, though it should be noted that the trade between ports was usually by sea and not by land.

The main exports were the traditional hides, cloth, fish and timber, with wine, oil, spices, salt and iron being the main imports. In other words, exports were still basic necessities and raw materials, while imports were mainly manufactured goods and luxuries.

With the political disturbances of the Elizabethan period, the Munster rebellions, and the Nine Years War and the restrictions placed by the government on foreign trade there was a great decline in those ports relying mainly on trade with the Continent, that is, the western, southern and south-eastern ports, and a rise in the importance of the northern ports, notably Drogheda, Dundalk, Carlingford and Carrickfergus. Their main trading contacts were with Chester and Liverpool, to whom they became subordinate and their exports were mainly yarn and tallow and lacked the variety of earlier trade.

64. SEVENTEENTH-CENTURY TRADE

Despite the decline in Irish trade with the Continent which occurred in the late sixteenth century it was still cosmopolitan in outlook in the late seventeenth century. A study of the main import, wine, has shown that links with the Continent were still very strong. Although Anglo-Irish trade was increasingly dominant in Irish commerce, wine, salt, hops and iron were still imported from abroad, while Ireland continued to export fish, hides, wool, linen and provisions.

The map shows the wine trade in 1614–15, and demonstrates the increasing trading contacts with Britain and the new importance of the northern ports. The strong links between the south-western ports and Spain and France still persisted, although a sizeable proportion of the imported wine was carried in English ships. This indirect dependence on England is shown in the contemporary shipping figures. Of a total of 143 ships engaged in importing wine into Ireland, only 31 were Irish; of the remainder, 51 were English and 31 Scottish.

As the century progressed, Ireland became increasingly dependent on trade with Britain. Irish cattle became an important export, and proved too successful for its own good. From about 1621 there was economic pressure on the English Parliament to control the import of Irish cattle because of the threat it was posing to the English farmer.

These efforts did not succeed initially, and until the 1640s Irish trade was reasonably successful; wool and butter also became important exports. During this period the agricultural potential of the country was just beginning to be exploited. For the first time there was a sustained period of peace in the country, and woodlands were being cleared in large numbers throughout Ireland. The increasing concentration of Irish exporters on agricultural products restricted trade, since Europe had little need of agricultural products, and European outlets became fewer in number.

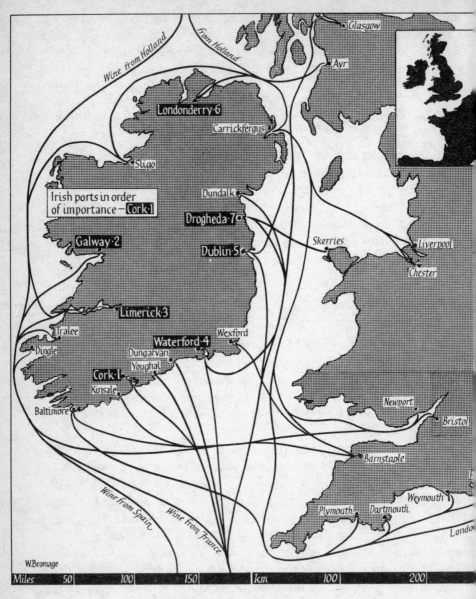

Wine from Holland

From Holland

Glasgow

Ayr

Londonderry·6

Carrickfergus

Sligo

Dundalk

Irish ports in order
of importance – Cork·1

Drogheda·7

Galway·2

Skerries

Liverpool

Dublin·5

Chester

Limerick·3

Tralee

Wexford

Dingle

Waterford·4

Dungarvan

Youghal

Cork·1

Kinsale

Newport

Baltimore

Bristol

Barnstaple

Wine from Spain

Wine from France

Weymouth

Plymouth

Dartmouth

London

W.Bromage

Miles   50   100   150   km   100   200

64. *Wine trade, 1614–15*

214

The wars between 1641 and 1652, the famine of 1652 and the plague of 1650 all contributed to the disruption of Irish economic life. The Cromwellian land confiscations inhibited agricultural and commercial stability. Customs revenue, which had reached £60,000 in the 1630s, had slumped to £12,000 in 1656.

A fundamental recovery was, however, in evidence by the end of the decade, and exports rose steadily. Dependence on the English market was increasing; the demand for cattle and wool continued. Irish beef was shipped to the British colonies in the West Indies.

In 1663, the poor state of the market for cattle in England led to the passing of a bill imposing heavy duties on Irish cattle or sheep imported from July to December each year. In 1667 a bill was passed which forbade the importing of any Irish cattle, sheep, pork or beef. Heavy as was this blow to Irish trade, there were compensations in the increased demand for Irish wool. Nevertheless, Irish trade was in an unhealthy state at this time; there was little demand anywhere for agricultural produce.

The economic prosperity of many of the Irish ports was affected by these and other measures, including the Navigation Acts of 1671–85, which forbade the importing of many products, including sugar and tobacco, except indirectly from England. Many ports began to sacrifice their earlier importance to increased centralisation. Dublin, Cork and Belfast grew enormously in size and importance, while there was a marked decline in the importance of Carrickfergus, Youghal, Kinsale and many other similar smaller and less well placed ports.

Despite the measures discriminating against Irish trade, exports continued to expand until the mid 1680s. Ulster was developing a prosperous linen industry. However, yet again, peace proved transitory, and with the outbreak of war in 1689 Irish trade once again suffered. The steady recovery of the mid 1690s was accomplished largely by famines in France and Scotland which produced an artificial demand for agricultural produce. This recovery was not to progress unimpeded, however. Mainly because of the alarm shown by English merchants at the competitiveness of Irish wool, a bill was passed by parliament in 1699 which outlawed the export of woollen cloth from Ireland overseas; prohibitive duties already made it uneconomic to export Irish woollen goods to England. Direct interference by the English government with Irish trade was to continue during the eighteenth century (65).

65. EIGHTEENTH-CENTURY TRADE

Although the laws discriminating against Irish trade were serious in their effect on Irish prosperity, they were only a part of a general economic decline. A revaluation of the Irish currency brought about a fall in prices at home, which, coupled with a slump in European markets occasioned by war, had a serious effect on the Irish export trade. Occasional years of recovery during the next few decades were accompanied by harvest failures and a gradual fall in the value of foreign trade. Only the linen trade was really prosperous; by 1730 it made up over a quarter of all Irish exports. Recovery during the 1730s depended largely on the linen trade and on a high demand in the colonies for Irish products, particularly beef and butter. This provision trade was hindered by a series of embargoes on trade with countries hostile to England which affected Irish trade with France, though not with her colonies. In 1776 a general embargo was placed on the provision trade except to Britain and her colonies. From this came the Irish provisions trade's ultimate dependence on Britain.

The linen trade was largely dependent on England from 1696 when duties were abolished on Irish linen entering England. During the eighteenth century Irish linen became supreme in English markets. From making up about 23% of exports to Great Britain in 1698, linen had reached 80% sixty years later. The woollen industry improved also with the abolition in 1739 of all duties on its entry into England and the repeal in 1779 of the 1699 act. Another important factor in improving Irish trade was the demand for cattle, beef and butter in England in the 1750s which led to the suspension of the Cattle Acts and those prohibiting the export of beef and butter in 1758 and 1759 and their repeal in 1776.

The centralisation of the ports which had been occurring during the seventeenth century was virtually complete by the mid-eighteenth century. A comparison between the ports' relative importance in the early seventeenth-century wine trade and their importance in the 1750s illustrates the position (64). Of the ships employed in Irish trade during 1753, Dublin had the lion's share, with 2,360,

216

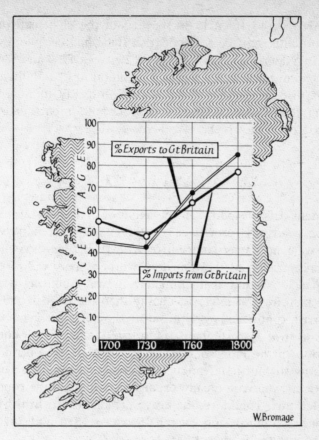

65. *Eighteenth-century trade*

Cork was second with 732, Belfast third with 468, Waterford fourth with 208, Drogheda fifth with 200 and Dundalk sixth with 179. No other port had more than 100 ships. The eastern and northern ports concentrated on the export of linen and Cork and Waterford on the provisions trade. Irish shipping was classed as British and could trade with Britain and the colonies directly. Basically then, the story of Irish trade during the late seventeenth and eighteenth centuries is of contraction of foreign trade, mainly due to British protectionism. But British support for the linen trade and a special position in the British market was a considerable compensation.

By 1779, under pressure from the Volunteers, England had no option but to concede 'free trade', which meant the opening of the colonial trade to Ireland. By the end of the eighteenth century, therefore, although the scope of Irish trade had become restricted, it was in a flourishing state otherwise. Between 1700 and 1800 Irish exports went up in value from £1·2 million to £7·6 million, while imports rose even more from £1·2 million to £11 million. The increasing dependence on Great Britain for both imports and exports is illustrated in the graph.

66. PRE-FAMINE TRADE

The main Irish exports of the eighteenth century were linen, woollen goods and provisions. By the end of the century woollen goods were no longer competitive with their English counterpart. The concentration of the industry in urban areas and its inferior craftsmanship meant that ultimately it was producing a product higher in price and lower in quality than the English alternative, although it continued largely to satisfy the home market.

One feature of Irish trade before the famine is the enormous expansion in the provisions trade, an anomaly in a period when there was so much starvation throughout the country. The linen industry continued its steady expansion. Although the contraction of foreign trade continued, the heavy demand of the British market for linen continued, and overall, between 1810 and 1825 linen exports increased by over 100%.

Although the best period for the provisions trade was during the Napoleonic wars, its growth continued. By the 1830s, 700,000 tons of agricultural produce were being exported annually. Although Dublin was still the premier port, handling 28% of all exports and imports, with Belfast having 15%, Cork 13% and Waterford 12%, the strength of the first two was in linen, while the latter two specialised in provisions. Estimates of the value of the exports and imports handled by the major ports during the 1830s indicate their specialisations.

The message of these figures is clear. The south-eastern, southern and western ports were heavily dependent on a single export, either provisions or cereals. With the advent of the famine of the 1840s this trade was to collapse catastrophically. The north-eastern and northern ports were healthier, since the three main ports had linen

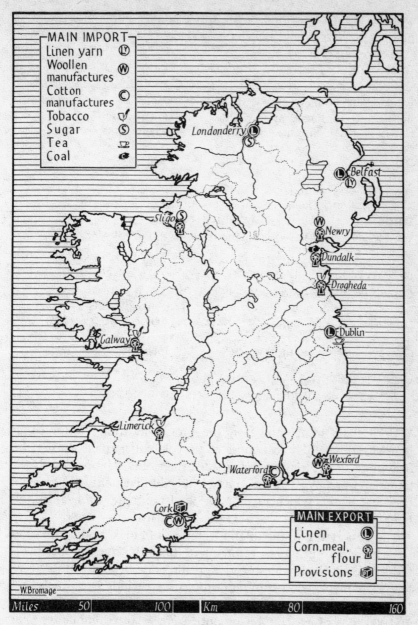

MAIN IMPORT
Linen yarn Ⓛⁱ
Woollen Ⓦ
manufactures
Cotton Ⓒ
manufactures
Tobacco Ⓥ
Sugar Ⓢ
Tea
Coal

Londonderry

Belfast

Sligo

Newry

Dundalk

Drogheda

Galway

Dublin

Limerick

Waterford

Wexford

Cork

MAIN EXPORT
Linen Ⓛ
Corn, meal,
flour
Provisions

W.Bromage

| Miles | 50 | 100 | Km | 80 | 160 |

66. *Pre-famine trade*

as their main export and of the three smaller ports, only Dundalk had a very heavy dependence on food exports.

Port	Main Export	% of Total	Main Import	% of Total
Londonderry	linen	30%	sugar	6%
Belfast	linen	62%	linen yarn	26%
Newry	corn, meal flour	33%	woollen mfs	10%
Dundalk	corn, meal flour	62%	coal	18%
Drogheda	corn, meal flour	34%	tobacco	31%
Dublin	linen	29%	tea	12%
Wexford	corn, meal flour	56%	woollen mfs	19%
Waterford	corn, meal flour	43%	cotton mfs	30%
Cork	provisions	69%	cotton and woollen mfs	32%
Limerick	corn, meal flour	52%	tobacco	22%
Galway	corn, meal flour	86%	tobacco	21%
Sligo	corn, meal flour	50%	sugar	15%

Until the famine, however, the provisions trade continued to flourish, although it lost most of its colonial markets during the beginning of the century when the Americans captured the Newfoundland and West Indies market. Its main elements were bacon, beef and butter, which made up 45% of the trade, corn, meal and flour 37% and livestock 18% in the mid 1830s.

The importance of the inland waterways in making the provision trade possible must not be forgotten. Since the sources of agricultural produce were widespread, and the ports dealing with it were few in number, good communications were vital. The canals and navigable rivers were of great importance. During the 1830s, about 700,000 tons of agricultural produce were exported annually; total tonnage carried by all waterways was about 600,000, of which the vast majority must have been provisions.

After the famine the emphasis of the provisions trade changed.

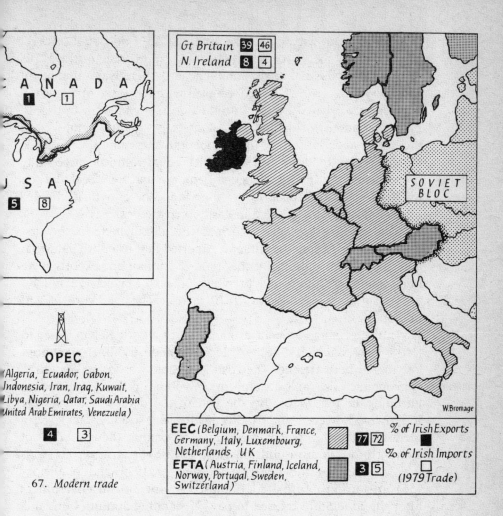

CANADA 1 ☐1

USA 5 ☐8

OPEC
(Algeria, Ecuador, Gabon,
Indonesia, Iran, Iraq, Kuwait,
Libya, Nigeria, Qatar, Saudi Arabia
United Arab Emirates, Venezuela)

4 ☐3

Gt Britain 39 ☐46
N. Ireland 8 ☐4

SOVIET
BLOC

W. Bromage

EEC (Belgium, Denmark, France,
Germany, Italy, Luxembourg,
Netherlands, UK   77 ☐72

EFTA (Austria, Finland, Iceland,
Norway, Portugal, Sweden,
Switzerland)   3 ☐5

% of Irish Exports ■
% of Irish Imports ☐
(1979 Trade)

67. Modern trade

Bacon, beef and butter declined in importance as exports, while
the livestock and corn trade increased.

67. MODERN TRADE

The agricultural emphasis of the Republic's trade is still evident in
its exports, but twentieth-century industrialisation has been extensive enough to broaden the base of her exports considerably.

After the famine, livestock became an important export as pastur-
age became a more important part of agriculture – largely because

221

of the steady growth in the size of farms. After an initial brief recovery during the 1850s and 1860s the export trade of the 1870s reflected an industrial crisis. Simultaneously there was a number of bad harvests in 1876–9, which, coupled with increased foreign competition exacerbated by the introduction of steam-ship transport, had a serious effect on the provisions trade. Matters improved in the 1890s and the setting up of cooperative creameries produced a stable dairy industry by 1900, which could compete successfully even against the new challenge of Denmark and New Zealand. The livestock trade continued to be important. The growth in the distillery industry was reflected in vastly increased exports.

Irish industry was very much export dominated; in the first decade of the twentieth century it exported half its entire industrial and agricultural output. By this time the important exports were linen, ships, distilling and brewing. Linen, of which 32 million yards had been exported in 1810, had reached a figure of 230 million.

With the change brought about by partition, the Republic had to face a new situation. The most lucrative industry, linen, had been lost to Northern Ireland. The Irish Free State was formed at a time of economic crisis and a slump in agricultural prices. Exports were declining in the 1920s. By the end of the decade matters were improving, however, and exports again rising steadily. The government maintained a policy of encouraging exports, though it did not attempt protectionism until the early 1930s. The crisis of the 1930s was a result of the Great Depression of 1929 and retaliatory measures against Irish trade imposed by the British government after the Free State refused to pay outstanding annuities on land. Anglo-Irish trade did not return to normal until 1938. The protectionism introduced by the Fianna Fáil government in the 1930s helped industry but injured the export trade; exports continued to fall throughout the decade and through the 1939–45 war. A similar fall in imports affected the supply of the raw materials and helped to reduce the output from industry.

After the war exports continued to be low. Agricultural output was too low to allow for high exports, and industrial output had not expanded enough to make significant export gains. There was little growth throughout the 1950s, but the 1960s proved to be a period of recovery (61).

With recent industrialisation, manufactured goods have replaced agricultural products as the largest category of Irish exports (£3,499 million in total). While food and livestock in 1979 accounted for 35% of total exports (meat 13%, dairy products 9% and livestock 4%), machinery and transport equipment provided 16%, chemicals 13% and other manufactured goods 24%. Machinery and transport equipment were 29% of total imports (£4,816 million), fuels 12%, chemicals 12% and other manufactured goods 30%. Overseas-financed factories in Ireland are highly export-oriented; by the mid-1970s their products accounted for nearly half of total manufacturing exports.

As far as the Republic's export markets are concerned, her reliance on British markets is lessening gradually. In 1924 84% of her exports went to Great Britain; the 1979 figure was 39%. Exports to the United States have risen from 0·5% in 1938 to 5%, while exports to the E.E.C. – only 4·6% in 1958 – reached 77% in 1979. In 1924 Great Britain supplied 69% of imports, but her share decreased in 1979 to 46%, while the United States' share has decreased from 11·4% in 1938 to 9%. Imports from the E.E.C. rose from 11·1% in 1958 to 72% in 1979. Figures for the E.E.C. have of course been drastically affected by its enlargement in 1973 to include three new members – Ireland, the United Kingdom and Denmark.

XI Social Change

For the mass of the people, life in Ireland before the eighth century was probably more agreeable than for over a thousand years afterwards. After the Celtic invasion had given way to a permanent settlement (IV) the life of the people was stable. The population was small and food ample and varied. Complex laws determined a man's position in society and dictated the work he did, the clothes he wore and the food he ate. Although restrictive, these laws served to protect those it bound and defend them where necessary. Although there were no towns and the inhabitants lived in small communities, they were not isolated. They had a strong cultural tradition, the druids being inheritors of an oral tradition as well as poets and lawyers. The staple diet of the people was meat, fish and corn, with milk and ale in large quantities. Feasts were quite common and musicians and poets provided entertainment at such gatherings.

By the eighth century, just before the Norse invasions were to disrupt the life of the community, Christianity had introduced certain changes into Irish life. Christians had brought a written culture which was cultivated in the monasteries with dedication and artistry. Small groups of people lived around monastic settlements. The country was almost totally agricultural, and the diet was expanded by the cultivation of crops. Houses, though primitive, were probably overall somewhat superior to those inhabited by many peasants during the nineteenth century. There continued to be a widespread popular culture; entertainments were provided at feasts and fairs and storytelling was a pastime of many members of the community.

It would be misleading to give the impression that the Ireland of this period was a land overflowing with milk and honey and peopled with merry and cultured farmers. Life was certainly difficult; work was hard for those who were required to perform it and there were serious agricultural recessions during the eighth century. Neither was the country wholly peaceful. Cattle raids, warfare between *tuatha* and personal violence were not infrequent. Nevertheless, for the majority of the people, it was a life of stability which in normal circumstances yielded adequate food, comfort and cultural diversity.

This life was to be considerably disturbed by the Norse raids, although many of the people were completely untouched by two centuries of intermittent warfare. The greatest social changes were brought about by the establishment of Norse and Norman towns; hitherto only scattered proto-urban settlements had existed. In the rural community conditions did not change so much. The Normans introduced feudalism, but it was not radically different from the social system which had pertained in earlier centuries, although its law was different from Brehon law and the introduction of primogeniture was an alien concept. Nevertheless, the serfs of the feudal system were similar to the slaves of the *tuatha* (IV). In the Gaelic areas the cultural traditions continued and the way of life changed little, although there was more disruptive military activity than in earlier centuries. In the Norman areas a new culture had been introduced which was primarily French in origin and which was to have an influence on the later literature of Ireland. Norman architecture was radically different from Irish architecture; stone churches, monasteries and castles were constructed throughout the country within a short time after the invasion.

The greatest social upheavals occurred during the thirteenth century when the bubonic plague killed about 14,000 people in 1348 alone. Outbreaks of the plague or Black Death occurred also in 1361, 1370, 1384 and 1398. Earlier in the century there had been epidemics of other diseases, a number of famines and the ruinous and destructive Bruce invasion (14). Of those who died from the plague, the Normans were the worst affected, since urban communities were the most vulnerable. It is estimated that almost half the colonists and their tenants were eliminated, and vast numbers in the towns, but while the plague brought some deaths to Gaelic

225

Ireland they were not sufficient in number to affect the fabric of society.

During the later middle ages there was a strong Gaelic cultural revival, in which many of the Norman colonists took a close interest. The itinerant poets were popular and revered members of the community who received patronage from both Gaelic and Norman lords. As far as the mass of the people were concerned, the cultural revival was of little relevance. Their lives were still virtually unchanged. Their houses were still primitive, their work hard agricultural labour and their food meat, corn and dairy products and their main drink ale – with wine for the middle and upper classes, and whiskey becoming popular. Their entertainments were popular festivals which occurred three or four times a year; more frequent enjoyments were dancing and storytelling.

The wars of the sixteenth and seventeenth centuries affected the lives of the common people, since they were so widespread, but a more significant social development was in the rapid rise in the population which began at the end of the seventeenth century. By the end of the eighteenth century the country was suffering from overcrowding, and the mass of the population were living in inferior conditions to those of their ancestors, and on a restricted diet. By the early nineteenth century meat and fish were rare items in their diet, and more and more families were beginning to rely on the potato for food, with milk as the only drink.

The social disasters of the nineteenth century are described in detail in this section and in section VII. Only massive depopulation could restore the living conditions of the majority of the Irish people to a tolerable level.

68. THE DEVELOPMENT OF TOWNS

Before the Vikings there existed round major monastic centres like Armagh, Clonmacnois and Clonfert, semi-urbanised communities probably composed mainly of craftsmen and labourers working at the monastery. The Vikings set up a number of coastal towns as strongholds and later as commercial centres. Of these foundations, Dublin, which was set up in the ninth century, became within a century extremely powerful and had dependencies as far north as Strangford Lough and as far south as Waterford. Limerick was

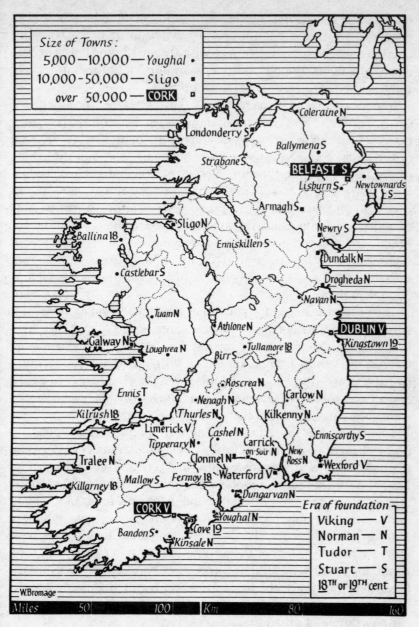

Size of Towns:
5,000–10,000 — Youghal •
10,000–50,000 — Sligo ▪
over 50,000 — CORK ▫

Coleraine N
Londonderry S
Ballymena S
Strabane S
BELFAST S
Lisburn S
Newtownards S
Armagh S
Sligo N
Newry S
Ballina 18
Enniskillen S
Dundalk N
Castlebar S
Drogheda N
Navan N
Tuam N
Athlone N
DUBLIN V
Galway N
Loughrea N
Tullamore 18
Kingstown 19
Birr S
Roscrea N
Ennis T
Nenagh N
Carlow N
Kilrush 18
Thurles N
Kilkenny N
Limerick V
Cashel N
Enniscorthy S
Tipperary N
Carrick on Suir N
Tralee N
Clonmel N
New Ross N
Wexford V
Mallow S
Fermoy 18
Waterford V
Killarney 18
Dungarvan N
CORK V
Youghal N
Bandon S
Cove 19
Kinsale N

Era of foundation
Viking — V
Norman — N
Tudor — T
Stuart — S
18TH or 19TH cent

W.Bromage

Miles 50 100 Km 80 160

68. *Irish towns, 1841*

227

occupied by the Vikings in the ninth century but did not become a proper town until the tenth century, when for many years its inhabitants waged sporadic warfare with Dublin. From being a dependency of Dublin, Waterford became an important town in its own right in the tenth century, as did Cork.

By the time of the Norman invasion therefore, Ireland had a small number of powerful coastal towns, but none inland. The Normans set up towns around their major castles and either the king or the lords of a liberty would grant them charters permitting them to set up a community court, elect a mayor and conduct certain kinds of trading. The proliferation of towns in Leinster and Munster is due to the fact that these provinces were the Normans' area of influence while Connacht and Ulster were mainly held by the Irish. The exceptions to this are Galway and Athenry in Connacht, founded respectively by the de Burgos and the de Berminghams, and Carrickfergus in Ulster, which was founded by John de Courcy.

The prosperity of most of the towns kept them loyal to the Dublin administration. Although there were large numbers of native Irish in the towns, there was a considerable hostility to them among the rest of the urban population and during the fourteenth century many attempts were made to limit the numbers of Irish in towns and to control their behaviour. Simultaneously, Irish communities were springing up outside the walls of the towns.

Towns outside the Pale were almost completely independent, many of them in practice controlled by a small number of powerful families, who went to all lengths to keep control in their own hands. With the Tudor conquest this independence was gradually eroded. There were some Tudor foundations as a result of the plantations, but the main wave of new foundations came with the Stuarts, particularly in Ulster. Since that period foundations have been very limited. Before the famine Ireland was primarily a rural community and only 20% of the population lived in towns or villages compared with 50% in England and Wales. It took the disaster of the famine to bring the Irish people to the acceptance and even the welcoming of urban life.

In 1841 only 20% of the population of Ireland lived in towns. In the Republic in 1971 the figure had risen to 59% and in Northern Ireland to 55%. However, as a result of the massive depopulation of the country, this shift from a rural to an urban society was accomplished without much increasing the actual town populations. In 1841, 1,475,106 people lived in towns of over 500 population, while in 1971, for the Republic, the equivalent figure was 1,648,962. The main change has been therefore less in the size of town populations than in the concentration of the population in bigger towns. The map shows how variable the history of Irish towns has been during this period; many of the less important towns have lost many of their inhabitants to larger towns.

In 1841 there were only three towns with more than 50,000 inhabitants, Dublin (232,726), Belfast (75,308) and Cork (80,720). In 1971 there were three more within that category, Dun Laoghaire (52,990), Limerick (57,137) and Londonderry (51,617), while Dublin had grown to 566,034, Belfast to 358,991 and Cork to 128,235. In 1841, 4% of the population of the twenty-six counties lived in Dublin; in 1971, 23% lived there, while 35% lived in one of the four major towns of the Republic. The equivalent figures for Belfast are 5% and 26%.

The Republic's plans for regional industrialisation were intended in part to reverse the alarming decline in population of inland towns and the equally alarming increase in the population of the large towns. Over the past few decades most of the smaller towns have increased in size, but until the 1970s their growth was slower than that of the larger towns. Recent figures show an encouraging reversal of previous trends: between 1971 and 1979 the population of towns between 1,000 and 5,000 inhabitants grew by 11%, while that of towns over 50,000 (excluding Dublin, which actually fell by 4%) grew by only 6%.

The smaller towns perform a vital function throughout the country by providing employment and commercial and social contact for the surrounding rural communities. It is crucial for the future of rural Ireland that the reversal of the decades of decline continues.

229

Size of Towns:
5,000 - 10,000 — Youghal ·
10,000 - 50,000 — Sligo ▪
over 50,000 — **CORK** ▫

Coleraune+138
LONDONDERRY +241
Letterkenny+141
Ballymena+220
Strabane+98
Newtownards+
BELFAST
←+378
Lisburn+336
Sligo+18 Monaghan+27·
Newrv-5
Ballina+20
Enniskillen+15
Dundalk+121
·Castlebar+26
Drogheda+24
Navan+18
Athlone+82·
Mullingar+102
DUBLIN — 143
Ballinasloe+21·
Naas+42·
C T
DUN
LAOGHAIRE
Galway+70.
Tullamore+18
Droichead Nua+714
+1305
Portlaoighise+78·
Bray+
400
Ennis+16
·Nenagh-40
Carlow-1
Arklow+116
Thurles-6
Kilkenny-35
Enniscorthy-6
LIMERICK
+28
Carrick-55
-on-Suir
NewRoss+3
Tralee+17·
Clonmel-6·
·Wexford+18
Mallow-5·
Waterford+45
Killarney+6·
Youghal-43
Dungarvan-64
CORK
+59
Cobh+39

Figures shew percentage change
in population 1841–1971
+ increase — decrease
C = Clondalkin } founded
T = Tallaght } since 1841

—W.Bromage—

Miles | 50 | 100 | Km | 80 | 160

69. *Towns, 1841–1971*

230

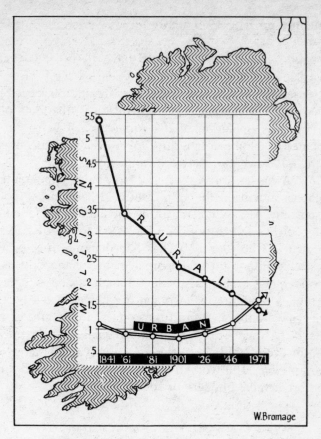

70. *From a rural to an urban society*

70. FROM A RURAL TO AN URBAN SOCIETY

The extent to which Ireland has moved from rural to an urban society is somewhat deceptive. Irish society is in fact less urban in character than the rest of the British Isles, but the speed with which the rural population has declined has exaggerated the social consequences of the change.

In 1841 5% of the population of Ireland lived in cities of more than 50,000 while the equivalent figures for England were 30%. By 1911 the percentage had risen to 15% for the twenty-six counties, 31% for Northern Ireland, while Wales was 27%, Scotland 40% and England 51%. Since that date the rate of urbanisation in most of the British Isles has slowed down considerably but Ireland is

231

still catching up. The 1971 figure of 33% urbanisation is still not high.

Although Ireland will probably have to become even more urbanised in the future, the social problems have been severe. In other parts of the British Isles, where urbanisation has been gradual, and the overall population has risen steadily, urbanisation has not meant rapid depopulation of the rural areas, whereas in Ireland the population of the towns in 130 years has risen only slightly while there has been a massive rural depopulation.

Taking towns as centres of 1,500 or more population, in the Republic, as shown on the graph, since 1841 the urban population has risen only 41% while the rural population has fallen by 74%. Although such a fall in population was economically necessary for the survival of the country, it has had demoralising social consequences. One important social problem in Ireland now is that of a preponderance of males in the rural areas and females in the major towns. Modern Irish women are not attracted by rural life and they have emigrated from the country in far greater numbers than have the men. In 1971, in the Republic there were only 88 women for every 100 men in the rural areas, while there were only 93 men for every 100 women in the towns. This sexual imbalance has had predictable but serious social consequences.

71. POPULATION CHANGES: 1841–51

From 1841 to 1851 the population of Ireland dropped from 8,175,124 to 6,552,386, a fall of 20%. Since by 1845 the figure was probably closer to 8,500,000 the fall is over 23%. The fall was due to death and emigration, mainly resulting from the Great Famine of 1845–8. Estimates can be made of the number of deaths, but all figures must be examined with caution. In many areas of the country death was so common that bodies were thrown into communal graves without any records being kept.

The map shows the changes in population in all the Irish counties and it can be seen how variable the changes were. The figures can give a misleading idea of the severity of the famine in certain areas. There is no question but that the west of Ireland was the worst affected and yet there are even more severe falls in some of the midlands counties. One reason for this is that the slightly

DONEGAL 14

LONDON-DERRY 14

ANTRIM 11

TYRONE 18

FERMANAGH 26

ARMAGH 16

DOWN 11

MONAGHAN 29

SLIGO 29

LEITRIM 28

CAVAN 28

LOUTH 16

MAYO 29

ROSCOMMON 31

LONGFORD 29

WESTMEATH 21

MEATH 23

9% INCREASE DUBLIN

GALWAY 27

KING'S CO 24

KILDARE 16

WICKLOW 22

CLARE 26

QUEEN'S CO 27

CARLOW 21

TIPPERARY 24

KILKENNY 22

WEXFORD 11

LIMERICK 21

WATERFORD 16

KERRY 19

CORK 26

PERCENTAGE DECLINE IN POPULATION BY COUNTY 12

W.Bromage

Miles 50 100   Km 80 160

71. *Population changes, 1841–51*

233

better-off tended to emigrate first. In the case of the completely penniless, unless public assistance was forthcoming they could not emigrate until a relative or friend gave them the money. Therefore the drop in population in the poorer counties generally relates to a disproportionately heavy death rate.

The census of 1841 and 1851 give a number of interesting figures on the changes in population from province to province, as follows:

Province	1841	1851	% Fall
Ulster	2,389,263	2,013,879	16%
Leinster	1,982,169	1,682,320	15%
Munster	2,404,460	1,865,600	22%
Connacht	1,420,705	1,012,479	29%

During the following decade, when the mass deaths had ceased, and emigration was the main reason for population decrease, the proportions were:

Province	% Fall in population between 1851 and 1861
Ulster	5%
Leinster	13%
Munster	19%
Connacht	10%

Another valuable statistic relates to deaths during this period. Recorded deaths between 1841 and 1851 came to a total of 1,622,738. Of the total deaths recorded, men made up 56%.

The 1851 Census provides a painstaking analysis of the death statistics, although admitting that many must have gone unrecorded. Changes in the age groups between 1841 and 1851 are also significant. Children under ten were the group affected most; there were 34% fewer one-year-olds in 1851 than in 1841, 38% fewer one to five-year-olds and 25% fewer five to ten-year-olds. For ten to twenty-year-olds the decrease is only 10%. Remembering that the years 1845–51 were those of the majority of deaths, the effect on the one to ten-year-old population is grim.

72. POPULATION CHANGES: 1841–1871

No accurate estimates can be made of the Irish population before the nineteenth century. It seems likely that by the eighth century

234

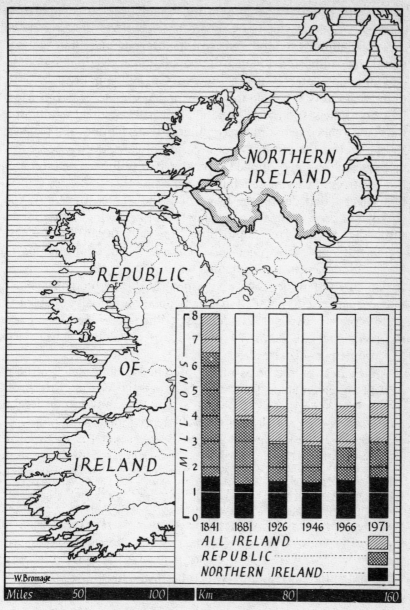

72. *Population changes, 1841–1971*

there were about half a million inhabitants; giving a population density of about sixteen per square mile. In 1659 an estimate of the population was produced, which although inaccurate gives a useful indication. It estimated the population at over half a million and although later evidence suggests (Sir William Petty in 1672 estimated 1,100,000) that this is an underestimate, it nevertheless indicates how static the Irish population had remained in almost a thousand years due mainly to continuous wars, famines and plagues. By the end of the century after a period of comparative peace this figure seems to have climbed to nearer two million. The estimates from sources of varying reliability, such as the Hearth Money Collectors, suggest that during the first half of the eighteenth century the population grew comparatively slowly, not achieving three million until the 1770s. The population explosion began in the late eighteenth and early nineteenth century, when a long period of almost unbroken peace, combined with what has been described as 'a gap in the famines' and a very high birth-rate brought about a massive increase in population. The population virtually doubled in the 50 years between 1791 and 1841. When it reached its highest recorded height of 8,175,124 in 1841, the population density was 254 people per square mile.

The figures for the areas of the present Republic and Northern Ireland are given below:

Date	Republic	% increase or decrease	N. Ireland	% increase or decrease	Ireland	% increase or decrease
1841	6,528,799	—	1,646,325	—	8,175,124	—
1851	5,111,589	−22%	1,440,797	−12%	6,552,386	−20%
1881	3,870,020	−24%	1,304,816	−9%	5,174,836	−21%
1901	3,221,823	−17%	1,236,952	−5%	4,458,775	−14%
1946	2,955,107	−8%	1,334,168	+8%	4,289,275	−4%
1961	2,818,341	−4%	1,427,000	+7%	4,245,341	−1%
1971	2,978,248	+6%	1,527,593	+7%	4,505,841	+6%
1979	3,368,217	+13%	—		—	

Ireland is the only country which has had a declining population during the last century, and for the Republic, the trend has only been reversed over the past two decades. The area of the country which became Northern Ireland, being much more industrialised than the south, suffered less during and after the famine, and its population has remained relatively stable over the century. While in 1971 the population of the Republic was only 46% of that of 1841, the Northern Irish population had dropped by only 7%. However, the Republic's 1979 census revealed a substantial increase in the population which reflected the economic successes of the 1960s and 1970s.

73. THE DEPOPULATION OF THE WEST

In this century a major social problem has been the depopulation of the west of Ireland. The continual drain of people from the west to the big cities or abroad has contributed to a deepset demoralisation. The 1979 census figures suggest that efforts to reverse the trend through job creation schemes are at last bearing fruit.

The effects of the famine varied considerably in different provinces, but the west of Ireland, and Connacht in particular, suffered more than any other part of the country. By 1926 the population of Leinster had dropped to 58% of the 1841 figure; by 1979 it had risen to 88%. The 1926 population of the whole of Ulster was 65% of that of 1841; the 1971 figure was up to 73%. The 1926 population of Munster was 40% of that of 1841; the 1979 figure was still only 41%. The 1926 population of Connacht was 39% of that of 1841; the 1979 figure was still lower, at 29%. However, the economic successes of the 1970s have had some impact in the west of Ireland. Foreign investment has provided jobs in manufacturing industry, while E.E.C. subsidies have greatly increased the prosperity of Irish farmers. The map shows important changes in the population of five of the western counties, compared to Co. Dublin. Although the figures for the 1970s are encouraging, the west still suffers badly from underpopulation, and the allied problem of a disproportionately small number of women and a low marriage rate. In 1941, there were more females than males in each province. In 1979 in the Republic, Leinster was the only province with more women than men, having 2% more, while Connacht had 6% fewer, and the country as a whole had 1% fewer. This has been caused primarily by three factors: first, the excess of male over female births; second, the much higher emigration rate of women in the 1960s; and third, the similarity between male and female life expectancy in Ireland, which is unusual for Western society in which women usually live longer than men.

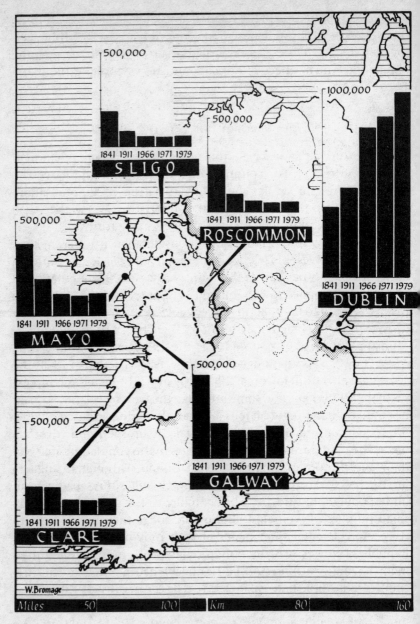

73. *The depopulation of the west*

238

The Republic has a marriage rate which is very much lower than that of the rest of the British Isles. In recent years it reached its nadir in 1960, when there were only 4·4 marriages per thousand population in the Republic compared with 7·0% for Northern Ireland, 7·5% for England and Wales and 7·7% for Scotland. Even though Irish fertility rates are consistently the highest in Western society, the unusually low marriage rates and high emigration kept the population in a state of decline until the 1960s.

74. MIGRATION: 1881–1979

Migration statistics are notoriously unreliable for Ireland before 1871, although some estimates can be made of the numbers of those who left the country before this time. In the main post-famine emigration period, 1845–55, almost 2,000,000 left the country for North America and Australia and probably about three-quarters of a million left for Britain. After 1855 the flood of emigrants began to wane somewhat, but it has nevertheless remained a way of life until the present day.

Throughout the second half of the nineteenth century the annual rate of emigration remained very high. Between 1871 and 1891 about 1,400,000 emigrated – an annual rate of about 70,000 of whom about 20% were from Northern Ireland.

It has theoretically been a great disappointment to the rulers of the Irish Republic that emigration continued at such a high rate even after independence, although in practice it has served to contain unemployment at home within reasonable bounds. Still, the depopulation of rural areas has forced the government to attempt to reverse the trend of emigration and provide economic and social incentives to keep would-be emigrants at home. It is not until the last decade that this policy has begun to succeed. Although emigration from Northern Ireland has been quite high, the losses of the Irish Republic have been much greater. Emigration from Northern Ireland has been reasonably steady during most of the century, as is evident from the stability of its population, but at its peak, in the 1950s, it lost over 90,000 people, about 6% of the population. During the same period the Republic lost over 400,000 or 14% of the population.

Since the early 1960s there has been a noticeable reduction in

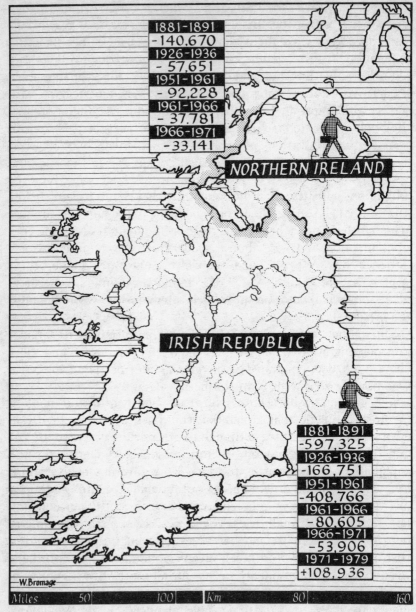

1881-1891
-140,670
1926-1936
- 57,651
1951-1961
- 92,228
1961-1966
- 37,781
1966-1971
- 33,141

NORTHERN IRELAND

IRISH REPUBLIC

1881-1891
-597,325
1926-1936
-166,751
1951-1961
-408,766
1961-1966
- 80,605
1966-1971
- 53,906
1971-1979
+108,936

Miles 50 100 Km 80 160

74. *Net migration, 1881–1979*

emigration from both parts of Ireland, and this has had a pronounced effect on the population figures. During the 1970s the Republic at last reversed the pattern of net emigration, but the sexual imbalance is still worrying; male migration exceeded female by 22%. From 1926–36, 1946–51 and 1961–71 women have been emigrating in far larger numbers than men – about 20% more. Also, the emigrating women tend to be better educated than the men. In recent years among Irish emigrants to Britain, about 20% of the women have joined the professions, compared with only about 2% of the men. To a considerable extent this is due to the economic problems which face a working woman in Ireland, where equality of pay and opportunity still get mainly lip-service (77).

75. EDUCATION: 1800–1971

The appalling illiteracy figures of the pre-famine period can be somewhat misleading, for it must be remembered that many of those who could not read or write retained some of the oral culture of previous generations. Nevertheless the relevant statistics for 1841, as shown on map 75a, indicate how backward Irish education was at this point.

At the beginning of the century, for the mass of the population, the only schooling available was obtained from 'hedge' schools, which were literally schools held in the open. With the founding of the Irish Christian Brothers, schools were introduced to the main towns and the Presentation Sisters and Ursuline Sisters opened girls' schools in urban areas also – catering exclusively for the Catholic population. There were a number of endowed schools for the Church of Ireland, and an educational body called the Kildare Place Society which offered non-sectarian education but was unacceptable to the Catholic church. This was typical of the kind of problem which arose in an era when education was the preserve of the church. In Ireland there were inter-denominational jealousies and deep mutual suspicions which mitigated against any kind of constructive cooperation. The Catholic clergy considered an illiterate flock preferable to one which had been subjected to the dangers of non-Catholic education. This conflict was to continue throughout the nineteenth and twentieth centuries in inter-denominational squabbles about education and was to frustrate the British govern-

241

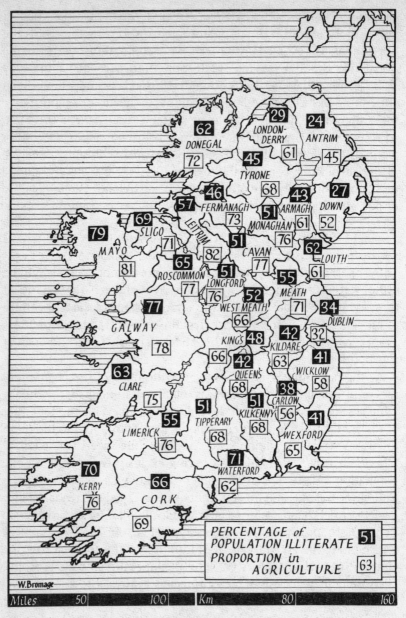

75a. *Illiteracy, 1841*

242

ment in many of their attempts to provide an education for the mass of the population.

In 1831 the whig government set up a national education system which vastly increased the scope of education throughout the country. From only 789 schools in 1831, there were 3,501 national schools twenty years later and during that period pupils increased by about 400,000 to over half a million. At the time of the famine, however, the disparity of educational opportunities between different provinces was very marked, with Ulster having about 40% of the schools and Connacht only 10%. The initial concentration of schools in urban areas meant that illiteracy was particularly high in rural areas, and tended to be closely related to occupation; map 75a shows the close correlation between illiteracy and the dependence on agriculture.

There was also a close correlation between illiteracy and religion as might be expected, since the mass of the population were Catholics. The relevant proportions of illiterates according to religion in 1861 were as follows:

Province	Roman Catholic	Protestant
Ulster	44·4%	15·2%
Leinster	39·9%	8·2%
Munster	48·4%	9·9%
Connacht	59·4%	13·9%
Total	45·8%	13·7%

The problem of illiteracy had been virtually beaten in Ireland by the end of the century. The illiteracy figures for the whole country are as follows:

1841	1851	1861	1871	1881	1891	1901	1911
53%	47%	39%	33%	25%	18%	14%	12%

In 1878 with the introduction of the Intermediate Education Act the problem of secondary education was tackled, since grants were made available both for private and state schools. In 1923 the Intermediate Board virtually went out of existence.

University education had been very limited, since the only university in Ireland was Trinity College, established in 1593, which had received Catholics only from 1793. In 1845 the Queen's Colleges (Ireland) Act provided colleges at Belfast, Cork and Galway.

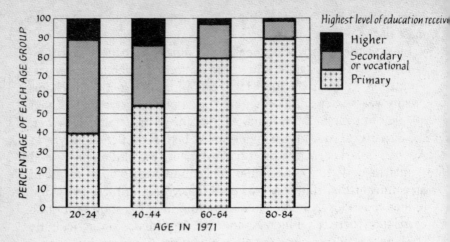

75b. *Educational advances: twentieth century (Republic)*

In 1854 the Catholic University was founded in Dublin with the future Cardinal Newman as Rector. It was reorganised in 1882 as University College, Dublin, and was controlled by the Jesuits from 1883. An examining body, the Royal University, set up in 1879, was empowered to confer degrees. In 1908 the National University of Ireland, comprising the three constituent colleges of Dublin, Cork and Galway was set up, and Queen's College, Belfast was made an independent university. All negotiations on university education were marred by long-drawn out disagreements, mainly between the clergy of the Catholic church, but a compromise solution was eventually reached.

There have been few educational changes since the setting up of the Republic until during the 1960s the government accepted that education was its responsibility rather than the church's. Free secondary education and university grants have been introduced and the government is more involved in education than in the past. Chart 75b illustrates educational advances in this century.

76. IRISH SPEAKERS: 1851–1971

The Irish literary tradition was almost exclusively oral in character, so that with the introduction of a written culture Latin and English began to predominate in education and culture. Latin was the

244

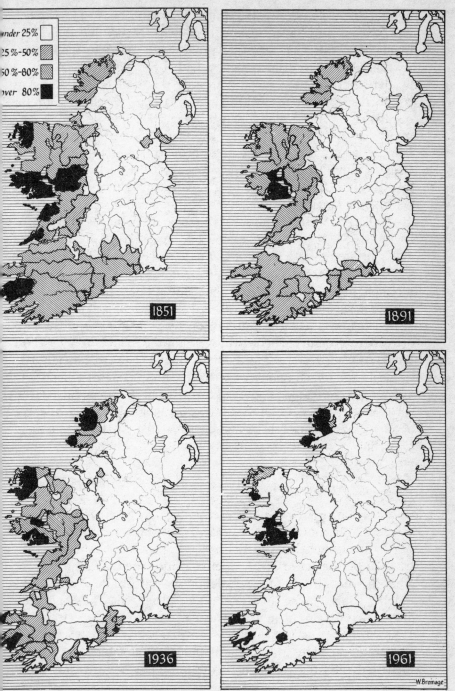

76. *Irish speakers, 1851–1971*

(Reproduced from *A View of the Irish Language*, ed. Brian Ó Cuiv, with the permission of the Controller, Stationery Office, Dublin.)

normal language of the Irish church for centuries. Norman French was spoken for a time, especially among the administrators, but English was the language of the professional classes by the late sixteenth century. The displacement of Latin by English was accelerated by the Reformation. Anyone with any educational, professional or commercial aspirations was required to learn English, with the result that by the Union English was spoken by the middle and upper classes while Irish was spoken by the mass of the rural population outside Ulster. Therefore, from the collapse of the traditional Gaelic culture and the disappearance of the Gaelic professional learned class, Irish ceased to be a language of culture and gradually became the language of the poor and the uneducated.

The decline of Irish continued throughout the nineteenth century. In 1851 25% of the population could speak Irish; by 1911 only 12%. Inspired by the work of German and French scholars on the Gaelic language, the Gaelic League, founded in 1893, made valiant attempts to revive the language and the culture. Their success was mainly academic – not practical.

In 1925 the Gaeltacht Commission was set up to consider those areas of the country where Irish was still the main language. Those areas coincided with the poorest ones. The Commission distinguished between two types of Gaeltacht. In the Fíor-Ghaeltacht, at least 80% of the population spoke Irish; in the Breac-Ghaeltacht, between 25% and 80%. Of those areas designated as Gaeltacht areas, despite government aid, the numbers of Irish speakers continued to decline.

Irish Speakers as Percentage of Total	1936	1946	1961
Fíor-Ghaeltacht	83·1%	76·3%	71·9%
Breac-Ghaeltacht	41·5%	33·8%	35·3%

In 1956 the Gaeltacht areas order redefined the Gaeltacht to cover areas in which most of the population spoke Irish; these areas were roughly equivalent in area to the Fíor-Ghaeltacht. The population of this new Gaeltacht in 1956 was 85,700, in 1961 79,323, and in 1971 70,568.

Despite, therefore, the financial inducements which the government provides, the Gaeltacht is declining fast. Theoretically about

27% of the Republic's population can speak Irish – the highest figure ever recorded, since that of 1851 was only 24·5%. It is cautionary to add, however, that those recorded as Irish-speaking are those who were taught Irish as a compulsory subject at school. It is doubtful if many of these ex-pupils can speak Irish with any ease once they have left school.

The basic reason why the Gaeltacht is dying is an economic one. Despite government grants, the younger generation do not wish to be restricted by their language to an extremely limited range of jobs or locations.

77. THE STATUS OF WOMEN: 1841–1979

Before the Great Famine in the 1840s, more than half the non-agricultural labour force was female; women were also valued workers on farms. The collapse in domestic industry that followed the famine, coupled with the shift from tillage to livestock which reduced the need for farm labour, produced a disastrous reduction in job opportunities for women. Except in Ulster, where factory work was available, most women were left with the options of domestic service, marriage, the convent, emigration or dependence on relatives.

The agricultural bias of the economy kept an enormous number of young men on farms awaiting their inheritance and deferring marriage; poor youths would usually marry only a woman with a dowry; a puritanical and materialistic society kept the sexes apart. By 1926, the year of the first census of the Irish Free State, only about 75% of women in their forties were married; half of these had husbands about ten years their senior. Chart 77a shows the pattern of female employment in the Republic between 1926 and 1971, a period that saw the vast majority of working women restricted to a small number of occupations which were badly paid and had no career prospects.

Although revolutionary leaders like Pearse and Connolly had supported the movement for female suffrage and in consequence women in Ireland had voting equality with men before their counterparts in most European countries, they had until recently little voice in public affairs. Most women who achieved prominence did so because of their family connections. With a few honourable

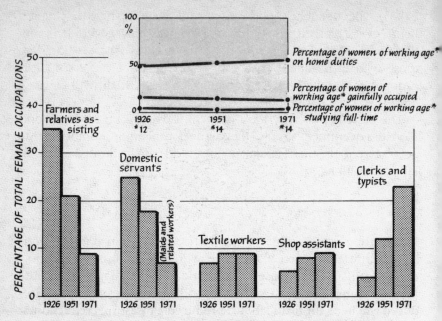

77a. *The status of women: occupations 1926–71 (Republic)*

exceptions, female members of the Dáil have got there only because of an act of piety by the electorate towards dead relatives (see chart 77b). They have usually been distinguished by silence and conservatism. Nor have women been present in other than derisory numbers in the Senate or local government.

Important advances have been made in the 1970s mainly because of pressure from without and below. The women's movement became a potent force world-wide in the 1960s and 1970s and the Republic, rather late and feebly, had to come to terms with it. In 1970 the government established a Commission on the Status of Women, which in 1973 made a wide range of recommendations for removing legal, financial or other discriminations against women. Many of these have been or will be implemented. For instance, the ban on the employment of married women in the civil service or local government has been abolished, and taxation and legal concessions have been secured. The E.E.C. is also a force for change.

The Republic still has a lower proportion of females in the labour force than almost any other European country. Equal pay and equality of opportunity are nowhere near achievement. Yet unques-

248

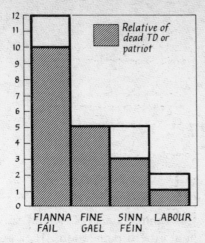

77b. *Women members of the Dáil, 1922–80*

tionably Irish women have made more progress in the 1970s than in the whole of the previous century. They are at last represented by an articulate and self-confident pressure group.

In Northern Ireland the women's movement has attracted far less attention, first because of the political turmoil of the 1970s and second because women in the province have historically faced much less discrimination than have women in the Republic.

XII Northern Ireland

In 1838 the Railway Commissioners of Ireland, surveying the whole country, said of the northern population, 'They are a frugal, industrious and intelligent race, inhabiting a district for the most part inferior in natural fertility to the southern portion of Ireland, but cultivating it better.' This is a traditional view of the Ulster people, taken by its largely Protestant commentators. Travellers, philanthropists and entrepreneurs coming to Ireland in the nineteenth century to try to solve its problems were wont to remark approvingly on the efficiency of the northern population compared to that of the rest of the country.

Ulster is very much the creation of the Scots. There is an irony in this in that the Irish were early colonists in Scotland when in the fourth century they set up the kingdom of Dál Riada. Intercourse between the province and western Scotland was always frequent. The old Gaelic families continued to dominate Ulster throughout the medieval period, despite John de Courcy's success in subduing limited areas of the province. The bond between the two countries was emphasised in the fourteenth century with the Bruce invasion, and during the next two centuries the Scots mercenary soldier (the galloglas) became a familiar feature in Irish military encounters.

Ulster did not really change until after the Nine Years War, when its strategic inviolability ceased. By the early seventeenth century garrisons were set up throughout the province, and it was ready for the planters. The province had remained independent after the rest of Ireland had been effectively conquered. It was rural; apart from Carrickfergus, there were no towns as we know them before

250

the Plantation. That this Plantation succeeded when the Tudor plantations failed was mainly due to the Scots' familiarity with Ulster. Western Scotland had always had a higher population than it could prosperously accommodate, and even without government incentives the Ulster lands attracted them. Most of the immigrants were landless and poor.

The seeds of future tragedy were sown during the seventeenth century. There were not enough settlers to work the land, so a large Catholic population remained to act as labourers or to occupy the inferior land, while, unlike the other provinces of Ireland there were enough settlers to make up a proportion of the population too substantial ever to be shifted or absorbed. The land-hungry Scots proved efficient at clearing forests, farming land and founding towns and industries.

With the outbreak of war between Charles I and the Scots, their Presbyterian brethren in Ulster, who had suffered under Sir Thomas Wentworth, supported them. When the 1641 rebellion broke out it was led by Ulster Catholics and the planters had their homes burned and some suffered torture and murder. The horrors of the rising were not forgotten; they were remembered and embellished in the Protestant memory. With the joining in alliance with the Irish of the Old English, who were also Roman Catholics, the religious element became the important feature distinguishing the royalists from the parliamentarians.

During the seventeenth century Ulster gradually became the most prosperous province in Ireland. Although domestic industries were not unique to Ulster, they were practised more seriously there and with superior craftsmanship. Immigrants like the Huguenots and the Quakers came to the north in comparatively large numbers and brought with them an expertise in textiles and a dedication of approach. With the Ulster Custom, which gave security of tenure and compensation to tenants, there was a stability in Ulster which was lacking in the rest of the country.

The religious division intensified with the war in Ireland between James II and William of Orange. The bitterness at their suffering coupled with the pride at their courage persists in the songs which are still sung about the relief of Derry, while for the Irish Catholics the defeat of the Stuarts represented the beginning of a period of serious religious persecution and mass emigration.

Despite their loyal support for the winning side, the Ulster Presbyterians experienced discrimination during the eighteenth century and many of them emigrated. Although history and prejudice prevented any kind of alliance with their fellow victims, the Catholics, it made them a more separate people in that a bitterness against England began to build up. Their increasing militarism was evident in the sectarian outrages of the eighteenth century, which began when, after 1782, Catholics were able to bid for land, and incensed their competitors for land by outbidding them. After the worst sectarian encounter (the Diamond) the Orange Order was founded. A typical oath of one of the early clubs was: 'To the glorious, pious, and immortal memory of the great and good King William, not forgetting Oliver Cromwell, who assisted in redeeming us from popery, slavery, arbitrary power, brass-money and wooden shoes.' Despite later attempts to moderate the movement, and to extend its proletarian base, such sentiments are its roots. Government policy in the 1790s (in the words of an English General) was to 'increase the animosity between Orangemen and the United Irish'.

The 1798 Rebellion and Emmet's rising of 1803 kept alive the fear of the Orange movement, as did the pressure first for Catholic Emancipation, for Repeal and finally for Home Rule, but during much of the nineteenth century it was not very serious. Fear of a sell-out over Home Rule became more and more potent however. Rudyard Kipling summed up the Ulster Protestant's attitude to Home Rule in a poem called 'Ulster 1912' when he wrote:

> 'The blood our fathers spilt
> Our love, our toils, our pains,
> Are counted us for guilt,
> And only bind our chains.
> Before an Empire's eyes,
> The traitor claims his price.
> What need of further lies?
> We are the sacrifice.'

In this poem are expressed the virtues and the deficiencies of the Ulster Protestants. Their history is that of a proud, industrious and courageous people developing a prosperous way of life out of devastation and misery. For centuries they have viewed the Catholics as a Fifth Column in their midst. They have little in common with their Catholic neighbours, except a common view that the two peoples cannot co-exist peacefully.

78. RELIGIOUS DIVISIONS

The Orange Order was founded in 1795 by Protestant peasantry to maintain the Protestant ascendancy. Within a year its usefulness in providing recruits for the yeomanry led to its acceptance by the gentry. The gentleman's lodge established to lead the Orangemen was based in Dublin. Southern landlords swiftly followed this lead and encouraged their Protestant tenants to form lodges. As map 78a shows, by the time the 1798 rebellion broke out, there were Orange lodges in almost every county. The Order's success in reviving the Orange spirit of 1690 made it a natural ally of the government in putting down the rebellion, but its fervour and the brutal sectarianism of many of its plebian supporters made it an embarrassment later. After its suppression in the 1830s it was abandoned by the gentry and the middle classes until its revival in the 1880s to resist Home Rule.

The Orangemen's emphasis on preserving the Protestant ascendancy, coupled with a change in the Presbyterian church from a liberal to a hard-line approach, set the basis for sectarian conflict in the north-eastern counties. During the nineteenth century, industrialisation attracted Catholics to Belfast; 10% of the population in 1800, they were 30% in 1830. Competition for jobs and houses exacerbated religious tensions, and serious riots in Belfast were often experienced from then on; religious segregation in employment and housing followed.

The Orange Order was the vital force in resisting Home Rule for a united Ireland and it was their leaders who dominated the Northern Irish parliament from its inception. Sectarianism flourished. The Unionists were never strong enough to do without the link with the Orange Order, which ensured Catholic hostility. Between 1921 and 1969, of the 54 Unionists who reached Cabinet rank in Northern Ireland, only three were not Orangemen. It is estimated that 95% of Unionists are Protestant and 99% of nationalists are Catholic. As far as religious divisions are concerned, 62% of the population are

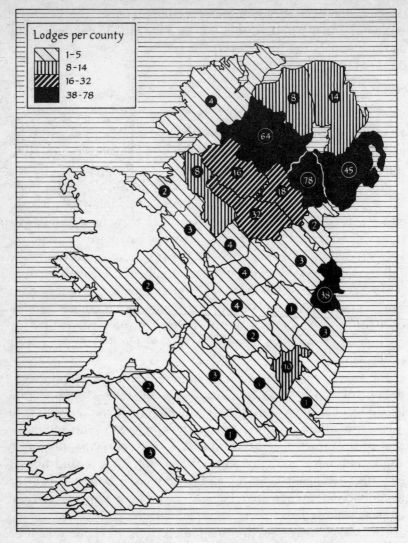

Lodges per county
1-5
8-14
16-32
38-78

78a. *The Orange Order, May 1798*

Protestant and 35% Catholic. Map 78b shows the distribution of Catholics throughout the state, with the countries nearest the border having the highest proportion. Conversely, three counties on the other side of the border, Donegal, Cavan and Monaghan, have the largest proportion of Protestants in the Republic.

Sectarianism has been exacerbated by segregated schooling;

254

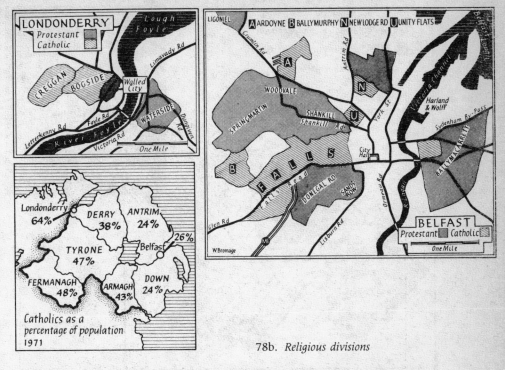

78b. *Religious divisions*

church leaders have been more concerned with maintaining rigid control over their flocks than with encouraging integration. Religious differences are not the only cause of the violence in Northern Ireland, but they are a major cause. Both states in Ireland discriminate against their minorities. In the Republic, Catholic morality has prevented non-Catholics from following their consciences in such matters as divorce and contraception. In Northern Ireland, the prevailing Protestant ethos has imposed on the Catholics such restrictions as Sunday observance, as well as actively discriminating against them in housing, employment and politics.

79. GOVERNMENT: 1921–69

The six north-eastern counties of Ireland, Antrim, Down, Armagh, Tyrone, Fermanagh and Londonderry, became the state of Northern Ireland as a result of the Government of Ireland Act of 1920. In area it is 5,452 square miles – only about 17% of the whole island, although the population hovers around 50% of the Republic's. The

255

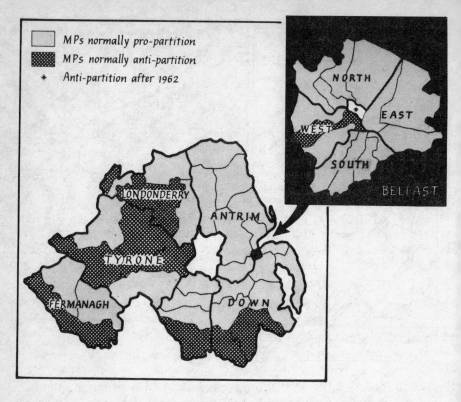

79. *Government: Stormont constituencies (excluding Queen's University), 1929–68*

Unionists accepted six counties rather than the nine (the six plus Cavan, Donegal and Monaghan) of Ulster because of the religious and hence the political split. Protestants in the nine were in a majority of 900,000 to 700,000 Catholics; in the six they were in a majority of 820,000 to 430,000, thus ensuring a substantial Unionist majority in Parliament.

Northern Irish nationalists believed partition to be temporary, hence initially they refused to recognise the new state and for the first few years their MPs refused to take their seats. This abstentionist policy left Unionists in full control of setting up the new state's institutions, so leaving Catholics at a permanent disadvantage. The police force, the Royal Ulster Constabulary (R.U.C.) and the part-time police, the 'B' Specials – armed to combat I.R.A. terrorism – were seen as instruments of oppression; the local government franchise was property not population-related; gerrymandering was common; proportional representation for parliamentary elections was abolished in 1929; the Catholic community opted out of the state secular education system; discrimination in housing and employment continued.

Unquestionably the Unionists set out from the beginning to discriminate in favour of the Protestant majority, but this they did through fear of the nationalist aspirations of the Catholics, a fear that was exacerbated by the latters' refusal for several years to accept the legitimacy of the state and later by de Valera's 1937 Constitution (32) which enshrined Catholic morality and a claim to the whole territory of Ireland.

The Government of Ireland Act reserved substantial powers (particularly in foreign affairs, finance and defence) to Westminster, where thirteen seats were allocated to Northern Ireland (reduced to twelve in 1948 with the abolition of university representation). Between 1922 and 1966 nine constituencies always returned Unionists (as did Queen's University constituency). Of the 62 Northern Irish MPs at Westminster during this period, 56 were Ulster Unionists. They were mainly professional or business men, unrepresentative of their own supporters and out of touch with their grass roots. They had little impact either at Westminster or in Northern Ireland. The politicians who mattered were in the Northern Irish parliament. The map shows the distribution of their support among the constituencies which existed between 1929 and 1968, during which period Unionists never took fewer than 34 of the 52 seats at any election.

Massive unemployment (25% on average) during the 1930s, coupled with bad housing, brought widespread sectarian riots which died down as employment prospects improved towards the end of the decade. The second world war brought an economic boom that reduced unemployment dramatically. The post-war British Labour government agreed to subsidise the extension to Northern Ireland of the new health and social welfare benefits; the Education Act of 1947 brought free post-primary education. By the 1950s Northern Irish Catholics, although still suffering from discrimination, were materially far better off than their counterparts in the Republic (a state of affairs that prevailed until the 1970s); a recognition of this led to the failure of the I.R.A. to gain support for their 1956–62 offensive.

257

In 1963, the inflexible and right-wing Prime Minister of twenty years, Lord Brookborough, retired. His successor, Terence O'Neill, had a policy of promoting reconciliation between the two communities and the two states. Although his efforts brought about much improved relations with the Republic, his domestic policies left the Catholic community unsatisfied. In 1968 the Civil Rights Association (C.R.A.) began a series of demonstrations against discrimination in housing and local government. Though the government agreed to a number of reforms, they came too late to stop the agitation. Instead they split the C.R.A. The radical student movement, the People's Democracy, whose leaders included Bernadette Devlin, pressed on. In January 1969 they organised a march from Belfast to Derry which was attacked violently at Burntollet Bridge by Protestant extremists, bitterly resentful of what they saw as O'Neill's compromising with traitors.

1969 saw a hardening on both sides. In the Stormont election of that year, 24 pro-O'Neill and 12 anti-O'Neill Official Unionists were returned. Unable to control the growing dissension in the Unionist party and under violent personal attack from popular Protestant hard-liners like Ian Paisley, O'Neill resigned, and his successor, James Chichester-Clark, took over the hopeless task of attempting reconciliation.

Sporadic violence took a new and unpleasant turn in August 1969 when rioting led to a three-day battle in the Bogside in Derry between the R.U.C. and the Catholic community. An invasion of the Falls area in Belfast by an angry Protestant mob led to seven deaths, with 3,000 Catholics losing their homes. On August 14 the British government sent in the army.

80. THE 1970s

In January 1970 the Provisional I.R.A. was formed, following a split between the followers of the socialist leadership (who became known as the 'Official' I.R.A.), who favoured an emphasis on political agitation, and those who favoured a violent approach. The Provisionals won support and recruits from the Catholic community, which, after a brief honeymoon, had come to see the British army as oppressors and the Provisionals as defenders. The Stormont govern-

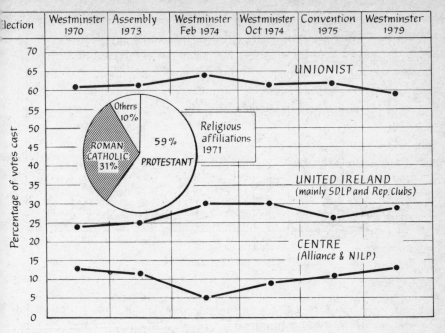

election	Westminster 1970	Assembly 1973	Westminster Feb 1974	Westminster Oct 1974	Convention 1975	Westminster 1979

80a. *The 1970s: political affiliations*

ment, under pressure at home and from London, introduced a series of important reforms that failed to stem the growing violence. By early 1971 the Provisionals were equipped with arms and explosives and had initiated a campaign of shooting and bombing with the intention of bringing about the collapse of the Northern Irish state. The Officials also began a similar campaign on a much smaller scale, but declared a cease-fire in 1972. After this virtually all acts of republican terrorism were the work of the Provisionals, until the emergence towards the end of the decade of splinter groups, notably the Irish National Liberation Army.

In March 1971 Chichester-Clark gave way to Brian Faulkner, who commanded the support of moderate Unionists. However, the credibility of the Northern Irish parliament was eroded when the newly formed moderate Social Democratic and Labour Party withdrew from it in a protest in July. The following month, in response to escalating violence and Protestant pressure, internment was introduced. It failed to reduce the violence and served only further to alienate the Catholic community.

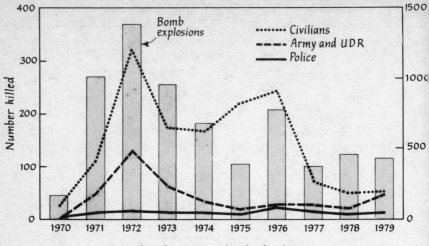

80b. *The 1970s: a decade of violence*

On 30 January 1972 – 'Bloody Sunday' – unarmed republican demonstrators were shot dead by British army paratroopers and the bitterness intensified. In March the Heath government prorogued Stormont and imposed direct rule. The following year the British government announced its plans for a power-sharing Executive to be formed from an elected Assembly. It held a tripartite (Britain, Northern Ireland and the Republic) conference at Sunningdale in December which agreed *inter alia* on the setting up of a Council of Ireland. Members of the Faulkner Unionists, the S.D.L.P. and the new centre Alliance party took office as members of the Executive on 31 December 1973.

By May 1974 the Executive had collapsed as a result of a massive loyalist strike against power-sharing and Sunningdale. Additionally, the February 1974 Westminster elections had resulted in the return of eleven extreme Unionists (anti-Sunningdale candidates had polled 51% of the vote). The Protestant community had become as hard-line as the Catholics. Extremism in politics was being mirrored in the emergence of a number of militant Protestant para-military organisations like the Ulster Defence Association and the Ulster Volunteer Force. Sectarian violence was rife; between 1972 and 1976, of 1,120 civilian murders, 569 were classified as sectarian.

In 1975 elections were held for a 78-member Constitutional Convention which the Wilson government hoped would make constructive proposals about how Northern Ireland should be governed. Yet again, a majority of electors opposed power-sharing, and this was reflected in the composition of the Convention and the proposals put by the majority to the British government in November 1975; these were rejected. In March 1976, the Convention was dissolved, as it was clear that there was no prospect of agreement between the United Ulster Unionist Coalition (U.U.U.C. – Official Unionists, the Vanguard Unionist Party and Ian Paisley's Democratic Unionist Party) and the S.D.L.P., who wanted power-sharing. After this the British government decided that there should be a settled period of direct rule before any new constitutional initiatives. In May 1977 a loyalist strike demanding the implementation of the Convention report failed. It brought about the dissolution of the U.U.U.C., as the Official Unionists refused to cooperate with those who had supported the strike.

In 1979 the Thatcher government put forward plans for a conference to discuss the devolution of powers to a Northern Ireland body. By mid-1980 little progress had been made in bringing the main political parties to any significant measure of agreement. Graph 80a shows how stable has been the vote in terms of the three main tendencies, Loyalist, Centre and United Ireland, and how closely related voting patterns are to religious affiliations. This rigidity demonstrates the difficulty of finding a political compromise.

Against this background of political trial and error by successive British governments, the men of violence on both sides continued their terrorist activities, with only occasional truces. As graph 80b shows, after the appalling figures of 1972, there was a slowing down in the effectiveness of the terrorists, due as much to a revulsion against them by the community as to improved and better organised intelligence work and more effective security measures. Sadly, the hopes generated in 1976 by the formation by Mairead Corrigan and Betty Williams of the Northern Ireland Peace Movement have been disappointed. Although the Peace People won support from both communities and its founders secured world-wide recognition with the award of the Nobel Peace Prize in 1977, dissent among the leadership and in the ranks have damaged the movement's image and reduced its effectiveness. The 1970s ended with less violence but possibly less hope; after so many failed initiatives, it is difficult to be

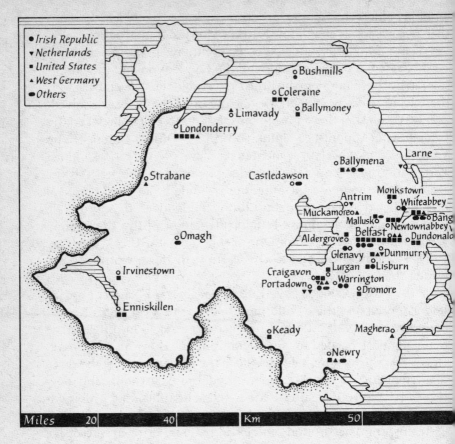

Bushmills
Coleraine
Limavady   Ballymoney
Londonderry
Larne
Strabane   Castledawson   Ballymena
Monkstown
Antrim   Whiteabbey
Muckamore   Bang
Mallusk   Newtownabbey
Omagh   Aldergrove   Belfast   Dundonal
Glenavy   Dunmurry
Irvinestown   Lurgan   Lisburn
Craigavon   Warrington
Portadown   Dromore
Enniskillen
Keady   Maghera
Newry

Miles   20   40   Km   50

81a. *Foreign investment, January 1980*

optimistic that a solution can be found that will be fair and acceptable to both communities.

81. TRADE AND INDUSTRY

The rise of the linen industry and of many of the other industries of Northern Ireland has been described elsewhere (60, 64, 65). By the early nineteenth century the transformation of industry in the province from domestic to factory-based production was in progress. Banking developed more extensively in Ulster than elsewhere and thus capital was more readily available. By this period Belfast, which had been in existence for only two centuries, was the second

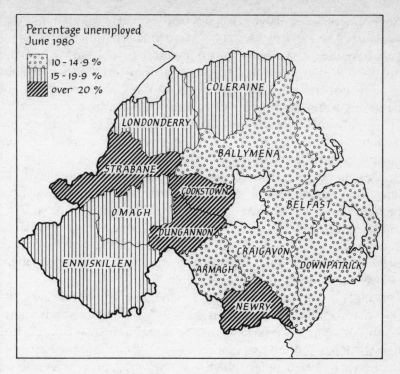

COLERAINE

LONDONDERRY

BALLYMENA

STRABANE

COOKSTOWN

BELFAST

OMAGH

DUNGANNON

CRAIGAVON

ENNISKILLEN

ARMAGH

DOWNPATRICK

NEWRY

81b. *Unemployment*

most important city in Ireland and had extensive trading contacts:
it centralised the trade in agricultural produce.

Since 1945, and particularly since 1960, there have been fundamental changes in the Northern Irish economy. The traditionally
important linen and shipbuilding industries have declined and the
governments' policy of encouraging industrial development geared
to broadening the state's industrial base has led to considerable
diversification. The four main groups of manufacturing industry are
engineering (employing over 30% of employees in manufacturing),
with products including ships, aircraft, electrical and electronic
equipment; textiles (employing about 20% of employees in manufacturing), with man-made fibres the most important products;
food, drink and tobacco; and clothing and footwear.

Like the Republic, with which it is in competition, Northern
Ireland has had as a prime policy objective the attraction of
foreign investment by means of financial and other incentives.

Government-assisted overseas (and cross-border) projects amounted to over 170 by 1980, of which 60% were financed from Great Britain, 20% from the United States, 7% from West Germany and 5% from the Republic. While these and other indigenous projects have brought jobs to Northern Ireland, they have tended to follow other factories in clustering round Belfast. Map 81a shows the distribution of foreign investment projects early in 1980 (those financed by Britain are too numerous to include). Map 82b shows how the imbalance in distribution of jobs has affected the pattern of unemployment, which in parts of the Province had by 1980 reached crisis proportions. It is an oversimplification to see this simply as discrimination against the areas with a high proportion of Roman Catholics. Firms find it convenient to be near large centres of population. In Britain there is a similar imbalance between the number of jobs available in the south-east and in parts of northern England, Wales and Scotland. But in Britain unemployment is lower and society much more stable.

Trade is important for Northern Ireland, which imports most of its raw materials and a large proportion of its finished goods and exports a substantial amount of its agricultural and industrial output. It is heavily dependent on two markets, Great Britain and the Republic. In the early 1970s (after which the relevant figures ceased to be available) Great Britain accounted for over 70% of Northern Irish imports and over 80% of exports, and trade with the Irish Republic accounted for about 10% of the total.

XIII Literature

It is convenient to study Gaelic and Anglo-Irish literature as two separate cultural developments. To do this without distortion, it is vital to be alive to the common inspiration of many writings in both English and Irish. An appreciation of Gaelic folklore and literature was necessary to Yeats, Joyce, O'Connor and many other lesser writers; to place such writers solely in the context of an Anglo-Irish tradition is to ignore the real roots of their inspiration.

The seventeenth century witnessed in Ireland the decline of an oral and written Gaelic literature and the rise of a great tradition of writing in English. Political upheaval had finally ended the poets' position of privilege. The bardic tradition was dying with the ruin of its aristocratic patrons. The seventeenth- and eighteenth-century poets were often reduced to manual labour or begging to survive. Dáibhidh Ó Bruadair (c. 1625–98), Séamus Dall Mac Cuarta (c. 1647–1732), Aodhagán Ó Rathaille (1670–c. 1728) and Eoghan Ruadh Ó Súilleabháin (1748–84), the most famous poets of this period, all experienced great physical deprivation and died in poverty, railing against a society which no longer acknowledged their privileged position.

The main feature of their poetry lay in their use of satire. In their different hands it could be a stiletto or a bludgeon, but with all of them their language showed traces of a great rhetorical tradition. A unique example of the *genre* came with Brian Merriman (c. 1747–1805), with whom Frank O'Connor considered 'Irish literature in the Irish language may be said to have died'. In his poem *The Midnight Court*, Merriman chose a broader satiric target than

265

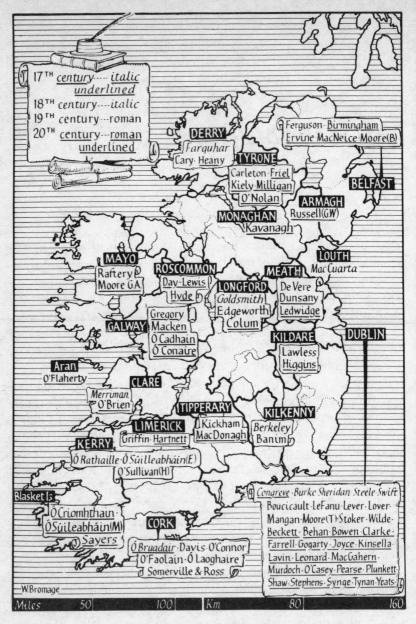

82. *Modern Irish literature*

his predecessors were wont to do, in flaying the marrying habits of the Irish. The earthy humour of the text, so true to the spirit of Irish folklore, led to its exclusion, for many years, from the accepted canon of Irish literature.

The economic and social disasters of the nineteenth century, coupled with the decline of the Irish language, brought a swift end to the Gaelic poetical tradition. The only other Gaelic poet with a reputation, albeit an indifferent one, was the itinerant Anthony Raftery (c. 1784–c. 1835) while original prose literature ceased with Humphrey O'Sullivan (1780–1837). The work of these men was not published until the Gaelic Revival at the end of the century, which was preceded by an antiquarian interest in the older language, which provided materials on which Yeats and his co-workers were to draw so fruitfully.

Despite the efforts of the Gaelic revivalists, little creative writing of lasting literary value has yet been produced in the Irish language. Outstanding is the novel *Cré na Cille* of Máirtín Ó Cadhain (1907–70), as are his short stories, and those of Liam O'Flaherty (1897) – better known for his creative work in English – and Pádraic Ó Conaire (1883–1928). The most distinctive writing of this century has been autobiographical, and of social rather than literary value. An t-Athair Peadar Ó Laoghaire (1839–1920) with *My own story*, Thomás Ó Criomhthain (1856–1937) with *The Islandman*, Muiris Ó Súileabháin (1904–50) with *Twenty years a-growing* and Peig Sayers (1873–1958) with *Peig*, were voices from the world of little or no property which had received scant attention in the novels of the 'Ascendancy' and of the nationalist writers alike. They are evocative and realistic reconstructions of a vanishing world, recorded elsewhere only in the collections of the Irish Folklore Commission. Brian O'Nolan (1912–1966), writing as Myles na gCopaleen, produced in *An Béal Bocht* a unique contribution to the satire for which the Irish tradition had been distinguished.

While creative work in the native language decayed, a distinctive literature emerged, which is termed 'Anglo-Irish'. The greatest names of eighteenth-century Anglo-Irish literature are dramatists, although much fine writing was produced by essayists and men whose contemporary reputations rested equally in fields outside literature. Among the latter category appear the political polemicist and satirist, Jonathan Swift (1667–1745), the essayists Richard Steele

(1672–1729), the philosopher George Berkeley (1685–1753) and the orator Edmund Burke (1729–97). The begetters of the great and still flourishing tradition of Irish drama were the fine comic writers William Congreve (1670–1729), George Farquhar (1677–1707), Oliver Goldsmith (1728–74), Richard Brinsley Sheridan (1751–1816), and later Dionysius Boucicault (1822–90). These writers came mainly from the Protestant middle class.

A new element was to enter Anglo-Irish literature early in the nineteenth century – introduced by the descendants of the native Irish who, with the viewpoint of the emerging Catholic middle class, showed attitudes that diverged from those of their more prosperous 'Ascendancy' contemporaries. This viewpoint was already evident in the work of Humphrey O'Sullivan who wrote in Irish a diary Pepysian in its concern for detail and solidly middle class in attitude and aspiration. Writers in this tradition include William Carleton (1794–1869), Michael (1796–1874) and John (1798–1842) Banim, Gerald Griffin (1803–40) and Charles Kickham (1828–82).

The concerns of these writers provide an interesting contrast to those in what is often pejoratively described as the 'ascendancy' or 'landlord' tradition. Foremost among these were Maria Edgeworth (1767–1849), Samuel Lover (1797–1868), Charles Lever (1806–72), Emily Lawless (1845–1913), George Birmingham (1865–1950) and Somerville and Ross (Edith Somerville 1858–1949 and Violet Martin 1862–1915). Many of these writers were later resented for appearing to laugh at 'Irishness' and their reputations have suffered accordingly in the past, although recently their work is being judged according to more objective standards.

Two distinctive novelists who fit into no earlier tradition were Sheridan Le Fanu (1814–73) and Bram Stoker (1847–1912) who proved themselves masters of mystery and horror.

The nationalist tradition in Anglo-Irish literature is generally seen to begin with Thomas Moore (1779–1852), whose collections of *Irish Melodies* proved immensely popular, both musically and politically. Aubrey de Vere (1814–1902) and more notably, Sir Samuel Ferguson (1810–86) based much of their poetic work on Irish history and tradition, thus providing a link with the later Irish literary renaissance. With the exception of James Clarence Mangan (1803–1849), the Young Ireland movement yielded writers like Thomas Davis (1814–45) and Lady Wilde (1826–96), whose poetry was more noted for its nationalistic fervour than for its quality. This was true also of later poets in this tradition, although Patrick Pearse (1879–1916), Joseph Mary Plunkett (1887–1916) and Thomas MacDonagh (1878–1916) had some genuine talent.

Since the late nineteenth century have emerged many of the giants of Irish literature – Yeats, Shaw, Wilde, Joyce, O'Connor and others. The great dramatic tradition has persisted with Oscar Wilde (1856–1900), George Bernard Shaw (1856–1950), John Millington Synge (1871–1910), Séan O'Casey (1884–1964) and Samuel Beckett (1906). Wilde, Shaw and Beckett left Ireland as young men and chose to be dominated neither in style nor content by their background, although their common anarchy of approach had its roots in the Irish dramatic tradition. Synge, Lady Gregory (1859–1932) and more recent dramatists such as John B. Keane (1928) found their inspiration in Irish country life, which determined the style and content of their plays. The works of O'Casey and later Brendan Behan (1923–64) had their roots in the Dublin slums. These were the first real interpreters of the Irish working class. St John Ervine (1883–1971), Hugh Leonard (1928) and Brian Friel (1928), are more broadly-based and cosmopolitan in aspiration.

The most important single literary development of the late nineteenth and early twentieth centuries was the emergence of the movement which centred around William Butler Yeats (1865–1939), drawing its inspiration from Gaelic literature and folklore. Its patroness, Lady Gregory, made a lasting contribution with her collections of folk beliefs and song, her versions of the Irish sagas and her role in the foundation of the Abbey Theatre. Other notable contemporaries were G. W. Russell (1867–1933), who wrote as 'AE' and was an important poet, and George Moore (1852–1933), possibly best remembered as the acerbic chronicler of the movement. Katherine Tynan (1861–1931) was a prolific and popular poet and novelist, while Oliver St John Gogarty (1878–1957), also a poet, chronicled literary and political Dublin. Contemporaries who made important contributions to the appreciation of Gaelic literature were Douglas Hyde (1860–1949), outstanding for his work as President of the Gaelic League, and Daniel Corkery (1878–1964) whose book *The Hidden Ireland* was to prove a major source of inspiration for generations of writers.

The Irish novel has flourished in the twentieth century. The giant of the *genre* is James Joyce (1882–1941), whose complex scholarship and wholly original talent were devoted to the immortalising of the Dublin of his adolescence. James Stephens (1882–1950) and Brian O'Nolan (1912–66) demonstrated also a remarkable and peculiarly Irish talent in their writings, Stephens in his fantasy *The Crock of Gold* and O'Nolan in his entire corpus of writing in both English and Irish. Of his English novels, O'Nolan's *At Swim Two Birds* displays his extensive classical scholarship, and a knowledge of Gaelic and English literature which is comparable with that of Joyce. The all-pervading wit and the anarchic originality of the book combine to make it worthy of comparison with any contemporary English novel.

Other Irish novelists of this century who have achieved an international reputation include Joyce Cary (1888–1957), Elizabeth Bowen (1900–73), Michael Farrell (1900–62), Walter Macken (1915), Iris Murdoch (1920), James Plunkett (1920), Brian Moore (1921), Aidan Higgins (1927), Edna O'Brien (1932) and John MacGahern (1935). Of these writers, all but Cary, Bowen and Murdoch are dominated in their books by their Irish background.

The short story has reached a new height in Irish literature. In a tradition which became popular with Lord Dunsany (1878–1957), it developed strongly, reaching its zenith with Michael O'Donovan, better known as Frank O'Connor (1903–1966), whose sensitivity, intelligence and humour were combined with a fine craftsmanship to produce stories of lasting merit. Other modern short story writers who have earned international reputations are Liam O'Flaherty, Séan O'Faolain (1900), Benedict Kiely (1919) and Mary Lavin (1912).

Less impressive have been developments in Irish poetry. Irish poets have been dwarfed by the achievements of Yeats, although writers of some distinction have emerged. Francis Ledwidge (1891–1917), Dunsany's protegée, was killed before his talent could mature. Padraic Colum (1881–1971), Austin Clarke (1896–1974) and Patrick Kavanagh (1906–67) achieved solid reputations as Irish poets, while the more celebrated Cecil Day-Lewis (1905–72) and Louis MacNeice (1907–63) left Ireland as young men and have been identified more with other poetic traditions. Of the many talented living Irish poets, Seamus Heaney (1939) has achieved the most international acclaim.

In examining the development of Irish literature over three centuries, the divisions within that culture should not be seen as being between writers in Irish and English. The important divisions are centred on the sources of inspiration, whether these were Irish or cosmopolitan, urban or rural, aristocratic middle class or working class. The truly Irish writer is distinguished by his interpretation of a whole tradition – not by the language he chooses as his medium.

Select Bibliography

The objectives of this bibliography are two-fold. Its primary purpose is to give to the general reader some guidelines on future reading on particular topics covered during the course of the book; it is in no way intended to be comprehensive. Its secondary purpose is to acknowledge my debts to various writers on whose work I have relied heavily.

GENERAL

The eleven volumes of *The Gill history of Ireland*, all published during the 1970s, edited by James Lydon and Margaret Mac Curtain, provide an excellent introduction to Irish history. The individual volumes are: Gearóid MacNiocaill *Ireland before the Vikings*, Donncha Ó Corráin *Ireland before the Normans*, Michael Dolley *Anglo-Norman Ireland*, Kenneth Nicholls *Gaelic and Gaelicised Ireland in the middle ages*, John Watt *The Church in medieval Ireland*, James Lydon *Ireland in the later middle ages*, Margaret Mac Curtain *Tudor and Stuart Ireland*, Edith Mary Johnston *Ireland in the eighteenth century*, Gearóid Ó Tuathaigh *Ireland before the famine, 1798–1848*, Joseph Lee *The modernisation of Irish society, 1848–1918* and John A. Murphy *Ireland in the twentieth century*.

The course of Irish history (ed. T. W. Moody and F. X. Martin, 1967) is a useful collection of essays by 21 Irish historians surveying the whole period. Robert Dudley Edwards *A new history of Ireland* (1972) is a thought-provoking analysis of the development of the Irish community. For the medieval period, A. J. Otway-Ruthven *A history of medieval Ireland* (1968) is a detailed study of Norman Ireland.

Easier going is James Lydon *The lordship of Ireland in the middle ages* (1972), which is thematic rather than chronological in approach. Volume III (1976) of *A new history of Ireland* (ed. T. W. Moody, F. X. Martin and F. J. Byrne) is essential reading for all aspects of the Tudor and Stuart periods (the other volumes have yet to appear). For the eighteenth century W. E. H. Lecky *History of Ireland in the eighteenth century* (1892) has not been displaced. Three outstanding general surveys of the modern period are J. C. Beckett *The making of modern Ireland, 1603–1923* (1966), Robert Kee *The Green Flag* (1972) and F. S. L. Lyons *Ireland since the famine* (1971).

In the field of historical geography T. W. Freeman *Pre-famine Ireland: a study in historical geography* (1957) and *Ireland: a general and regional geography* (1972) are of abiding value to social and economic history. Walter Fitzgerald *The historical geography of early Ireland* is a pioneering work. J. P. Haughton *et al.* (ed.) *Atlas of Ireland* (1979) is a magnificent and beautiful collection of maps of social, economic and historical as well as geographical interest.

On all topics for which specialist reading is recommended below, the relevant general works have much to offer.

CARTOGRAPHY

G. R. Crone *Maps and their makers* (1953) is a useful introduction to the subject. Interesting works are T. J. Westropp 'Early Italian maps of Ireland, 1300–1600' in *Proceedings of the Royal Irish Academy* xxx (1913), G. A. Hayes-McCoy *Ulster and other Irish maps c. 1600* (1964), John Speed *The history of Great Britaine under the conquests of ye Romans, Saxons, Danes and Normans* (1611), Robert Dunlop 'Sixteenth century maps of Ireland' in *English Historical Review* xx (1905) and H. G. Fordham *Some notable surveyors and map makers of the sixteenth-eighteenth centuries and their work* (1929).

MILITARY DEVELOPMENTS

An important general work is G. A. Hayes-McCoy *Irish battles: a military history of Ireland* (1969), while J. J. O'Connell *The Irish wars: a military history of Ireland from the Norse invasions to 1798* (c. 1928) is an original and valuable survey of Irish military development. Eileen McCracken *The Irish woods since Tudor times* (1971) provides interesting information of significance to any study of strategic problems, while also being an important economic study. A useful survey of the Vikings is P. G. Foote and D. M. Wilson *The Viking achievement* (1970) and for the Irish angle A. Walshe *Scandinavian relations with Ireland during the Viking period* (1922) is still useful. For the Norman period G. H. Orpen *Ireland under the Normans 1169–1333* (1911–20) remains the classic study. H. G. Leask *Irish castles and castellated houses* (1941) is informative on Norman castles.

O. Armstrong *Edward Bruce's invasion of Ireland* (1923) is a sound and detailed study of the invasion. For the Nine Years War, Cyril Falls *Elizabeth's Irish wars* (1950) and G. A. Hayes-McCoy 'Strategy and tactics in Irish warfare, 1593–1601' in *Irish Historical Studies* no. 7 (1941) are important. There are few good military studies of the seventeenth or eighteenth centuries. Sir Henry McAnally *The Irish Militia, 1793–1816* (1949) is thorough and T. Pakenham *The year of liberty. The great Irish rebellion of 1798* (1969) is comprehensive. O. Dudley Edwards and F. Pyle (eds) *1916: The Easter Rising* (1968), Charles Townshend *The British Campaign in Ireland, 1919–1921* (1975), Calton Younger *Ireland's civil war* (1968), Joseph Carroll *Ireland and the war years* (1975), E. Rumpf and A. C. Hepburn *Nationalism and socialism in twentieth century Ireland* (1977) and J. Bowyer Bell *The secret army: the IRA, 1916–1979* (1979) cover *inter alia* the military events of the twentieth century.

POLITICS

Eoin MacNeill *Celtic Ireland* (1921) and *Phases of Irish history* (1919) are still valuable for the early period. For the Norman period see Robert Dudley Edwards 'Anglo-Norman relations with Connacht, 1169–1224' in *Irish Historical Studies* no. 2 (1938), A. J. Otway-Ruthven 'The character of Norman settlement in Ireland' in *Historical Studies V*, edited by J. L. McCracken (1965) and D. B. Quinn 'Anglo-Irish local government, 1485–1534' in *Irish Historical Studies* nos. 1 and 2. *The Irish parliament in the middle ages* (1952) by H. G. Richardson and G. O. Sayles is a difficult classic. For Tudor politics see Nicholas Canny *The Elizabethan conquest of Ireland* (1976) and also Robert Dudley Edwards and T. W. Moody 'The history of Poynings' Law . . . , 1494–1615' in *Irish Historical Studies* no. 8 (1941) and D. B. Quinn 'Henry VIII and Ireland, 1509–34' in *Irish Historical Studies* no. 12 (1960). A. Clarke *The Old English in Ireland* (1966), H. F. Kearney *Strafford in Ireland, 1633–41* (1959) and J. G. Simms *Jacobite Ireland 1685–1691* (1969) are important for the study of political development during the seventeenth century, as for the eighteenth century are J. C. Beckett 'Anglo-Irish constitutional relations in the later eighteenth century' in *Irish Historical Studies*, 53 (1964) and R. B. McDowell *Irish public opinion, 1750–1800* (1944). For the nineteenth century some important political studies are R. B. McDowell *Public opinion and government policy in Ireland, 1801–1846* (1952), J. A. Reynolds *The Catholic emancipation crisis in Ireland, 1823–29* (1954), J. H. Whyte *The independent Irish party, 1850–59* (1958) and C. C. O'Brien *Parnell and his party, 1880–90* (1957).

For the later period there are interesting essays in C. C. O'Brien (ed.) *The shaping of modern Ireland* (1960) and T. D. Williams (ed.) *The Irish struggle, 1916–26* (1966). C. C. O'Brien *States of Ireland* (1972) is an absorbing personal view. B. Chubb *The government and politics of Ireland* (1970) is a useful study. Two important books on Ireland during the Second World War are J. T. Carroll *Ireland in the war years* (1975) and T. Ryle Dwyer *Irish neutrality and the USA* (1977).

RELIGION

For early Irish church history J. F. Kenney *Sources for the early history of Ireland: ecclesiastical* (1929) is the major work of reference, while Kathleen Hughes *The church in early Irish society* (1966) is an excellent and scholarly survey. M. and L. de Paor *Early Christian Ireland* (1958) is valuable on the material culture aspect and A. Gwynn and N. Hadcock *Medieval religious houses: Ireland* (1970) is an indispensable source on monasticism. A. Gwynn *The twelfth century reform* (1968) is a useful survey. For the Tudor period Robert Dudley Edwards *Church and state in Tudor Ireland* (1935) and Brendan Bradshaw *The dissolution of the religious orders* (1974) are essential reading. Valuable studies on Irish Catholics at home and abroad have been produced by J. Brady and P. J. Corish *The church under the penal code* (1971), Cathaldus Giblin *Irish exiles in Catholic Europe* (1971) and M. Wall *The penal laws 1691–1760* (1961). For the Protestants, see J. C. Beckett *Protestant dissent in Ireland 1687–1780* and R. B. McDowell *The Church of Ireland, 1801–70* (1975). For the later period *The Catholic*

275

church and Ireland in the age of rebellion, 1859–1873 by E. R. Norman
(1965), *Church State and nation in Ireland, 1898–1921* (1973) by
D. Miller and *Church and state in Ireland, 1923–1979* (1980) by J. H.
Whyte are the standard works.

THE IRISH ABROAD

Studies of the Irish abroad are patchy in range and quality. Useful
information is contained in James E. Handley *The Irish in Scotland,
1798–1845* (1943) and *The Irish in modern Scotland* (1947), K. O'Connor *The Irish in Britain* (1972), Lynn Lees' study of London
immigrants, *Exiles of Erin* (1979) and in the volumes of *A history of
Irish Catholicism* edited by P. J. Corish dealing with the catholic Irish
throughout the world. On the Irish-Americans, W. F. Adams *Ireland
and Irish emigration to the New World from 1815 to the famine* (1932) and
W. V. Shannon *The American Irish* (1963) are useful. T. N. Brown
Irish-American nationalism, 1870–1890 is an interesting analysis. P.
Keatinge *The formulation of Irish foreign policy* (1973) is a standard
work on international relations.

LAND

W. F. T. Butler *Confiscation in Irish history* (1918) is still a useful
survey but has on many aspects been outdated. T. W. Moody *The
Londonderry plantation* (1939), Karl Bottigheimer *English money and
Irish land* (1971) and J. G. Simms *The Williamite confiscation in Ireland, 1690–1703* (1958) are excellent studies of seventeenth-century
plantations. For the eighteenth and nineteenth centuries,
Barbara Solow *The land question and the Irish economy, 1850–1914*
(1971), James Donnelly *The land and the people in nineteenth-
century Cork* (1975) and Samuel Clark *The social origins of the Irish
land war* (1977) superseded all previous treatments of landlord/
tenant relations.

COMMUNICATIONS

For the history of early communications Colm Ó Lochlainn 'Irish
roadways' in *Féilsgríbhinn Eóin Mhic Néill* (1940) is pioneering.
Otherwise see K. B. Nowlan (ed.) *Travel and transport in Ireland*
(1973) and J. Stapleton *Communication policies in Ireland* (1974).

New work of considerable value has been produced in recent years by L. M. Cullen in *An economic history of Ireland since 1660* (1972), *Anglo-Irish trade, 1660–1800* (1968) and (ed.) *The formation of the Irish economy* (1969). For the earlier period there is a paucity of material. A. Stopford Green *The making of Ireland and its undoing, 1200–1600* (1908) is biased and should be treated with caution. A. K. Longfield *Anglo-Irish trade in the sixteenth century* (1929) is useful but limited. H. F. Kearney 'The Irish wine trade, 1614–15' in *Irish Historical Studies* 36 (1955) is the source for map 64. J. Meenan *The Irish economy since 1922* (1970) and R. Fanning *The Irish department of Finance, 1922–1958* (1978) are essential reading.

SOCIAL CHANGE

M. Dillon (ed.) *Early Irish society* (1954) is a useful collection of essays, while P. W. Joyce *Social history of ancient Ireland* (1903) and E. O'Curry *Manners and customs of the early Irish* (1873), if read with caution, are still valuable. Useful studies of the later period are E. MacLysaght *Irish life in the seventeenth century: after Cromwell* (1950) and L. M. Cullen *Life in Ireland* (1968) and *Six generations: everyday work and life in Ireland from 1790* (1970). Excellent recent surveys of particular issues are R. A. Butlin *The development of the Irish town* (1977) and M. MacCurtain and D. Ó Corráin (ed.) *Women in Irish society* (1978). An important study is K. H. Connell *The population of Ireland* (1950). For the more recent period, a great deal of valuable material is to be found in the censuses of Ireland. For the history of education useful recent books are D. H. Akenson *The Irish education experiment* (1969) and *A mirror to Kathleen's face: education in independent Ireland, 1922–1960* (1976) and E. Randles *Post-primary education in Ireland, 1957–70* (1976). For the Irish language, an excellent collection of articles is in Brian Ó Cúiv (ed.) *A view of the Irish language* (1969).

NORTHERN IRELAND

T. W. Moody *The Ulster question, 1603–1973* (1974) is a short authoritative summary of the historical background. On the economic

277

development of the north-east, E.R.R. Green *The Lagan valley, 1800–1850* (1949) is informative. H. Senior *Orangeism in Ireland and Britain, 1795–1836* (1966) and Aiken MacCelland *The Formation of the Orange Order* (n.d.) are good studies of that divisive force. For Northern Ireland politics, see John A. Harbinson *The Ulster Unionist Party, 1882–1973* (1973) and Patrick Buckland *The factory of grievances: devolved government in Northern Ireland, 1931–9* (1979). Of the many recent books on Northern Ireland the one to read in preference to all others is John Darby *Conflict in Northern Ireland* (1976) which does a first-class job in establishing hard facts and analysing them in a balanced and interesting way.

LITERATURE

There is a dearth of good general books on Irish literature. Douglas Hyde *A literary history of Ireland from the earliest times to the present day* (1967 edition with introduction by B. Ó Cúiv) and A. de Blacam *Gaelic literature surveyed* (1933) have not yet been replaced, although Myles Dillon (ed.) *Irish sagas* (1959), B. Ó Cúiv (ed.) *Seven centuries of Irish learning, 1000–1700* (1961) and D. Greene *Writing in Irish today* (1972) are useful additions. J. C. Beckett *The Anglo-Irish tradition* (1976) is a fascinating personal view of that culture. B. Cleeve *Dictionary of Irish writers* (3 volumes, 1967–71) is a convenient work of reference. See also F. S. L. Lyons *Culture and anarchy* (1979).

Index

This index should be used only as a supplement to the contents page and extensive cross-referencing. It is in no way intended to be comprehensive. Maps are not indexed, Figures in brackets refer to sections.

Britain – *cont.*
239, 241; trade with, 205, 207, 209, 213, (65), 264
British Commonwealth, 20, 162, 163
Brittany, 139, 212
Broghill, Earl of, 63
Browne, Archbishop George, 125
Bruce, Edward, 29, 36, (14), 225
Bruce, Robert, 52, 54
Brugha, Cathal, 78
Brú na Bóinne, 117
Buenos Aires, 150
Burgo, de, William, 51; Richard, 52; Richard, Early of Ulster, 54; and *see* Burke
Burke (de Burgo), family of, 37, 51, 228; Ulick, 36–7; MacWilliam, Earl of Clanrickard, 170
Butlers of Ormond, family of, 36, 51, 54, 90, (26); Edmund, 54
Butt, Isaac, 105, 107

Callan, battle of, 36
Canada, 146, 149
Capuchins, *see* religious orders
Cardiff, 151
Carew, Sir George, 57
Carlingford, 213
Carlow, 15, 18, 71, 83, 89, 95
Carmelites, *see* religious orders
Carrickfergus, city of, 42, 49, 51, 54, 132, 228, 250; siege of, 65; port of, 212, 213, 215
Casement, Sir Roger, 42, 73, 75
Cashel, ecclesiastical province of, 13, 48, 54, 85, 118, 122, 189; synod of, 89, 118
Castlebar, 41, 42
Castlereagh, Lord, 101
Catholic Association, 101, 103
Catholic Emancipation, (30), 252
Catholic Relief Bill, 103, 105
Cattle Acts, 215, 216
Cavan, 16, 19, 107, 172, 254; 256; industry in, 196
Ceannt, Eamon, (20)
Celsus of Armagh, 118
Celts, 84, 117, 224
Chamberlain, Austen, 109
Chamberlain, Neville, 80
Charlemagne, 141
Charles I, 38, (16), 251
Charles II, 63
Chester, 207, 213
Chichester, Sir Arthur, 174
Chichester-Clark, James, 258, 259

Childers, Erskine, 80, 109
China, 148–9
Christian Brothers, *see* religious orders
Christianity, (V), 135, 205, 224
Church of Ireland, 60, 119, (36), (39), 177, 241
Cistercians, *see* religious orders
civil war, Irish, 20, 33, (22), 160
Civil Rights Association (CRA), 258
Clan na Gael, 137, 158–9
Clann na Poblachta, 113
Clann no Talmhan, 113
Clanrickard, *see* Burke
Clare, 15, 18, 21, 43, 51, 60, 85, 103; transplantations to, 175
Clare, de, family of, 36; Richard FitzGilbert, Earl of Striguil, *see* Strongbow
Clarke, Thomas (20), 159
Clonfert, 122, 226
Clonmacnois, 122, 226
Clonmel, 63, 193
Clontarf, battle of, 34, 45, 85; meeting at, 104
Clontibret, battle at, 37, 57
Cobh (Queenstown), 42, 80
Cohalan, Judge, 160
Colbert, Cornelius, 75
Coleraine, 51, 54, 172
Collins, Michael, 77, (22), 109
Confederation, Catholic, 38, (16), 177
Congested Districts Board, 186, 198
Congregationalists, *see* dissenters
Connacht, kings of, 15, 85, 88, 89; province of, 18, 19, 33, 55, 85, 169, 228; rebellion in, 37, 52, 57; grants in, 51, 52; projected plantation of, 60; population of, 134, 234, 237, 243; transplantation to, 175; transport in, 193; agriculture in, 206
Connachta, 85
Connolly, James, (20), 247
Connor, battle of, 54
Coote, Sir Charles, 63
Cork, county of, 15, 18, 80, 89, 131, 137, 186; port of, 21, 27, 188, 212, 215, 217, 218; city of, 42, 45, 51, 63, 65, 77, 209, 229, 243; plantation in, 172; transport links, 189, 193; industry in, 197
Cornwallis, Lord, 42
Cosgrave, William, 110, 111, 113, 161
Counter-Reformation, 119
Courcy, John de, 51, 52, 228, 250
Cromwell, Oliver, 38, 62–3, 131, 215, 252

280

Land Court, 186
Land League, 107
Landlord and Tenant (Ireland) Act, 185
Lanfranc, Archbishop, 118
Laois, *see* Leix
Laudabiliter, 119
Lauzun, Count de, 41
League of Nations, 163
Leinster, province of, 15, 18, 47, 55, 85, 95, 131, 170, 228; kings of, 34, 47, 48, 84, 88, 89; rebellion in, 52, 57, 61, 69, 74; population of, 134, 234, 237, 243; industry in, 169, 196, 206; confiscations in, 175; transport in, 193
Leitrim, 18, 175, 186
Leix (Queen's County), 15, 18, 54, 95, 170, 171, 175, 196
Libya, 31
Limerick, county of, 15, 18, 51, 79, 89, 131; port of, 21, 27, 212; sieges of, 39, 65; city of, 42, 45, 47, 51, 85, 207, 226–7, 229; Treaty of, 66, 177; transport links, 188, 189, 191, 193
Lloyd George, David, 76, 109
London, 37, 172
Londonderry, county of, 16, 132, 172, 255; city of, 21, 229, 258; siege of, 39, 65, 66, 251; industry in, 196
Longford, 18, 19, 175, 196
Lough Swilly, 42, 71, 80
Louis XIV, 30, 42
Louth, 15, 18, 90, 95, 103, 191, 196
Loyal National Repeal Association, 104
Lynch, Liam, (22)

MacBride, John, 75
MacCarthy, family of, 36, 48, 51, 86, (26)
MacCracken, Henry Joy, 69, 71
MacDermott, Sean, (20)
MacDonagh, Thomas, (20), 269
MacDonlevy, family of, 51, 86
McGarrity, Joseph, 160
MacGillapatrick, family of, 47, 170
MacKenna, family of, 55, 172
MacLochlainn, family of, 86, 88, 89
MacMahon, family of, 37, 55, 172
MacMurrough, family of, 86, 92; Dermot, (12), 89
MacNeill, Eoin, 20, 73
MacSwiney, Terence, 76
Máel Mórda, 34
Maguire, Hugh, 55
Malachy II, 45, 85, 88

Malachy, St, 118, 122
Mallin, Michael, 74, 75
Markiewicz, Countess, 74, 75
Marlborough, Duke of, 65
Marx, Karl, 151
Mary Modena, 143
Mary, Queen, 15, 127, 168, 171
Mathew, Father Theobald, 199
Maynooth, 37
Mayo, county of, 18, 175, 186, 196; diocese of, 122
Meagher, Thomas Francis, 31, 104
Meath, 15, 18, 48, 93, 95, 191, 196; risings in, 52, 69; kings of, 84, 85, 86, 88, 89
Mellows, Liam, 74, (22)
Mesolithic people, 83
Methodists, *see* dissenters
Mitchel, John, 31, 104
Molyneux, William, 100
Monaghan, 16, 37, 55, 103, 172, 196, 254, 256
Monro, General Robert, 38, 61, 62
Montgomery, Hugh, 174
Moran, Cardinal, 148
Mortimer, Roger, 54, 55
Mountcashel, Lord, 42
Mountjoy, Lord (Charles Blount), 38, 57, 58
Moyry Pass (Gap of the North), 33, 38, 55, 58, 191
Mulcahy, Richard, 78, 110
Munro, Henry, 71
Munster, province of, 15, 18, 33, 34, 51, 55, 92, 169, 170, 228; kings of, 15, (24); rebellions in, 30, 37, 41, 57, 63, 212; confiscations in, 175; transport in, 193; industry in, 206; population of, 234, 237, 243
Murphy, Father Michael, 39

Nation, The, 104
National Volunteers, *see* Volunteers
Navigation Acts, 215
Needham, General Francis, 39
Neolithic people, 83, 117
neutrality, (23)
New Departure, 158–9
Newgrange, 83
Newman, Cardinal, 244
New Ross, 63, 71, 212
Newry, 33, 51
New Stone Age, 83
New Zealand, 222; emigration to, 136, 150
Niall of the Nine Hostages, 85, 139

Nine Years War, 30, 34, 38, (15), 206, 212, 250
NORAID, *see* Irish Northern Aid Committee
Normans, 15, 29, 34, 36, (13), (14), (25), (26), (27), 136, 225, 226; invasion, 34, 36, (12), 168, 188; and the church, 119, 122; and trade, 205, 207; and towns, 209, 225, (68)
Norse, *see* Vikings
Northern Ireland, state of, 16, 20, 167, (XII); government of, 78, 187; and second world war, 82; 1970s crisis, 114, 164, (80); and religion, 119–20; agriculture in, (55); communications in, 193, 195; trade, 207, 222; population of, 231, 236, 237

O'Brien, family of, 13, 15, 36, 37, 48, 52, 54, (24), (26), 170; Murrough (Lord Inchiquin), 38, 61–2, 63; Murchertach, 88, 89; Turloch, 89
O'Brien, William Smith, 31, 104
O'Byrne, family of, 54, 92
O'Carroll, family of, 37, 86
O'Connell, Daniel, (30), 105
O'Connell, J. J., 78
O'Connor, family of, 52, 86, 88, (26), 170; Rory (high-king), 36, 47, 48, 51; Felim, 54; Turloch, 89
O'Connor, Rory, (20)
O'Donnell, family of, 29, 37, 86, (26); Aodh, 54; Hugh, 38, (15), 172
O'Duffy, General Eoin, 113
O'Farrell, family of, 37
Offaly (King's County), 15, 18, 51, 95, 171, 175, 196
Offaly, Lord, *see* Fitzgerald, Thomas
O'Hanrahan, Michael, 75
O'Higgins, Kevin, 110
O'Mahony, John, 157
O'More, family of, 54; Rory, 60
O'Neill, family of, 29, 36, 37, 54, (26), 170; Hugh, Earl of Tyrone, 34, 37, 38, (15), 170, 172; Brian, 36; Shane, 37, 172; Owen Roe, 38, 61–3; Sir Felim, 60; Turloch Luineach, 172
O'Neill, Captain Terence, 258
Orange Order, 39, (17), 69, 252, (78)
Orange, William of, *see* William of Orange
Ormond, territory of, 51, (26); first Earl of, 93; first Duke of, 38, (16), 131; *see also* Butler
O'Rourke, family of, 48, 54, 86
Ossory, 15, 47

O'Sullivan, family of, 58, 92
O'Toole, family of, 54, 92; St Laurence, 118

Paisley, Ian, 167, 258, 261
Pale, 34, 37, 89, (27), 125, 129, 170, 171, 188, 228
Paletines, *see* dissenters
Palladius, 120
Parnell, Charles Stewart, 104, (31), 159
Parsons, Sir William, 60
partition, 19, 20, 255–6
Patrick, St, 120, 121
Patriot parliament, 98–9
Peace Conference, 109
Peace People, 261
Pearse, Patrick, (20), 247, 269
Peel, Sir Robert, 103, 104, 106
Peep-O'-Day Boys, 39, 66
penal laws, 65, 101, 131, 143, 169, 177, 178
People's Democracy, 258
Perry, Anthony, 39
Petty, Sir William, 27–8, 132, 175, 236
Philip II of Spain, 41
Pilltown, 36
Pipard, Roger, 51
Plunkett, family of, 37
Plunkett, Joseph, (20), 269
Poynings's Law, 96, 100
Premonstratensians, *see* religious orders
Prendergast, Maurice de, 47
Presbyterians, *see* dissenters
Presentation Sisters, *see* religious orders
Preston, family of, 37; Thomas, 38, 61–3
Ptolemy, Claudius, 24–5

Quakers, *see* dissenters
Queen's County, *see* Leix
Queenstown, *see* Cobh

Raleigh, Sir Walter, 41, 172
Rathbreasail, synod of, 118
Rathmines, battle of, 62
Redmond, John, 73, 108
Reformation, 96–7, 119, 122, (36), (37), 136, 246
religious orders, (35); *and also* Cistercians, 119, 127; Franciscans, 127; Dominicans, 127; Jesuits, 127, 143; Capuchins, 129, 138; Carmelites, 129; Christian Brothers, 149, 241; Presentation Sisters, 241; Ursuline Sisters, 241
Republic of Ireland Act, 20

Walter, Theobald, 51; *see also* Ormond
Waterford, county of, 15, 18, 79, 89, 95,
    172; port of, 21, 43, 188, 212, 217,
    218; city of, 45, 47, 48, 191, 193, 209,
    226, 228; siege of, 63; constituency of,
    103
Wellington, Duke of, 103
Wentworth, Sir Thomas (Lord Strafford),
    60, 98, 174, 251
West Indies, 25, 151, 175, 215;
    emigration to, 146
Westmeath, 18, 57, 85, 103, 175, 196
Westminster, 98, (29), 108, (30), (31),
    257, 260; Statute of, 161
Wexford, county of, 15, 18, 47, 48, 71,
    74, 89, 92, 95, 175; port of, 21, 209,
    212; city of, 45, 62

Whiteboys, 66
Wicklow, 18,. 34, 54, 71, 92, 93, 95, 191
Wild Geese, 42, 66
William of Orange, 30, 39, (17), 100,
    131, 251, 252
Wilson, Sir Henry, 78
Wilton, Lord Grey de, 41
Windsor, Treaty of, 51
Wyndham Act, 186

Yellow Ford, battle of, 37, 57
Yelverton's Act, 179
York, Richard, Duke of, 36, 95, 96
Youghal, 55, 63, 209, 212, 215
Young Irelanders, 31, (30), 157

Zubiar, Pedro de, 41